THE ORIGINS OF SCIENTIFIC ECONOMICS

The Origins of
Scientific Economics

WILLIAM LETWIN

Massachusetts Institute of Technology

Doubleday & Company, Inc.
Garden City, New York
1964

The Origins of Scientific Economics was originally published
in England by Methuen & Company Ltd. in 1963.

Library of Congress Catalog Card Number 64–15339
Copyright © 1963 by William Letwin
All Rights Reserved
Printed in the United States of America
First Edition in the United States of America

PREFACE

THE POPULAR NOTION that Adam Smith invented economics has always discomfited those historians of economic thought who, like all true historians, feel a strong urge to trace things back to their utmost beginnings. The work of discovering origins that predate the apparent original was begun soon after Smith's time by such of his followers as James Mill and J. R. McCulloch. Being inclined to view economic theory as a particularly elegant way of demonstrating the merits of *laissez-faire*, they concluded that whoever advocated free trade must be something of an economist, and they located several writers during the seventeenth and early eighteenth centuries who had advocated it so forcefully as to qualify them, in their eyes, as considerable economists. As economics became more elaborate and refined, interest in its history became more intense, and the historians slowly succeeded in proving that not only medieval churchmen, moralists and merchants, but even ancient philosophers had commented on economic matters. More recently still, some have penetrated beyond classical antiquity to find that ancient Chinese sages and Babylonian lawgivers made wise pronouncements on economic subjects. Having by now located the beginning of economics at the very beginnings of history, they rested confident of having achieved their calling's highest goals.

This resting place, though convenient, is ill-chosen; the historians both halted too soon and went too far. In a sense economics has always been known. It is so vital in the life of merchants, moralists and statesmen that they could never have done their work without understanding its basic principles. In the same way builders have always known physics.

Most men of course know such things without being aware that they know them. Some few may become conscious of fragments of their knowledge and may make incidental remarks that can be recognized as striking foresights by anyone who is searching for such prodigies. But great skill and wise insights existed long before science, and neither makes up science. The science of economics, like all sciences, had to be created.

The distinguishing characteristic of a science is that it is an explanatory system. It rests on a small number of principles. It is capable of explaining, or predicting, many diverse phenomena of a certain sort. It accounts for them by tracing them logically (or, what is equivalent, mathematically) to the restricted group of principles or laws. All such explanatory systems are scientific theories, even though they may vary widely in their quality. A theory that cannot predict accurately or explain thoroughly will nevertheless still be a scientific theory, though a poor one, if only it is of the proper form. Some particular economic theory, for instance, may be weak because it explains wages but not the level of employment; it may be imprecise because it predicts that in certain circumstances wages will rise but cannot tell by how much; but if the explanation and prediction follow necessarily from a few principles that explain many other phenomena as well, it is nevertheless a scientific theory. On the other hand, the mere isolated statement of one of those principles, or even an exhaustive list of all of them, is not a scientific theory, any more than a long career of astute guesses shows that a capable businessman who made them was instructed in economic theory.

A scientific theory, being a system, cannot grow by mere idle accumulation, but must be produced by an act of invention. There can be no period when a science is partly in existence: someone either has or has not brought together into an orderly whole enough principles and effects to qualify as a science, however rudimentary and fallacious. In the case of economics, although its fundamental principles had all been dimly recognized for centuries, the connections between them and their logical implications were not set down until the end of the seventeenth century. Then, as is often the case with inventions, a number of men devised slightly different but basically similar theories within a few decades. Before 1660 economics did not exist; by 1776 it existed in profusion.

It would seem quite natural that the invention should have taken place at the end of the seventeenth century, and in England, since seldom has a community been so fervently interested in both trade and science. But this plausible surmise has little to do with explaining the rise of scientific economics. For it is remarkable that the inventors had none of that detached objectivity that goes by the name of 'scientific attitude'. They created scientific theories, yet they generally did not do so deliberately, nor did they do it even for the sake of knowledge, but rather their scientific accomplishments were a by-product of their efforts to convince others to accede to certain economic policies.

To show how these practical, and often mercenary objectives led certain men to build a new science, the first social science, is my chief purpose.

In such an undertaking, the word 'economic' is bound to assume a variety of meanings. I have used 'economics' in the restricted sense of 'scientific economic theory', and 'econo mist' in the related sense of one who works with scientific economic theory. I have used the adjective 'economic' in a much broader sense, an 'economic' question or problem being one that would now fall within the scope of 'economics', an 'economic writer' being a man who deals with such problems—whether he does so with or without the aid of 'economics'—and 'economic thought' being the set of ideas, whether scientific or not, of men who have considered such questions. The only one of these distinctions which must be treated with care is that between 'economic theory' and 'economic thought'; I have used the former as a special case within the latter, that is, as a synonym for 'scientific economic thought' or 'economics'.

In quoting writers of the seventeenth and eighteenth centuries, I have generally modernized spelling and punctuation. In citing their works, I have often abbreviated the titles; full titles can be found by referring to the Bibliography and the bibliographic aids referred to there.

I gratefully acknowledge permission granted by the President and Fellows of Harvard University to use material from my monograph, *Sir Josiah Child, Merchant Economist* (Cambridge, Kress Library Publication No. 14, 1959), and by the Editors of *Economica* to use material from my article, 'The Authorship of Sir Dudley North's Discourses on Trade', N.S. 18 *Economica* 35 (1951).

I acknowledge also the generous aid of the Sloan Research Fund at the School of Industrial Management of the Massachusetts Institute of Technology, the American Philosophical Society, and the Social Science Research Council.

CONTENTS

PART I

The Old Style

Chapter 1

SIR JOSIAH CHILD: MERCHANT
ECONOMIST

I

INTERPRETING THE PAST in the light of its future is a temptation difficult for historians to resist. Historians of economic thought have been particularly vulnerable to it, especially in studying the beginnings of modern economics. They have tended to take Adam Smith as a starting point and hunt backward through time in pursuit of his anticipators, treating anyone who showed the slightest resemblance to Smith as fair game. In this way a number of seventeenth-century economists have come to be classified as forerunners of economic liberalism and of classical economic theory. One of the best known of them is Sir Josiah Child.

This judgment of contemporary writers must be radically revised, however, if they are considered in relation to their own time and circumstances rather than to what followed. When seen in his proper setting, Child does not appear to be a great economist. He looks instead like an advocate rather than theorist, a purveyor of patent remedies, an interested party vainly asserting his objectivity, an imperfect copyist rather than a vigorous innovator, and only an occasional liberal. If despite this his work remains of the greatest interest, it is because of what it shows about the difficulties that faced economic writers of his time, and the inadequacy of the old methods for dealing with them. More than any other writer, he illuminates the setting in which theoretical economics grew up.

Child's economic doctrines were aimed directly at solving the economic problems that faced England during the decade after the Restoration. In the background of all these problems was the commercial rivalry of Holland. The Dutch were rapidly replacing the English in branches of foreign trade they had long been accustomed to consider England's exclusive preserve; and the extraordinary efficiency of Dutch merchants threatened to destroy altogether the prosperity and power which the English had come to attribute to extensive foreign commerce and the great merchant marine it supported. The sense of rivalry and its effect on England's economic well-being was expressed in a popular jingle, 'Make wars with Dutchmen, Peace with Spain, Then we shall have money and trade again.'[1] War with the Dutch broke out in 1664, and continued during the next three years, at enormous cost and with discouraging defeats for both sides.

In the midst of the war, two further calamities badly disrupted England's economy and even more the public confidence. During the summer of 1665, the Plague reached a peak of violence, with the result that about 100,000 died of it in London alone. The following year was marked by the Fire, which raged in London for three days 'as if it had a commission to devour everything that was in its way', and which succeeded in consuming about a quarter of the city's houses and property worth perhaps £10,000,000. By 1667 complaints of depression were heard everywhere. The plague was said to have caused an 'infinite interruption to the whole trade of the nation'.[2] Poverty and pauperism were increasing, according to a somewhat earlier observer who produced as evidence the vast number of 'poor men, women, and hunger-starved children lying in every corner. . . .' The value of land was supposed to have dropped greatly; 'that rents decay', wrote a government official, 'every landlord feels'. And these complaints, which may seem to rest on nothing more solid than hearsay, are borne

[1] Burnet, I, 389.
[2] Quoted by Andrews, 85.

out by evidence that prices in general dropped off sharply between about 1665 and 1670.[3]

The Government, in all its parts, reacted quickly to the crisis. The House of Commons late in 1667 appointed a Select Committee on the State of Trade, including a number of its senior members and all the merchants of the House. In 1668 the King established a new Council of Trade, a large body of statesmen and merchants responsible for advising him on all economic questions. And in 1669 the House of Lords appointed a committee of its own 'to consider of the causes and grounds of the fall of rents and decay of trade within this Kingdom'.[4] The formation of these groups reflected the belief that economic policy was partly at least a matter of expert knowledge; indeed the practice of continuously maintaining within Government a group of specialists on economic affairs, and more specifically, the beginnings of the Board of Trade, can be traced from this moment.

In the activities of the Council of Trade and the Lords' Committee, and perhaps in those of the Commons' Committee as well, Josiah Child played a leading part. The views which he urged in all of them are summarized in his pamphlet, *Brief Observations concerning trade, and interest of money.*

'Observations' is a somewhat misleading title; 'proposals' would have been more to the point, since the main purpose of the pamphlet is to advocate that the rate of interest be reduced by law from a maximum of 6 per cent to 4 per cent or less. The practical purpose of the pamphlet is indicated moreover by the fact that it was written, so Child said, during the summer of 1665, to persuade some friends in Parliament, 'who were pleased to take copies of it, for their more

---

[3] *Short Notes and Observations drawn from the present decaying condition of this Kingdom in count of trade* . . . (1662), 4; [William Coventry], 'An Essay concerning the decay of rents and the remedies' [c. 1670], Add. MSS. 32,094, f. 243; E. B. Schumpeter, 'English Prices and Public Finance, 1660–1822', *Rev. Econ. Stat.*, XX (1938), 21–37. E. H. Phelps Brown and Hopkins, 'Seven Centuries of the Prices of Consumables', N.S. 23 *Economica*, 296, 313 (1956).

[4] *C.J.*, IX, 15 (4 Nov. 1667). On the Council of Trade, see pp. 23 ff., below, and Andrews, *passim*. L.J., XII, 254 (25 Oct. 1669).

deliberate consideration and digestion of the principles therein asserted'. But it was published in 1668, the year when a Bill to reduce interest from 6 per cent to 4 per cent was before the House of Commons, and the coincidence suggests that its publication, like its writing, was intended to have an immediate effect on policy. The course of debate —which was inconclusive, as Parliament adjourned shortly —suggests moreover that the advocates of the Bill were using Child's arguments, or more exactly, arguments similar to them, for they were by no means originally his.[5] But if the effect of the *Brief Observations* on this proceeding is too intangible to trace, the influence of the pamphlet and of Child on the Lords' Committee is perfectly plain.

The Lords' Committee decided at the outset that the best way of investigating the decay of trade was to invite testimony from members of the Council of Trade. But as the hearings continued through the autumn of 1669 they turned into an examination of Child's views, interlarded with debates between Child and some of his colleagues on the Council.[6]

Child began his analysis of the decay of trade by listing those branches of commerce that had declined. England's trade in Newfoundland fish was smaller than it should have been. Foreign sales of English cloth had not been increasing, and a recent tax imposed by Louis XIV had reduced exports to France. The Baltic trade was impaired, partly because commercial treaties gave Baltic merchants free access to England without assuring reciprocal advantages to English merchants. Exporters of English cattle still faced the competition of Irish cattle, which, now that the law prohibited their export into England, were being sent to the colonies instead. Besides, Irish goods were no longer being carried in English ships, for an Englishman could 'hardly put in a ship into any Irish port, being stopped up by the Dutch'. There were other reasons for these difficulties, such as the Plague, the Fire, laws like the statutes of bankruptcy and of appren-

[5] B.O., 17; C.J., IX, 79, 86 (11 and 22 Apr. 1668); *Diary of John Milward* (Robbins ed., 1938), 253, 269.
[6] M.B. The minutes are calendared in H.M.C., *Eighth Report* (1881), Part I, Appendix, 133 ff.

ticeship, and a shortage of money, made worse by so much coin being shipped out of the country or locked up in the safes of London bankers.[7]

The difficulties could be remedied and the nation made more prosperous, Child insisted, if England imitated the policies that had made the Dutch so formidable. They, unlike the English, maintained the quality of their goods by careful inspection, rewarded inventors for publishing their discoveries, built small and efficient ships, educated their children to commerce and put their poor to work. They made the most of their capital by maintaining public banks and pawnshops, encouraging the easy use of bills of exchange, maintaining public registers of title, which enabled landowners more easily to sell or pledge their property, and by practising frugality in their public as in their private affairs. They also encouraged trade by relieving it of burdens that English merchants were still forced to support: their customs were low, commercial litigation was simplified by the law merchant, all men were readily admitted to the privileges and freedom of cities, and liberty of religion prevailed, so that they regularly gained by persecution elsewhere. Their greatest advantage in trade, however, was a low rate of interest, and England could reproduce it by passing a law to reduce the maximum from 6 per cent to 4 per cent.[8]

The proposal to reduce interest rates, the same one that the Commons had considered a year earlier, particularly interested the committee, who set a day to consider it in detail. On that occasion, Child, again a principal speaker, opened by asserting that a low rate of interest always enriched a country. The generalization was immediately contradicted by speakers who maintained that low interest was the effect rather than the cause of riches, this being the chief argument that had been made against the Commons' Bill, as well as the most telling one that was directed against

---

[7] M.B., 2–6. The ambiguous phrase concerning Irish ports suggests either a blockade, which seems unlikely since the two nations were now at peace, or, as the H.M.C. calendarist understood it, that Dutch merchantmen were so thick in the Irish ports that an English one could find no anchorage or cargo.

[8] M.B., 2–6.

the *Brief Observations* by other economic writers.[9] Nor was the experience of Holland, on which Child depended so heavily, altogether in his favour. Thomas Grey, for instance, explained that interest was low there because the Dutch had a great deal of money but little land. He reasoned presumably that money which could not be used for buying land would be offered instead for loan, bidding down the rate of interest, and he cited as further evidence that interest rates were particularly high in Scotland and Ireland, where there was much land and very little money. Colonel Titus then argued that since low interest was a consequence of wealth, it would be futile or worse to aim at it by law. If a statute were passed, its effect would be to make usurers call in their loans. Traders would be ruined, and mortgages foreclosed; gentlemen who needed to borrow would be forced to break the law, although when they loaned money they would get only the legal rate, and ultimately they would be ruined. 'In all monarchical and aristocratical governments the first pulling down thereof has been lowering of interest.'[10]

In answer, Child denied that loans would be called in if the interest rate were reduced by law. Usurers had little choice; they could lend their money, buy land with it, or let it lie dead, but surely they would take 4 per cent rather than nothing if the law allowed them no more—this much he had said earlier. Since his adversaries also maintained that the Dutch, who took advantage of the difference in interest rates by investing money in England, would withdraw it if the rate were forced as low as in Holland, Child insisted that there was not as much as £10,000 of foreign money in

[9] Edmund Waller, opposing the Bill to reduce interest during the Commons' debate, said that 'it was not the way to make money plentiful nor land at a better rate . . . for it [is] with money as it is with other commodities, when they are most plentiful then they are cheapest, so make money plentiful and the interest will be low': Milward, *op. cit.* n. 5, p. 6 above, 270. The earliest pamphlets that pronounced this view in opposition to the *Brief Observations* were *The Interest of Money Mistaken* (1668) and Thomas Manly's *Usury at Six Per Cent Examined* (1669); it became, of course, the generally accepted position of classical economics.

[10] M.B., 13 ff.

England. And he met the argument that interest was the effect of wealth rather than of law by rehearsing the power of legislation. The Act of Navigation had improved trade; and three previous statutes had reduced the maximum rate of interest to 10 per cent, 8 per cent, and 6 per cent; why then should not another one reduce it still further?[11]

The committee was convinced; thirteen of the fourteen present voted to introduce a Bill to lower interest to 4 per cent; and by 24 November, the Earl of Essex reported to the House that the committee also recommended Bills for a register of deeds and for naturalization.[12]

The House soon took up the question of interest, and resolved that they too would like to hear the experts. The opening speaker against the Bill, Colonel Titus, enlarged on the arguments he had offered before the committee. If the Bill were passed, loans would be called in, and great harm done. Mortgaged lands would be forfeited to the usurers; young merchants, whose credit was their treasure, would be forced to give up trading; widows and orphans, whose subsistence was the interest of their money, would be damaged; no money could be raised to meet public emergencies. Any advantages of passing the Bill were future and conjectural. The nation had never been in better condition than when the rate was 10 per cent; with each reduction in interest rate the value of land had declined. Money was a commodity, like coal, and like it would become scarce if it were priced too low.

Titus' testimony called attention once more to the supply of loan funds, and the House asked the experts to 'show upon conjecture as near as may be what quantity of foreign money is now in England'. Titus answered that the London goldsmiths said it was a great deal: according to Alderman Bucknel, about £100,000 of it had been deposited with him and his partners, and Mr Meynel said he had about £30,000. Another witness said Mr Dericost always had more than £200,000 of Dutchmen's money, and similar statements of other London bankers were reported. The figures far ex-

11 *Ibid.*
12 *L.J.*, XII, 273–4.

ceeded Child's estimate, and weakened that part of his case.[13]

But Child concentrated on rebutting the statement that England had been better off when interest rates were higher. The facts showed, he said, that there was now much more money in England. Larger wedding portions were given with daughters and greater sums with apprentices; customs receipts had risen, as had rents in London; the city was being rebuilt in a luxurious manner; and merchant shipping had increased a hundredfold in the past seven years. It was typical, he said, to complain of the present and commend what was past, but there could be no doubt that England was, despite 'seeming scarcity', in the midst of 'real plenty'. This point he had been careful to make at the outset of the committee's hearings, when he began by saying that England was much wealthier than people thought; and it was a keystone of his argument, for he had little other proof that low interest rates were beneficial. The cure was confirmed by experience; some of it, he insisted, had already helped, more would make England strong enough to overcome even the Dutch.[14]

The Lords seemed once again to have been persuaded by Child, and as a committee of the whole, they voted that lowering interest would increase the value of land, those being the terms in which the question was put. But on the next day the House rejected the report of the committee of the whole, and the measure died.[15] Proposals for a register of title and some measure of religious toleration were equally fruitless, so that on this occasion Child's efforts were unsuccessful.

That Child failed to achieve his goals is of less interest than that his goals were political. It might seem that the normal bent of his mind cannot be deduced from what he said before a legislative body, since he was obliged to offer them practical advice. But Child was not out of his element

[13] House of Lords MS. Minute Bk. 4, 26 Nov. and 1 Dec. 1669 (H.L. Rec. Off.). Cf. L.J., XII, 277 (26 Nov. 1669).

[14] Ibid.

[15] House of Lords MS. Minute Bk. 4, 2–3 Dec., 1669; L.J., XII, 279, 280, 284.

in those circumstances. He was not a scientist but a man of
affairs interested in promoting certain policies.

II

Child's method was not to argue from general principles to
particular policies, but rather to insist that if certain policies
had been effective in the past they would have equally good
consequences in the future. He called those policies the
'causes' of the desirable 'effects', but he never attempted to
demonstrate that between those causes and effects there was
any necessary relation.

The nature of his method is evident from the very opening
of the *Brief Observations*. The work was intended to prove,
he wrote, that the means whereby the Netherlands prodi-
giously increased their trade could be imitated by almost
any other country, and with special ease by England. Although the larger part of the text is devoted to showing why
England should reduce the rate of interest, the full discussion of this most vital method is preceded by a brief catalogue
of fourteen other Dutch practices.[16]

But by far the best explanation of their prosperity was the
lowness of interest, which seldom exceeded 3 per cent, and
even during the war did not rise above 4 per cent. This, said
Child, was 'the *Causa Causans* of all the other causes of the
riches of that people, and . . . if interest of money were
with us reduced to the same rate it is with them, it would
in a short time render us as rich and considerable in trade
as they now are'. To reinforce the reputation of this empirical remedy, Child then traced its effects in the past and
in other lands, replied to certain objections, and finally
identified those Englishmen who would benefit from it. The
historical account maintained, in short, that since Parliament passed the first law to reduce interest, England steadily
became richer. Several pages are filled with such evidence
as this: 'Let us ask the aged whether five hundred pounds
portion with a daughter sixty years ago were not esteemed a

[16] B.O., 3 ff.

larger portion than two thousand pounds is now; and
whether gentlewomen in those days would not esteem themselves well clothed in a serge gown, which a chambermaid
now will be ashamed to be seen in; whether our citizens
and middle sort of gentry now are not more rich in clothes,
plate, jewels and household goods, etc. than the best sort of
knights and gentry were in those days; and whether our best
sorts of knights and gentry now do not exceed by much in
those things the nobility of England sixty years past, many
of whom then would not go to the price of a whole satin
doublet, the embroiderer being yet living who had assured
me he had made many hundreds of them for the nobility
with canvas backs.' These comparisons from English history
are followed by a geographical survey to supply further evidence for the generalization that 'all countries are at this
day richer or poorer in an exact proportion to what they pay,
and have usually paid, for the interest of money'.[17]

But this collection of facts, as Child recognized, still left
the crux of the matter unsolved. 'It remains that we enquire
carefully whether the abatement of interest be in truth the
cause of the riches of any country or only the concomitant
or effect of the riches of a country, in which seems to lie the
intricacy of the question.' After discussing this point with
the most ingenious men he knew and reading all the books
he could find, he decided that low interest is the cause of
wealth.[18] He rested his case on fact and authority, and instead of offering any positive demonstration that his conclusion was correct, he only refuted objections to it. The
objections he refuted, moreover, pointed out the practical
difficulties that would follow from the policy of lowering interest, rather than questioning the theoretical conclusion
that low interest makes a country rich.

The first objection was that if interest were reduced,
Dutch and other foreign investors would call home their
loans. Child answered that this would not happen if it were
reduced to 4 per cent, since the foreign investors could earn
only 3 per cent at home, and that even if they did withdraw
their funds, England would benefit because the lender al-

17 B.O., 7–10.
18 Ibid., 10–12.

ways enriches himself at the expense of the borrower. More-over, if a law for transferring bills of debt were passed at the same time, any funds withdrawn by the Dutch would not be missed. The second objection was that reducing the rate of interest would increase the price of land, thereby raising rents, the price of farm products and eventually the price of all goods, thus making life more difficult for the poor. Child seemed to agree that it would raise prices, but maintained that the poor would benefit, since, as a general principle, 'wherever provisions are for continuance of years dear in any country the people are rich, and where they are most cheap throughout the world, for the most part the people are very poor', the explanation being that the poor work harder when prices are high and become lax when they are low. To the third objection, that English usurers would call in their loans, Child answered that they would not, or that if they did, landowners would not suffer, for the price of land would have risen so much that it would be worth their while to sell it and pay off the mortgages.[19] To those who maintained that the King could not borrow enough money when the legal rate was 6 per cent and would have greater hardship if it went down to 4 per cent, Child replied that when the King borrowed from corporations, he only paid the legal rate and that he could always raise more money by borrowing from private lenders at rates above the legal one—if he had to pay 10 per cent when the legal rate was 6 per cent, he would have to pay only 6 per cent if the legal rate were lowered to 4 per cent. To the last objection, that a reduction would harm widows and orphans who lived on interest, Child replied that the executors of their estates need not lend the money but could invest it in land or com-merce, where its value would increase if interest were re-duced; but whatever happened, the loss to these persons, 'being but two per cent, is inconsiderable in respect of the great advantage [that] will accrue to the nation in general'. Throughout this set of answers Child insisted that lowering the rate of interest either would not reduce the supply of

[19] *Ibid.*

loan funds or that a reduction in the supply of loan funds would be beneficial.[20]

Finally, Child undertook to say who would benefit from the policy. His conclusion that loans would cost less and lands rise in price made him predict great improvement in the position of the King, the nobility and gentry, merchants and farmers; and since English merchants could compete more successfully for foreign trade, the benefits would spread to mariners, shipwrights, porters, clothiers, packers and all sorts of labouring people that depend on trade; only the 'griping dronish usurer' would be harmed. The method adapted from the Dutch would transform the English from 'dwarfs and pigmies in stocks and experience' into 'Samsons and Goliaths' able to defeat their potent adversaries.[21]

To persuade his readers that his policy would work, rather than to discover why it did, was Child's aim, and in pursuing his purpose he neither borrowed nor devised any explicit general theory, even as a method of persuasion. His argument, as he frankly conceded, turned on whether low interest is the cause of national wealth or rather its effect; yet in defence of his view he had nothing better to say than that he and other men believed it was the cause. He inferred that this was so by tracing the supposed sequence of events, without making any effort to explain how the presumed cause brought about the presumed effect, or to show that the two events were not merely coincidental, that the presumed cause was not instead an impediment or perhaps really the effect.[22]

Child's facts themselves were of mixed quality. Some of what he said, to be sure, was common knowledge. Everyone agreed that since the beginning of the century the

[20] B.O., 12.

[21] Ibid., 13–16.

[22] Later, when replying to criticism on this point, Child adopted the position that low interest is at the same time a cause and an effect of national wealth; which is a tenable position, logically and economically. It was rather incidental to Child's argument, namely that 'a low stated interest by law may be a cause of riches'; but whether or not the analysis was correct, it was a sort of analysis that did not recur in Child and was altogether absent from the Brief Observations. See N.D.T., 62–64.

Dutch had become the wealthiest nation in Europe, or one of the wealthiest. Everyone knew or believed that the Dutch followed some of the policies Child attributed to them, that they were, for instance, penurious and that their merchantmen sailed unarmed. But not all of Child's assertions were so widely believed, and indeed his critics denied that the Dutch followed what he described as their central policy, asserting on the contrary that they did not restrict the rate of interest by law.[23]

When such doubts were raised about his assertions, Child replied by reiterating them, putting the burden of proof on the critic, questioning the critic's experience, intelligence and good faith, and appealing to authority. This mode of argument was in keeping with his method, for his factual statements were seldom founded on concrete evidence that he could cite. Instead they were almost exclusively borrowed from other writers. It is hardly too much to say that the *Brief Observations* is merely a compendium of statements made by a series of authors whom Child followed more or less closely, but never with acknowledgment.

The sources on which Child drew were part of a great mass of books and papers in which Englishmen tried to account for the amazing commercial success of the Dutch and urged that their policy be adopted as a model for English policy. This literature, which reached its highest point in Sir William Temple's *Observations upon the Netherlands*, stemmed from *Englands Safety, In Trades Encrease*, written in 1641 by Henry Robinson, a London merchant and pamphleteer remarkable for the liberality of his views on religious as well as economic affairs, and the most influential among the many earlier admirers of the Dutch.[24] In *Englands Safety*, Robinson advocated and discussed at some length seventeen methods by which England could improve the conditions of commerce. In discussing each method Robinson explained why it would be useful, and incidentally, only incidentally, examined its use by the great com-

[23] This rebuttal is made for instance by the author of *Interest of Money Mistaken* (1668); see Child's answer, *N.D.T.*, 59–60.

[24] Sir William Temple, *Observations upon the United Provinces of the Netherlands* (1668). Robinson: Kress, 597.

mercial powers, France, Venice, or if it so happened, the
Netherlands. The Dutch had not yet reached that pre-
eminence in trade that made later English writers quite naturally take them as a model adequate in itself. When that
time came, Robinson's successors simply attributed to the
Dutch those policies that Robinson had advocated on their
merits, and it was in just this spirit that Child borrowed
from him.

Of the fifteen policies that Child advocated, ten were taken
from Robinson.[25] A number of them, where the substance
of Child's remarks was the same as Robinson's, evidently
came down to Child through other writers, who followed
and slightly modified Robinson's views, and all of whom,
like Child, neglected to acknowledge the source. But other
of Child's arguments so closely resemble Robinson's, not only
in meaning, but also in the choice of words and order of
presentation, that Child must have written them with Robinson's text in sight, or the memory of it clearly before him.

The faithfulness with which Child drew from Robinson
is clearest in his rebuttal of arguments against lowering the
interest rate. Robinson took up three objections. The first is
that as soon as the rate was reduced in England, foreigners
would cease sending money to England for loan; to which
he replied, 'it were good they brought none at all, being
better to have a little trade with a greater profit to be divided
amongst ourselves, than a larger trade with less benefit on
it, and that chiefly to go to strangers'. Child also refuted
objections, also considered this one first, and, though he
began by pointing out, as Robinson did elsewhere, that the
foreign lenders would not withdraw their funds as long as
they earned more in England than at home, he concluded
in a very similar vein to Robinson's: 'But if they should call
home all the money they have with us at interest, it would
be better for us than if they did it not, for "the Borrower is
always a Slave to the Lender" and shall be sure to be always
kept poor while the other is fat and full.'

The second objection that Robinson considered was that
English usurers would call in their loans, to which he an-

[25] See Appendix II.

swered that they would not, for although they preferred more interest to less, they preferred less to none at all. And to the third objection, that land would rise in value, Robinson answered that it would not rise as much as might be supposed and that, in any event, a rise in the price of land is quite desirable. Child gave the same answers and merely reversed the order of the objections. Robinson's order was a reasonable one, for both his first and second objections are special cases of the argument that if interest rates are lowered, the supply of loan funds will decrease—because of the reaction, first, of foreign lenders, and second, of domestic lenders—and the third objection naturally follows these, on the argument that after usurers call in their loans, they will invest their funds in land instead, and thereby bid up its price. But the sequence in which Child presented the objections is much less satisfactory. He arranged them at random, and this, as well as what he chose to omit in condensing Robinson, shows that while he understood well enough what Robinson was driving at, he failed to see the economic reasoning—implicit, though barely beneath the surface—that dictated the order in which Robinson had presented the argument.

Robinson was a source not only for Child, but also for other writers on whom Child drew. In 1651 a pamphlet, *The Advocate*, was published, under the signature 'Philopatris', by Dr Benjamin Worsley.[26] What Worsley took from Robinson was everything useful to his own particular purpose, namely to advocate the Navigation Act, of which he considered himself a chief architect. In view of his pur-

[26] Philopatris [Dr Benjamin Worsley], *The Advocate* (1651; Kress, 837). The attribution to Worsley depends on his statement to Lady Clarendon, that he was 'the first solicitor for the act for the management of trade and navigation and . . . writ the advocate in defence of it': Bod. Lib. Clarendon MSS., 75, f. 300; cited by C. M. Andrews, *Colonial Period of American History* (1938), IV, 60. It is confirmed by Sir William Petty, who in *Reflections upon Some Persons and Things in Ireland* (1660), 89, refers to *The Advocate* as having been written by his enemy Worsley and describes it as a 'frippery and long-lane of threadbare notions concerning trade'. Furthermore, *Free-ports, and the nature of them stated* (1651), obviously by the author of *The Advocate*, is subscribed 'B.W.'.

pose, he paid a great deal of attention to the Dutch skill in managing their merchant marine, a skill that he considered the principal cause of Dutch enrichment and the principal danger to England's international trade. He therefore greatly elaborated on Robinson's bare statement that the Dutch had many ships, and it is his fuller explanation of Dutch shipping practice that Child in turn followed, as a comparison of the texts shows.

Worsley set forth part of his argument in three stages:[27]

> 1. Few merchants' ships among the Hollanders were ships of much defence . . . and so they were neither at so great a charge . . . in building them, nor did carry a proportion of men or victual . . . answerable to English shipping of the same burthen.
>
> 2. Several trades they did drive in fleets with great . . . vessels, having never a gun at all in them . . .
>
> 3. Those their fleets were . . . carefully and constantly attended with a convoy at the public charge.

Child, without formally indicating the stages, retained them in the structure of his abbreviated statement:[28]

> Their contriving and building of great ships to sail with small charge, not above one third of what we are at, for ships of the same burthen in England; and compelling their said ships (being of small force) to sail always in fleets, to which in all times of danger they allow convoy.

The close correspondence is emphasized by the recurrence of the catchwords, 'charge', 'burthen', 'fleets' and 'convoy'.

The only bit of information that Child added to Worsley's statement was the number, one-third, which he gave as the relation of Dutch to English shipping costs. It is a rather surprising number, since experts on the question had long been saying, as with one voice, that Dutch shipping costs were one-half or two-thirds of the English.[29] Child's esti-

---

[27] *The Advocate,* 3; cf. Appendix II.

[28] *B.O.,* 4.

[29] Violet Barbour, 'Dutch and English Merchant Shipping', *Econ. Hist. Rev.,* II (1930), 2, reprinted in E. M. Carus-Wilson (ed.), *Essays in Economic History* (1954), 239–40, 249.

mate may differ only because of a typographical error or because he misread a text that said the Dutch shipped cargo at one-third less cost than the English, or because he was convinced that the general view was mistaken. This last possibility might be excluded in the case of other writers, since no explanation or supporting evidence is offered for an unusual view, but in this instance it is difficult to assess the meaning, as Child not infrequently asserted, without more support, equally novel and contested facts. Although there was no other material that Child took directly from *The Advocate,* his association with it continued. He and Worsley collaborated for years on the Council of Trade and still later he composed—so some said—a pamphlet whose only signature was Philopatris.[30]

The remaining prescriptions that Child presented were taken from several other writers. Among them, those whom he laid under the heaviest contribution were Samuel Lambe, who himself had closely followed Dr Worsley, and Sir William Petty, the only one of his authorities to be mentioned by name.[31]

To call Child's borrowings plagiarism would be to impose standards foreign to the period and the enterprise. To borrow from old books was a common practice among men who were still inclined to think that old books were the best books and agreement with authority the surest sign of truth. The practice was widespread among economic writers as well as others, and so was the failure to acknowledge the loan; for footnotes are an obsession of scholars, and mainly of modern scholars.

But in Child's case there is the additional consideration that he wished to seem original. Yet originality was a quality dangerous for Child to claim, since his remedy had little to recommend it except its past successes. The discomfort that Child felt on this score, and the means he took to ease himself, appear in an explanation appended to the *Brief Observations.* He was sure, he said, that the abatement of interest was the best remedy for the situation,

[30] See Appendix I.
[31] Samuel Lambe, *Seasonable Observations* . . . (1657); [Petty], *Treatise of Taxes and Contributions* (1662). Cf. Appendix II.

Which notwithstanding, I should not have presumed to expose it to public censure on my own single opinion, if I had not had the concurrence of much better judgments than my own; having never seen anything in print for it (though much against it) until the latter end of January last, at which time a friend whom I had often discoursed with upon this subject met with, by accident, a small tract to the same purpose, wrote near fifty years ago, which he gave me; and I have for public good thought fit to annex it hereunto verbatim.[32]

Child's conclusion therefore allows him to claim originality for the *Brief Observations*—'every paragraph whereof was writ by me . . . many months before ever I saw or heard of this or anything else writ or printed to the like purpose'[33] —while still producing among his credentials the independent testimony, fifty years old, of the author whose tract he appends to his own. If, however, the claim to originality is to prevail among the historians of economic thought, it must rest on something more than the prescriptions and the arguments that he merely borrowed and reproduced without adding to them anything useful of his own.

III

Aside from being thought original, Child wanted also to be considered objective. His writings, like those of all economic writers of his time, abound in assertions of good faith: 'My ends have only been to serve my country, which I can with a sincere heart declare, in the presence of God and men.'[34] But a reputation for objectivity was very difficult to achieve in the seventeenth century. Being designated an expert did not automatically assure anyone that the expert's proposals were disinterested. On the contrary, most men evidently be-

[32] B.O., 17. The pamphlet to which he refers, *A tract against Usurie*, was published anonymously in 1621 by Sir Thomas Culpepper. Soon after Child revived it from oblivion, Culpepper's son republished it (1668; Kress, 1217).
[33] B.O., 18.
[34] N.D.T., 75–76.

lieved that anybody's recommendations on economic affairs ought to be examined suspiciously, because they might always be directed rather by the writer's private interests than by a disinterested concern for the public good. This scepticism was often justified. Many pamphleteers expected, as merchants, to gain immediate financial benefits from the policies they espoused as experts. When so many words were spent solely to fill authors' pockets, and when merchants in particular were believed to put nothing before their own interests, it was easy to condemn any writer on economic questions as a special pleader. The circumstances of Child's career made him especially vulnerable to that attack. His mercantile, religious and political associations all suggested that there might be ulterior motives to his economic arguments.

Child's career as a merchant, which began in the usual way, soon brought him into contact with public affairs.[35] The earliest remaining evidence of this connection is from 1650, Child's twentieth year, when he undertook to carry ships' provisions from Plymouth to Lisbon on behalf of the Parliamentary fleet.[36] By 1653 he was acting as an agent for the Admiralty Commissioners, and within two years became Deputy to the Navy's Treasurer at Portsmouth, a post he continued to hold until the Restoration, and one chief responsibility of which seems to have been to arrange for

[35] There is considerable confusion about Child's parentage and early career. H. R. Fox Bourne, *English Merchants* (1886), 231, citing Collins' *Peerage*, Lodge, *Peerage of Ireland*, I, 57, and Morant's *Essex*, maintains that Child's father was a 'London merchant', who acquired considerable wealth, bought property in Bedfordshire, and was appointed Sheriff of Bedfordshire in 1648. There is nothing, however, in the official records to identify Richard Child the Sheriff as Josiah's father. The only information on Child's youth is Evelyn's bare statement (16 March 1683) that Child had served an apprenticeship, from which scant information Macaulay drew a picture of Child in a 'humble position', 'sweeping one of the counting houses of the City', *History* (1914, Firth ed.), V, 2096.

[36] *C.S.P.D.* (21 May 1650), 172. The entry describes Child as 'merchant', but the context suggests that he may have been supercargo, a position in which young men were often placed soon after their apprenticeship; cf. *Lives*, II, 300.

the provisioning and victualling of ships.[37] During the same period, he also rose high in the civic administration of Portsmouth, becoming a burgess in 1655, mayor's assistant in 1656, and mayor in 1658. These, or perhaps other, unknown political activities are said to have aroused a suspicion of disloyalty, so that commissioners appointed by Charles II removed Child in 1662 from Portsmouth Corporation. That he was out of favour for some reason is suggested by the fact that for about three years following he apparently had no dealings with the Navy.[38]

But from 1665 on he began again to sell supplies to the Navy, and there is evidence that he was becoming a specialist in this branch of commerce. He contracted to furnish the Navy with timber in various forms, especially with masts that he imported from New England.[39] He sold the Navy its beer, and to make a better thing of it, bought a brewery in Southwark, whereupon he was commissioned brewer to the King as well; he still had ample supplies, some of which he exported and some of which he offered to the East India Company.[40] Altogether, he became prominent enough among dealers in ships' supplies so that Pepys urged him to submit a tender for the Navy victualling contract, which, a few years later, he did, though at first unsuccessfully.[41] From this time on, nevertheless, Child was recognized as an expert in naval affairs.

But he was regarded as an expert of very distinct political bias. This was amply revealed when he was suggested in 1669 for a position on the Navy Board. The Duke of York, then High Admiral, opposed the appointment, which he

[37] C.S.P.D. (10 June 1653), n. 76; 1655, 431, 489; 1658–59, 326; 1659–60, 496, 501, and passim.

[38] R. East (ed.), Extracts from records . . . of Portsmouth (1891), 315, 355.

[39] C.S.P.D., 1665–66, 129–130, 301, 381; 1666–67, 390; 1667–68, 107, 259, 576.

[40] C.S.P.D. (30 Apr. 1666), 371; Child et al. to Oxinden (9 Mar. 1665): Add. MSS. 40,700, f. 149; E. B. Sainsbury (ed.) Calendar of the Court Minutes of the East India Co., 1664–67, 294 (1 Mar. 1667).

[41] Pepys' Diary (7 Oct. 1665); C. Treas. Bks., II (1667–68), 403, 409, 420 et seq.

understood as one of Buckingham's manoeuvres to under-
mine his authority by placing members of the anti-court
party in the Navy's governing body. Accordingly, he was
'pretty stiff' against Child, as Pepys observed, the more so
since he considered merchants incapable of governing the
Navy well even when their political affiliations were less
suspect. At a later meeting of the Navy Board, the Duke
reiterated his antagonism, which was echoed by Captain
Cox, who reported that Child 'was talked of for an unfair
dealer with masters of ships, about freight'. They were chal-
lenged only by the co-Treasurer of the Navy, Sir Thomas
Littleton, another Buckingham candidate and sometimes
Child's business partner, who declared that 'he never heard
any honest man speak ill of Child'. The rebuff merely succeeded in angering the Duke and reinforced his determination to keep so confirmed a Whig as Child off the Board.[42]

One of the facts that most discredited Child in the eyes
of the Duke of York was his membership on the Council of
Trade. Extremists among the Court Party suspected the
Council of being part of a conspiracy organized by Buckingham and Shaftesbury to make Parliament master over
the King, by first depriving him of money and then doling
it out only for purposes of which they approved. What stood
in their way was the income from certain taxes whose proceeds had been permanently assigned to Charles as part of
the Restoration settlement; whatever was collected in customs, chimney-taxes, and certain excises was the King's without Parliament's leave and free of their control. But as the
amount collected was variable, the income from customs in
particular rising and falling with the volume of foreign
trade, the opposition could quietly constrict the King's power
by impeding the flow of commerce. This was the reason,
according to Roger North, always suspecting Whiggish
machinations, why such representatives of the faction as
Paul Foley were willing to say that 'all foreign trade was
loss, and ruinous to the nation'. Their paradoxical view,

---

[42] Pepys' *Diary* (25 Sep. 1668, 2 Apr., 5 Apr., 3 May, 10 May,
1669). Child, Papillon and Littleton were partners in bidding for the
Navy victualling contract in 1668: Pepys' *Diary* (24 Aug. 1668 and
passim).

North insisted, had an obvious meaning: 'the mortal evil of foreign trade was the great supply it brought to the crown, by which it could be supported, without being continually at the mercy of the parliament for supplies.'[43]

In order to carry out their purpose, North continued, Buckingham and Shaftesbury had persuaded the King that since commercial questions arising before the Privy Council were generally referred to merchants, they should once and for all be made the province of a separate council of merchants chosen for their good sense and impartiality. The devious ministers intended, of course, to pack the council with their own adherents. 'This plausible project,' North maintained, 'was put in execution, and the leaders of the fanatic party in the City, as Love, Child, etc., were the commissioners; for so it was plotted.'[44]

The roster of the Council of Trade at least partly bore out North's suspicion. To be sure, about thirty of the forty-six members were noblemen and high officers of the crown, and even North would not have believed that the Duke of York, the Lord Keeper, Lord Privy Seal, the Secretaries of State, and all the other Privy Councillors, had entered into a conspiracy against their master. But North could have argued that those dignitaries were mere embellishment, for it was the ten or twelve merchant members who really were the Council, wrote its reports, advised the King, and gave evidence before parliamentary committees and the Government. And their convictions were bound to inspire mistrust among supporters of High Church and strong prerogative, among everyone who considered religious heterodoxy and parliamentary supremacy as the two ingredients of rabid republicanism.[45]

[43] Lives, I, 310–11. Cf. Examen, 461–62.

[44] Examen, 461–62.

[45] The full membership of the Council, as given in House of Lords Record Office, H.L. Papers (1669), 215d, was:

The Duke of York, Prince Rupert, The Lord Keeper (Orlando Bridgeman), The Lord Privy Seal (Roberts); The Dukes of Buckingham, Albemarle, and Ormonde; The Earls of Devonshire, Bridgewater, Sandwich, Ossery, Anglesey, Carlisle, Craven, and Lauderdale; Viscount Halifax; Lords Arlington, Berkley of Berkley, Berkley of Stratton, Holles, and Ashley; Thomas Clifford, George Cartrett, John

William Love, whom North identified as a co-leader with
Child of the fanatic party in the City of London, undoubtedly deserved the distinction. He was one of four citizens
whom the City elected to Parliament in 1661 with cries of
'No Bishops! no Lord Bishops!' an outlook that convinced
Pepys they were 'so far from being episcopal that they were
thought to be Anabaptists'. Love was an official spokesman
for nonconformity, as for instance, during the debate in
1673 of a Bill for toleration, when the House expressly delegated him to find out what the dissenters thought of the
measure. Another member of the Council, John Shorter,
had a similar reputation. According to Luttrell, he was a
'great Presbyterian'; Evelyn called him 'an Anabaptist very
odd ignorant mechanic'; and in 1681 he was Whig candidate for Mayor of London. Still another, Dr Benjamin
Worsley, not a merchant but a great proponent of the Council of Trade and secretary to its successor in 1672, was
forced to resign from that post in June 1673 because he refused to take the oath of conformity. John Birch, a Cromwellian colonel, was also a Presbyterian; and Silius Titus,
another Cromwellian colonel, was made a Privy Councillor,
so Evelyn said, to assuage the Independents; in Parliament
both were known as leading spokesmen of the Country
Party. Associated with them was Thomas Papillon, who distinguished himself as a Whig on many occasions and became a figurehead of the Opposition after 1681, when,
despite being elected Sheriff of London by an overwhelming
majority, he was ousted at the insistence of the Court in
favour of its Tory nominees. The majority of the merchant

Trevor, William Morris, William Coventry, Thomas Osborne,
Thomas Littleton, Henry Blount, George Downing, Andrew Riccard,
William Thomson–Baronets or Knights; Silius Titus, William Gar-
roway, Henry Slingsby, Thomas Grey, John Birch and William Love,
who are described as esquire; Dr Benjamin Worsley; John Buckworth,
Thomas Papillon, John Page, Josiah Child, Thomas Tite, Benjamin
Albin and John Shorter. The last seven were explicitly listed as 'merchants'. Riccard, Thomson, Birch and Love were merchants, though
listed among gentlemen, and Worsley was included for his interest
in commercial policy, while Blount, a traveller, was included as an
expert on foreign places. The others, except only two or three, were
appointed *ex officio*.

members of the Council—and all but one of those whose religion and politics can be traced—were Whigs or nonconformists or, in North's term, fanatics.[46]

The councillors were also closely associated in business. Three of them, Papillon, Shorter and John Page, were at various times Child's partners; four, if Sir Thomas Littleton, whose appointment to the Council was probably *ex officio*, is included.[47] The East India Company was heavily represented: by Sir Andrew Riccard and Sir William Thomson, who between them shared the governorship of the Company for ten of the twelve years from 1660 to 1671; by Thomas Papillon and Benjamin Albin, who were directors; and by Child, who, though not yet an officer, had some connections with the Company.[48] The Levant Company was represented by two of its leading members, Love and John Buckworth, and by Riccard, who presided over it as well as the East India Company—a joint rule that indicated how closely the great mercantile enterprises of the City were interwoven.[49]

[46] LOVE: Pepys' *Diary* (20 Mar. 1661); Burnet II, 8n. SHORTER: Narcis. Luttrell, *Brief Historical Relation* (1857 ed.), I, 411; Evelyn, IV, 562 (29 Oct. 1687). WORSLEY: Andrews, p. 98. BIRCH: *D.N.B.* TITUS: Evelyn (12 July 1668); see the party affiliations as assigned by Basil Henning (ed.), *Parliamentary Diary of Sir Edward Dering* (1940), Index. PAPILLON: *Pap. Mem., passim.*

[47] PAPILLON: *Pap. Mem.* Shorter was Child's partner in the mast trade: *C.S.P.D.*, *1667–68*, 235. JOHN PAGE participated with Papillon and Child in the East India trade: Add. MSS. 40,700, f. 149 (9 Mar. 1665). Page, moreover, was mayor of Plymouth in 1655–56, while Child was a burgess; *C.S.P.D.*, *1655*, 45, 188, 197, *1655–56*, 477; East, *op. cit.* n. 38, p. 22 above, 315, 355. Like Child he dealt in ships' provisions: *C.S.P.D.*, *1656–57*, 551. He later engaged in the Spanish trade: *C.S.P.D.*, *1668–69*, 229; 1673, 577; *1673–75*, 18. He became a member of the East India Company (*C.S.P.D.*, *1673*, 296) and served as a director in 1680, 1681 and 1683: Add. MSS. 38,871, ff. 7b, 8.

[48] Hunter, II, 201, n. 3, and *passim*; *Pap. Mem.*; on ALBIN: Ct. Bk. 25A, f. 8 (8 June 1666).

[49] LOVE: *Examen*, 461. BUCKWORTH was Deputy Governor in 1681: A. Bryant, *Pepys, Years of Peril* (1936), 357; he appeared as the Turkey Co.'s representative before the Privy Council in 1682: Ct. Bk. 33, f. 5a. RICCARD was Governor of the Turkey Co. from 1654 to 1672: Wood, Appendix IV; he was an early investor also in the African Company, of which both Child and Buckworth were subsequently officers: K. G. Davies, *Royal African Company* (1957).

It was this very grouping of East India and Turkey merchants which, according to North, brought the Council to an end. All had been going well until a dispute broke out between the two companies, the Turkey Company asserting that the other was infringing its exclusive privileges. When the matter was referred by the King to the Council on Trade, a furious argument developed among them and especially between Love and Child. 'Whereby it appeared most plain to the King, that they were a pack of K[nave]s, and there was no grain of justice or ingenuity among them, but all partiality and selfishness, agreeing in nothing but the common notion of trade, which is to serve themselves at the cost of everybody else.' The dispute to which North was apparently referring took place in 1670, and the Council of Trade seems virtually to have ceased operating after that time.[50] There was little ground for hoping, in any event, that a council of merchants could give disinterested advice on mercantile policies that vitally affected their interests.

Actually, in 1670, Child was not yet an authoritative spokesman for the East India Company; he was not even properly part of it, though he had been skirting its edges for some time. As early as 1659, the Company, on the recommendation of Major Robert Thomson, placed an order with him to provision their ships. By 1664, his connection with the Company seems to have been closer, though still nebulous, for several directors were delegated to inquire whether he had been admitted to membership. In the following year, he joined with Thomas Papillon and two others in trading with India on their private account, carrying their goods by licence on the Company's ships. His influence within the Company was still limited, for the honour and profit of being the Company's Brewer, which Child requested in 1667, were bestowed on another.[51] Not until 1671 did he become a stockholder. But between June 1671 and November 1673, he suddenly bought up £12,000 worth of shares,

50 *Examen*, 462; Wood, 103; Andrews, 95.
51 Sainsbury, *Calendar*, 1655–59 (*op. cit.* n. 40, p. 22 above), 350, 355; 1664–67, 105, 294; Add. MSS. 40,700, ff. 149, 67b (9 Mar. 1665, and Mar. 1666).

which made him probably the largest single holder.[52] He
was immediately chosen a director, and from 1674 until his
death twenty-five years later was re-elected every year but
one.[53] In 1681, he was elected Governor, and from then on
his policy and the Company's policy were one, so that he
became the symbol as well as manager of the Company's
rapidly increasing power.

In 1673, just when Child was buying up East India Company stock, there were other signs that he was flourishing.
He was elected to Parliament, and bought the famous house
at Wanstead, which he continued to improve at great expense and to live in for the rest of his life.[54] It is tempting
to speculate whether all these changes represented only a
new style of life or a sudden increase in fortune. What
suggests that it may have been the latter was that in 1672,
he, Papillon, Littleton and several others were partners in
the Navy victualling contract, which may have become par-

[52] The purchases are recorded in Sainsbury, *Calendar*, 1671–73,
307 ff. at their nominal value, twice the paid-up value. As the Company had a paid-up joint stock at this time of £370,000, and every
£250 of stock (paid-up) entitled the owner to one vote, by 1673
Child had about 2 per cent of the stock and 24 votes. In 1681 the
East India Company's opponents alleged, as evidence of excessive con-
centration of control, that one member (Child) had at least 80 votes,
to which the Company replied that none had as many as 60 votes;
the latter, taken literally, means that by then Child owned just short
of £30,000 worth of stock: *Allegations of the Turkey Co.* (17 Aug.
1681) and *The East India Company's Answer* (1681) 2, 3, 8; Philopatris, *Treatise* (1681), 32, 43. Since a defender of the Company
would tend, if anything, to understate the number of Child's votes,
Scott's observation (II, 153) that the number was 'probably a great
exaggeration' must be dismissed, especially since the record shows that
Child had nearly 50 votes as early as 1679. In 1691, by which time
the total stock of the Company had doubled to £740,000, Child's
holdings had increased to £51,150, by far the largest single block:
K. G. Davies, 'Joint-Stock Investment in the Later Seventeenth Century', *Econ. Hist. Rev.*, 2nd Ser., IV (1952), 296–97, quoting a list
of individual holdings in India Office Records, Home Miscellaneous
I. Cf. *Sir John Banks* (1963), by D. C. Coleman, whose aid on
this point had been invaluable.

[53] H. Yule (ed.), *Diary of William Hedges* (1888), II, cxii.

[54] Hunter, II, 286.

ticularly profitable when the third Dutch war broke out.[55] In any event, from this time on, Child began to enjoy the reputation of uncommon wealth.

But his increasing wealth and his new responsibilities in the East India Company did not at first alter his politics, and the events of 1676, the only year after 1674 when he was not re-elected a director of the Company, confirm the estimate that the Duke of York and Roger North made earlier of his party attachment. On 17 April 1676, just as the East India Company began its annual elections, its governor, Sir Nathaniel Herne, received a letter from Sir Joseph Williamson, Secretary of State. The King had heard, wrote Williamson, that it was proposed to elect Child Governor and Papillon Deputy Governor, and had commanded him to inform the Company that 'They are persons that have behaved themselves very ill towards his Majesty, and that therefore his Majesty should take it very ill of the Company if they should choose them'. Agitated debates followed the receipt of the letter, and the Company's officers scurried to and from Whitehall. Finally Charles said that he had not meant to interfere with the Company's privileges, which was ironic, for they knew as well as he that their privileges depended solely on a royal charter that could be cancelled almost at will. Recognizing this, they adopted a resolution of gratitude to the King, 'under the beams of whose sun they had prospered, and without which they would wither and decay', and refrained from electing those upon whom the shadow of the King's displeasure had fallen.[56] Gossip had it that the King was persuaded to intervene by some members of the Company who wanted to strengthen their hand in its internal affairs.[57] But repeated emphasis on the King's

---

[55] C. Treas. Books, IV (1672–75), 148 and passim; C.S.P.D. (8 Apr. 1672) and passim. The scale of the contract is indicated by the bill Child and Papillon submitted at the end of 1673, showing £82,000 due to them; Bod. Lib., Rawlinson MSS. A 193, f. 194.

[56] Accounts of the incident are given by Yule (op. cit. n. 53, p. 28 above), II, cxiii; Hunter, II, 183 f.; and Pap. Mem., 78–80.

[57] John Verney to Sir H. Verney (26 Apr. 1676) in H.M.C. Rept. VII, App., 467. See also Two Letters concerning the East India Company (1676), 1: 'The last post brought me news of . . . factions and divisions in the East India Company . . . and adds that

personal displeasure makes it seem more likely that the explanation lay in national politics and particularly in the attempt to impeach his chief minister.

Early in 1675, the Lord Treasurer, Danby, in order to
strengthen the Crown, had introduced in the House of
Lords a Bill to reinforce the Test oath. It would have extended the oath to Members of Parliament and would
have required them, as well as all officers under the Crown,
to declare that any resistance to the King was unlawful and
that they would not attempt to alter the existing government
of Church or State. Dissenters, some latitudinarians and
moderates, enemies of prerogative, and the parliamentary
opposition in general joined forces to defeat the Bill; but
fearing it might pass the House of Lords, they prepared a
second line of defence in the Commons. There the Opposition denounced Danby and, supported by some of his rivals,
introduced articles of impeachment. They charged him with
usurping powers beyond those of his office. They gave as
one example his behaviour during a trial at which Danby
was trying to enforce a royal proclamation. When the de-
fendant cited certain Acts of Parliament as authority for his
action, Danby had—so the articles of impeachment maintained—'in utter contempt of the law, uttered the arbitrary
expression, "that a new proclamation is better than an old
Act", several of His Majesty's subjects being present; and
upon his lordship's report to the Privy Council the person
in question, being a foreigner and not obeying such proclamation but pursuing his right at law, was banished the Kingdom'. The witness, a reluctant witness, to this incident was
a certain Thomas Salter, who, after being urged, hectored
and offered indemnity by some Opposition Members of Parliament, finally signed a paper to say that he had heard
Danby speak the words. Later, after the attempt at impeachment had failed, Salter renounced his affidavit; and in an
interview with Danby, who was gathering evidence that
witnesses had been suborned, described the tactics of the
Opposition. He named among those who had played upon

one of the factions had induced his Majesty to interpose by letters in
the election of their governors and committees, and to prohibit their
choice of some persons by name. . . .'

him not only Sir Thomas Littleton and Henry Powle, who headed the attack in the House, but also Papillon and Child. It was at the next elections of the East India Company that the King made his attack in turn on Papillon and Child.[58]

The point of the lesson was not lost on Child. Whether the baronetage conferred on him in 1678 was to reward a promise of compliance, or whether it was something altogether different, is impossible to say.[59] But a few years later, when Child brought the Company largely under his control, the main strategy of its domestic politics became a close alliance with the court based on exchange of favours. At a moment when the Crown was able to override its Whig opponents, as it did during the last years of Charles II and the reign of James II, it was sensible enough for the Company to make at least a show of loyalty, no matter what the directors and Child privately hoped for the nation. And indeed, there is no direct evidence that Child shed his prin-

[58] Andrew Browning, *Thomas Osborne, Earl of Danby* (1944), I, 159, n. 4, and Chap. IX; II, 74–75. Salter to Danby (14 May 1675), in H.M.C. *Supp. Rept. on Lindsey MSS.* (1942), 10–12. That the King's intervention was not intended to stand as an attack on the Company as such is indicated by the fresh Crown Charter granted 15 October 1677, which stated that 'diverse transactions having happened, where the proceedings of the governor and company may be liable to some question, how far they are warranted, by the strict letter of the said charters . . .', therefore all the previous charters are reconfirmed: Scott, II, 139. Khan (194) explains the affair as royal retaliation for Child and Papillon's failure 'to supply the Navy with provision' when they held the victualling contract of 1672. In fact there was no such failure, but only a protracted delay in presenting their final accounts, or more probably, in persuading the Treasury to reach some settlement; see the sources cited in n. 55, p. 29 above. The accounts, in any event, were still not settled twenty-five years later: *Pap. Mem.,* 88–90. Why should the King have chosen 1676, rather than any other year between 1672 and 1685, as the appropriate time to show his displeasure?

[59] The Crown of course had a financial interest in creating baronets, each of whom, on being installed, paid into the Exchequer a sum sufficient to maintain 30 foot soldiers in Ulster for three years at 8*d.* a day, or £1,095 'which with fees, doth commonly arise to £1,200'; Chamberlayne, *Angliae Notitia* (1682), Pt. I, p. 306. Child paid his fee 20 July 1678: *C. Treas. Bks.,* V, 1062. If Charles II created 426 baronets, as has been said, the fees totalled over half a million pounds.

ciples for commercial advantage, though the opponents of
his policy were ready enough to accuse him of doing so; in
fact, the worst that they could establish was that he did work
with the ministers, for the time being successfully.

The occasion that called forth the first gesture of gener-
osity toward the King was an attack on the Company's
monopoly, one of those frequent attacks that became fiercer
as the Company established a firmer control over its trading
stations abroad and thereby a more powerful voice at home.
The chief antagonist, the Turkey Company, which had been
watching its own monopoly decay as a result of the other's
successes in an adjacent and sometimes overlapping area, became especially vexed when piracy in the Mediterranean
and tyranny in Turkey reached a peak, so that trade became
more risky and costly than usual. The Levant merchants
were so outraged, particularly by the exactions of the Grand
Signor, that they decided to retaliate with a boycott; and this
decision was all the more congenial—so at least Dudley
North, the Tory among them, suspected—because, as Whigs,
the merchants were not displeased with the decline in customs duties that their action would bring about. Recognizing
the danger, Charles threatened that should the Company
refuse to carry on the trade, others might be found to replace them. Upon this, they quickly conceded that they
would continue to send out annual ships if they could and
that if 'the continuance of their oppressions' stopped them
they were willing to declare the trade open to anyone at all.
But hardly had they concluded the arrangement than the
East India Company arrested several of their ships on the
ground that they had invaded its exclusive territory, and it
is not difficult to imagine the angry and yet plaintive tones
in which the Levant merchants would have asked the Privy
Council how they could continue to serve the King when
their best efforts were crushed by the exorbitant pretensions
of their rivals.[60]

As the dispute about detention of a few ships was only a
sign of conflicting claims between the two monopolies, the

[60] *Examen,* 462–66; Wood, 102–5; Privy Council Register, P.R.O.,
P.C. 2/69, f. 145 (10 Nov. 1680), f. 172 (27 Dec. 1680), f. 302
(16 June 1681).

Privy Council decided in June 1681 to review the whole problem. The Turkey Company submitted a paper, prepared by Sir John Buckworth and Dudley North, pleading that they be preferred to their rival.[61] They alleged in the first place that their business was more beneficial to the nation, because they exported about £500,000 worth of woollen goods and other English products and imported a great deal of raw silk and cotton that was subsequently worked up in England, all of which, exports and imports alike, gave employment to English labourers. The East India Company, on the other hand, injured the nation by exporting vast quantities of gold and silver, deprived English workmen of labour by importing finished calicoes and silk cloth, and sold at low prices the 'deceitful sort' of raw silk that they brought from India, to the 'infallible destruction of the Turkey trade'. Secondly, they said, the East India Company was much too exclusive. Their own, a regulated company, was open to any qualified merchant on payment of a small fee, whereas the East India Company, being organized on joint stock, could be entered only by buying some of a very small number of shares, whose ownership was, in fact, 'confined to the narrow compass of some few persons'. And the third great complaint was that the joint stock was too small to carry on the trade.

To supplement the stock, worth at most £370,000—so the Turkey Company's complaint continued—the East India Company had borrowed over £650,000 from the public. For the use of these funds, they paid only 3 per cent or 4 per cent, although they earned vastly more; and while they enjoyed these profits, they were immune from loss, since the Company, rather than its members, was the formal borrower and it alone was liable for repayment. In contrast, the Turkey Company, as such, had no capital and did no borrowing, but each member supplied his own capital and would

61 Privy Council Register, P.R.O., P.C. 2/69, ff. 302, 313, 329, 342, 346 (16 June–15 Aug. 1681); Ct. Bk. 33, f. 5a; *The Allegations of the Turkey Company and others against the East India Company . . . presented to the . . . Privy Council, the 17th of August 1681. Together with the answer of the said East India Company thereunto, delivered in writing the 22nd instant . . .* (Kress, 1526).

himself suffer the losses in case of failure. These comparisons proved, they maintained, that the Turkey Company
was more worthy of encouragement, and so they petitioned
the King's aid. They prayed that he might reconfirm exclusive right to trade in the Red Sea and all dominions of the
Grand Signor and to have free access to those areas by the
most convenient passages, despite any pretended privileges
of the East India Company; and they asked further that he
forbid the East India Company to import raw or wrought
silks into England. But if these requests should be thought
unreasonable, they petitioned that he order the East India
Company to put on sale additional stock so that the Turkey
merchants, who were losing their own trade to the East India merchants, could 'have some reparation by partaking of
theirs'.

The East India Company presently responded in a paper
drawn up by Child, Papillon, and others.[62] As to the first
allegation, they said that although the Privy Council could
undoubtedly discover the truth by checking the customs
house records, they themselves were certain they exported
more and better cloth than the Turkey Company, amounting recently to about 19,000 pieces a year, and that the Turkey Company was no less culpable than they themselves in
exporting gold and silver. As to the organization of their
trade, the experience of all European countries showed that
trade with the East Indies was best carried on by joint-stock
companies. To this, Child's favourite argument on the subject,[63] they added that their Company was by no means
so exclusive as the others alleged. If anything, it was more
open than the Turkey Company, for while the latter admitted only qualified merchants, such as had served appren-
ticeships, theirs was open to any Englishman at all that chose
to buy its stock. Furthermore, they denied that its stock was
so closely held as alleged; there were, they said, 600 share-
holders, and contrary to the assertion that a single share-
holder had over 80 votes—that is, owned over £40,000 of

[62] *Answer* . . . , printed with *Allegations* . . . , *op. cit.* n. 61, p.
33 above; the authors are identified in Ct. Bk. 32, f. 140a (19 Aug.
1681).
[63] N.D.T., Chap. III.

shares—no one owned as many as 60, although it would not matter if he did, because the Company's work benefited not only its owners and its employees, but many others. To the assertion that the Company lacked capital, they replied that, although the value of their joint stock was £370,000, their present stock in trade—their working capital—was at least £1,700,000. This was ample, and the Company did not wish to borrow, doing so only to oblige or not offend those who pressed them to accept loans even at so low a rate of interest as 3 per cent. Finally, they said, it could hardly be taken as a defect that they paid so low a rate. 'Whether a higher or lower interest be nationally disadvantageous or beneficial is an ancient theme which hath been learnedly and judiciously bandied in all ages and in most parts of the civilized world; and some of us have had the honour to argue that point before your lordships in the noble house of peers, where your lordships upon the question (as we remember) did resolve that the abatement of interest would tend to the increase of trade and advance the value of the lands of England.' This reference to the debate of 1669, and the disingenuous failure to mention that the House finally rejected the proposal to lower interest,[64] was one of several parting shots intended to convince the Privy Council that although the Turkey Company had suffered by the East India Company's activities, the rest of the nation had benefited.

Although there was little to choose between the two arguments considered in the abstract, the East India Company was evidently far more successful than its rival, and there were sound reasons in policy for giving it a good deal of leeway. But, as usual, the dispute was greatly complicated by political controversy. The East India Company was under criticism not only by its commercial rivals, but also by all those who believed that only Parliament had the right to grant monopolies,[65] or maintained that a joint stock company was too restrictive a form even for a monopoly, or felt that malpractice and fraud alone could have raised the price

[64] See above, p. 10.
[65] The argument was founded on the Statute of Monopolies (1624). See, for instance, *Two Letters concerning the East India Company* (1676; Kress, 1422), 5–6, 10.

of the Company's shares to almost three times their par
value. Nor was the court at this moment acting as a cham-
pion of corporate privilege. It had, on the contrary, adopted
the design of threatening municipal corporations with *Quo
warranto* suits unless they sent to Parliament men more
amenable than those who had just finished impeaching
Danby. And if the charters of great and ancient cities could
be revoked on flimsy pretexts, how would a young company
that had unmistakably exceeded its authority be able to with-
stand such attack? Surrounded by all these dangers, the
Company tried for a time to propitiate all the powers.

The Company made a concerted effort, for one thing, to
put its case before the public. It concluded its reply to the
Turkey Company with a request that the Privy Council
grant permission to publish the papers, and proceeded to
publish them immediately, with or without permission.[66] It
had already reprinted, just when the controversy began, a
pamphlet written, at Papillon's request, by Robert Ferguson,
the plotter, whose argument is summarized in the title, *The
East-India-Trade a most profitable trade to the Kingdom,
and best secured and improved in a company, and a joint
stock*.[67] And in the summer of 1681, it printed another
pamphlet written under the pseudonym of 'Philopatris'—
and since attributed, incorrectly, to Child—in which the author maintained that if the Company held its charter by
Act of Parliament 'it would be much better for the Kingdom in general'; that he, unlike most of the stockholders,
favoured extending the stock; and that this was as opportune
a time as any for Parliament to make whatever alterations

[66] *Allegations, op. cit.* n. 61, p. 33 above. The Privy Council Register does not record permission to print the papers, and the author of
An Arrest on the East India Privatier (1681), asserted that it was
printed without the Turkey Company's consent. The date of the
Arrest, 16 Sep. 1681, shows that the *Allegations* were published no
more than three weeks after the India Company submitted its answer to the Council.

[67] The pamphlet was originally published in 1677 as answer to the
Two Letters of 1676, and Ferguson was paid a gratuity for its composition by the East India Company; see Ct. Bk. 30, f. 185 (7 Feb.
1677). It was reprinted in 1680. See Appendix I.

it saw fit in the Company's constitution.[68] But the Company did not intend to commit itself to Parliament exclusively, and in order to balance this appeal to the popular party, the directors decided on 28 September 1681, that it would be 'highly for the Company's service that a present be made unto the King's Majesty of 10,000 guineas'.[69]

Although the directors and stockholders unanimously concurred in offering this gift to the King, the Company was by no means so unified in its attitude toward the proposal to widen the stock. One group of directors, Child at their head, opposed the measure; another, led by Papillon, favoured it. At first, Papillon's views were in the majority, and two days after voting the gift, the directors decided, though only after 'a very great debate', to suggest a plan for a new stock. Their representatives were to inform the Privy Council 'that they should be willing that this stock should be enlarged by a valuation of all their concerns, and a new subscription thereupon, or by 3 years notice according to his Majesty's charter, whenever his Majesty should find it for his own and the Kingdom's advantage'. Sir Joseph Ashe presently reported that having informed some privy councillors of the proposal to extend the stock, they replied 'that it was not fit to offer this when we made the present but the King should be made acquainted with it and in due time we should hear from him'. However, Papillon made another effort on 11 November, when the directors met to consider their petition for a proclamation against interlopers. The draft, apparently prepared by Papillon, recited some of the arguments they had submitted to the Council, prayed for relief against the interloping merchants who invaded their domain, and ended with a new offer of reorganization: 'And your petitioners do in all humility declare their willingness after three years from the 10th April next, if your Majesty shall please so to direct, to put a conclusion to the present Joint Stock, and in the meantime to lay open a book of subscription for all that will adventure in a new joint stock, to

[68] Philopatris, *A Treatise wherein is demonstrated . . . that the East India trade is the most national of all foreign trades . . .* (1681). See Appendix I.

[69] Ct. Bk. 32, f. 162a.

commence at the expiration of the said term, on such conditions as your Majesty shall think indifferent.' In the debate that followed, Child argued that the proposal was futile, since when it had last been made Sir Joseph Ashe 'said
the King would not do it'. It was replied that there was no
record of this answer—as indeed there is not—at which
Child became furious and exclaimed that the clause was
'brought in to do us a mischief'. Papillon, as he wrote in his
laconic notes on the incident, 'vindicated himself'. But the
directors now decided with Child to omit the offer, and
that they were correct in considering it superfluous, on this
occasion at least, became clear a few days later when
Charles signed the proclamation. The gift, the proclamation,
and the defeat of Papillon's plan were the first signs that the
Company was revising its earlier politics and reaching an
accommodation with the court.[70]

From this time on, the long association between Child and
Papillon dissolved at the same rate as the Company's alliance with the Government grew firmer. In 1682, Child was
re-elected Governor while Papillon was superseded by
Child's early supporter, Robert Thomson. A few weeks later,
when Child reported to the directors on the meeting of the
Privy Council that closed the dispute between the two companies, he remarked 'the satisfaction his Majesty and Council seemed to take in the present management of the affairs
of the Company'. That satisfaction must have increased in
1683, after Papillon failed to be re-elected a director and his
brother was discharged from the Company's employ. By
June of that year, it was being said that the Company intended to exclude all Whigs from membership, and this
report, though exaggerated in fact, certainly represented the
Company in the light it preferred to be seen.[71]

[70] Ct. Bk. 32, f. 162b (30 Sep. 1681), f. 164b (5 Oct. 1681), f.
165b (7 Oct. 1681); Pap. Mem., 82–83; A Proclamation for the re-
straining all his Majesty's subjects but the East India Company to
trade to the East Indies (16 Nov. 1681).

[71] Ct. Bk. 33, f. 1a (11 Apr. 1682), f. 5a (3 May 1682). Papillon failed to be re-elected on 17 April 1683, and his brother George
Papillon, was dismissed on 25 April (Ct. Bk. 33, ff. 134, 136b); on
the relation of George to Thomas, see Pap. Mem., 12; N. Harley to
Sir Edward Harley (2 June 1683), in H.M.C. Portland II, 236.

During the short reign of James II, the Company continued to enjoy its alignment with the Court. James II reconfirmed their charter and gladly took gifts in the form of Company stocks or bought stocks on his own account.[72]

But immediately after the Revolution, the association that had until then been such a benefit became a hindrance most unwelcome to a body that had to fight off a Whig Parliament (which put such men as Papillon in charge of investigating East India Company affairs) as well as a new Whig East India Company, founded by the interlopers and others who sought easy access to the profits of that trade. The practised criticisms of the old Company were now reproduced in a great series of pamphlets and orations, and a sharp attack was launched against Child and the old Company.

Hardly had the Convention Parliament opened its sessions before Child was called upon to defend himself against a charge of high misdemeanour for having arrested an interloping ship, the *Phoenix*. He pleaded the proclamation against interlopers as a defence, and eventually cleared himself. During the next years, a long series of other attacks was launched at the Company's management.[73] In this vulnerable situation, the Company evidently considered Child's reputation something of a liability, enough so that it was thought useful or necessary to suggest that he would soon relinquish his hold on the Company's reins. A pamphleteer, writing in defence of the Company, therefore let it be known that, although a single-handed rule had always been the principle of success in the Company's affairs, Child would soon withdraw from the management, 'being wearied with the fatigue of it, and want of health occasioned thereby', and indeed, it was hardly a matter of choice, he being 'near

[72] Papillon reported to the House of Commons that £3,000 of stock 'was purchased and transferred' to James during 1684, and 'that £7,000 stock more . . . to make up the former £3,000 stock to be £10,000 stock, was transferred . . . to King James his account . . . the 30th of November 1687'. C.J., X, 154 (28 May 1689). The wording leaves it ambiguous whether the stock was purchased or given as a gift, though the latter seems to be implied.

[73] Bod. Lib. Rawlinson MSS. A 170, ff. 148–75 (July 1689); Scott, II, 150 ff.

sixty years of age and sickly'. Despite this, however, Child
continued as a director of the Company during the few remaining years of his life; though he did give up his part in
the active management.[74]

At his death, he left behind a prodigious fortune,[75] and
a striking web of family alliances with the nobility. His
brother-in-law became the Duke of Chandos, a grand-
daughter the Duchess of Bedford, and a grandson the Duke
of Beaufort. But his connections were more elevated than
his personal reputation. Evelyn thought him an 'overgrown
and suddenly monied' man, 'most sordidly avaricious'. Burnet, less antagonistic, after praising his ability, and discount-
ing the envy and jealousy which his remarkably skilful
leadership of the East India Company brought down on the
Company and himself, yet concluded: 'he was vain and
covetous, and a thought too cunning, though to me he
seemed always sincere.'[76]

[74] *Answer to all the material objections against the present East
India Company* (n.d.) Child was born in 1630, so that the statement
about his age, if exact, must have been made in 1690 at the latest;
the context shows that the pamphlet was written no earlier than 1688.
The same argument is advanced in 'Humble Answer of the Governor . . .' (1692), in *Somers' Tracts*, 3rd Series (1751), III, 189. Cf.
Papillon to Child (22 Oct. 1698) and Child to Papillon (22 Oct.
1698), in *Pap. Mem.*, 88–90. Cf. Child to Robert Blackborne, Secretary of the Company (7 Nov. 1693): 'I have discontinued our courts
so many years that I am not willing to be at any hereafter, but whenever the company please to make use of any advise or experience I
have I shall serve them faithfully so far as will consist with my resolved retirement.' Bod. Lib. Rawlinson MSS. A303, f. 265.

[75] His will disposed of landed estates in the form of manors and
smaller holdings chiefly at Wanstead, Halstead, Cannon, and Pars-
lowe, in Essex, and various real estate in London; of which the total
value appears to have been about £150,000, yielding an income of
about £7,500. (Child regularly capitalized landed income at 5 per
cent.) There were cash bequests of about £20,000, and a residue
of property in the form of mercantile goods and East India Company
stock whose value is not given. (The will is at Somerset House: Prerogative Court of Canterbury, 111, Pett.) It is known that in 1691
Child's East India Company stock amounted to over £50,000 in face
value (cf. n. 52, p. 28 above), and assuming that he held this amount
until his death, it follows that his total estate was well in excess of
£200,000.

[76] Evelyn, IV, 305–6 (16 Mar. 1683); Burnet, *History of My Own
Time* (1823), IV, 403–4.

To many other observers, Child seemed anything but sincere. He was a merchant, and a merchant was always suspect, but never as suspect as when he urged the State to adopt a policy which obviously benefited merchants, while its supposedly beneficial effect on the nation was more remote and dubious. This long-standing attitude towards merchants was bound to colour the view taken of Child's advocacy in 1668 of a lower rate of interest. Child himself asserted that English merchants would compete more successfully with the Dutch if their interest charges were to be lessened by law, which was but to confess that Child hoped to gain by the change. The only persons who would obviously stand to lose were lenders, and it was out of the question that Child, at this time an active importer and trader, only later to be described as a 'suddenly monied' man, should have been a lender. The chief proposal of the *Brief Observations* seemed, to those who insisted on thinking in such terms, a piece of pure special pleading.

As for the auxiliary points of the *Brief Observations,* the other fourteen signs of Holland's commercial wisdom, they too could be explained in this way. Of course a merchant might think it laudable and desirable that merchants should be seated on Councils of State, that their ships should be convoyed at the public expense, and that special law courts with special laws should be maintained for their convenience. The argument for toleration, advanced not only by Child but also by Papillon and most of the other merchants who testified before the Lords' Committee of 1669, could also be explained away as an interested plea, a mere reflection of their own non-conformity, a request that they be admitted to new privileges, disingenuously dressed as an argument that the revision would improve the nation's trade.

There were other virtues of Holland, virtues that Child urged England speedily to adopt as policies, but whose connection with Child's personal interests was not so easy to detect. But the chief point was that all these virtues were the virtues of Holland and there was very good reason why a man like Child should take the trouble to extol Holland. It was one of the common attributes of a member of the Faction, an adherent of the Shaftesbury group, a fanatic—as sound royalists identified Child in 1668—that he should laud a republic, whose laws were directed at commercial supremacy, and whose constitution was equally antagonistic to royalty and to established religion. These fanatic merchants were not so enamoured of Holland that their avarice might not drive them to wish it defeated by arms, and old Royalists like Clarendon were disgusted by how mercenary were the motives that brought on the Anglo-Dutch War of 1665.[77] But envy and emulation do not lie far apart, and the reasons why London merchants hoped to see Holland beaten were the same as those which made them want to see Holland's policies established in England. So ran the Tory argument, and the Whiggish merchant was put to endless trouble reasserting his loyalty to the Crown and, if not loyalty to the Church, at least his willingness to abide by the laws against dissent until they could be repealed—shortly, he hoped.

How deep and entrenched the suspicion of merchants had become is evident from the manner in which the *Brief Observations* was republished in 1690. It reappeared as a *Discourse about Trade*, which included several additional chapters, one of which argued strongly in defence of the East India Company's monopoly as essential, lawful, and a great contribution to the public good.[78] The occasion for publishing it at that moment seems to have been that Parliament was once again considering a Bill to reduce interest from 6 per cent to 4 per cent.[79] But it might at the same time have served to defend the Company just when it was under concentrated attack, and to put before an energetic, reforming Parliament the whole of Child's programme of liberalizing legislation, including revision of the laws on religion, inheritance, property and apprenticeship. Moreover, the defence of the Company, when surrounded with such proposals, might itself be improved by their nobility. But there would evidently be no point in spoiling the effect by identifying these views with Child. The *Discourse* was, therefore, published anonymously. During the twenty years

---

[77] Cf. Charles Wilson, *Profit and Power* (1957).
[78] See Appendix I.
[79] *C.J.*, X, 433, 440, 484 (Oct.–Nov. 1690), 550 *et seq.* (1691).

that had passed since the *Brief Observations* was first published, many would have forgotten it and its author's name, if indeed they had ever known who 'J.C.' was.

Moreover, the publisher, in his Preface to the *Discourse*, obscured the authorship further by an elaborate smoke-screen. The manuscript, he explained in the first place, had come into his hands 'very accidentally'. Having discerned in it 'much experimental truth and reason', he had solicited permission to print it, which the author had granted, though, it was made to appear, with the utmost reluctance. The author would not allow his name to be divulged. 'But this I may truly say,' continued the publisher, 'he is no trader, neither pays any use [interest] for money but receives a great deal yearly, and hath to my knowledge a considerable estate in lands, and therefore the most invidious cannot conceive he had any private or selfish end in the following discourses.' The reader, it was clear, might be expected to raise invidious questions.

The publisher's comment, supposed to still all doubts, was a wonderful mixture of fact, fancy and *non sequitur*. It was less than candid to say that Child was not a merchant, even though it might be true that he had given up trading on his own account in order better to conduct the Company's trade. He may well by now have been a lender rather than a borrower, and have had no incentive on that score to see interest reduced; though the Company, on the other hand, was a very considerable borrower,[80] so that what he was apt to gain as chief investor in the Company might easily exceed the losses he would suffer as a lender. This seems plausible enough on its face; and it is quite certain that had Child's name been attached to the *Discourse*, critics would quickly have drawn the conclusion that this was in fact his motive. Moreover, although the publisher was telling nothing but the truth when he said that Child had a considerable estate in land,[81] the implication that Child was, therefore, indifferent to the interest rate is false; for Child himself asserted that the value of land inevitably rises when interest rates fall. Finally, the greatest flaw was, of course, an omis-

[80] Scott, II, 128–65.
[81] See above, n. 75, p. 40.

sion; the publisher neglected to mention that the author had some connection with the old East India Company.

The effect that this revelation would have had is easy enough to judge, for in 1693 the *Discourse* reappeared as *A New Discourse of Trade,* with Child's name prominently displayed on the title page. Why he should have left the shelter of anonymity, if shelter it still was, is not clear. But he did, and recrimination followed quickly. His critics, overlooking his protestations of objectivity, insisted that his 'private interest is so great in the East India trade . . . that I doubt [fear] he is no competent judge of the public interest of the nation'. They noticed that he favoured regulated companies in general, but excepted the East India trade from the rule on the grounds that peculiar conditions required it to be managed by a joint-stock company; and they explained that 'his private interest has led him to contradict himself and his own propositions . . . and showed the world how difficult a thing it is for some men to be impartial where private interest comes to stand in competition with the public'.[82]

There is no persuasive evidence for or against the presumption that Child wrote to advance his private interests. Child may have been proposing what he sincerely believed to be in the public interest; he may have been utterly cynical; his motives may have been mixed; there is no way of telling. The presumption arose readily, because he was a merchant writing about economic policy. Had he been a lawyer, theologian or poet, the doubts of his sincerity would not have arisen quite so spontaneously; though they might have done had he been, for instance, a poet advocating public support of poets. But whether in his particular case the suspicion was justified or not, it was characteristic; and economic writers had not yet devised any means by which they could decisively refute the accusation of mercenary intent.

[82] *The Interest of England Considered* (1694), 66. *Discourse concerning the East-India Trade* [1693] (Brit. Mus. 100 n. 40), 2.

IV

In time, and with frequent reprinting of the *New Discourse,* Child came to be the most widely read of seventeenth-century English economic writers. Eventually, historians of economic thought, reading the *New Discourse* but forgetting who its author was, enrolled him among the early forerunners of Adam Smith; he was, they said, an advocate of *laissez-faire,* albeit of a fragmentary and unformed sort, and also a great innovator of abstract economic theory. Their view has a foundation, though a slight one, in that some of Child's words resemble some of Smith's; but Child's outlook, considered as a whole and in its own setting, was radically unlike Smith's in policy and theory alike.

The utterances that have led to Child's identification as a free-trader are very near the surface of his work. Child has been credited, for instance, with a very advanced attitude toward immigration. He did certainly mention among the laudable policies of the Netherlands 'their toleration of different opinions in matters of religion'; by reason of which, he pointed out, 'many industrious people of other countries, that dissent from the established government of their own churches, resort to them with their families and estates, and after a few years' cohabitation with them, become of the same common interest'.[83] And elsewhere in the *New Discourse* Child advocated that England should imitate this policy, should moreover freely admit foreigners to naturalization, and among them even Jews.[84] That this policy should be described as liberal and humane is reasonable enough, but that it has anything to do with the doctrine of *laissez-faire* is questionable. In Child's version, at least, it follows from the principle that the first general rule for the enlargement of trade is to 'increase hands in trade',[85] and this rule, when translated into the proposition that national wealth increases as population increases, is easily recognizable as a

[83] *B.O.,* 5.
[84] *N.D.T.,* Chap. VII.
[85] *N.D.T.,* 168.

conventional mercantilist principle. It is true that some mercantilists opposed easy naturalization, for many reasons,[86] but all of them accepted the basic principle; and if Child differs in this, it is not because he disowned mercantilism but because he took a position that might perhaps be described as The Higher Mercantilism.

The same is true of his declaration, so liberal in appearance, that the monopolistic privileges of cities, guilds and trading companies should be abolished, and that the laws preventing the practice of a trade without serving an apprenticeship be repealed.[87] He urged that foreign trade—except that with the East Indies—be opened to anyone who chose to engage in it; and the argument is studded with catchwords suggestive of *laissez-faire*. In answering the objection that if everyone were allowed to trade many would ruin themselves, he wrote, 'Caveat Emptor, Let particular men look to themselves'. In answer to the further objection that they would not export enough English manufactures, but would be inclined instead to export money, he responded that they 'are like all other men (led by their profit) and if it be for their advantage to send out manufactures, they will do it without forcing'.[88] So far the analysis is distinctly free-trade in its bearing, but this is merely an appearance. A free-trader would have continued, in the well-known manner, that if the unlicensed trader exported coin, it would be just as well, for the nation could not long suffer either a deficit or surplus of money, and in any case the object of trade was neither to have a 'favourable' balance nor to accumulate bullion. But Child took quite an opposite position, and accepting as axiomatic that accumulation of bullion is the object of foreign trade, maintained that the unlicensed trader would be

[86] Papillon, for instance, told the Lords' Committee of 1669 that there ought to be free naturalization for all, with one proviso, 'that they be such foreigners as might and would incorporate into the nation . . . for that otherwise, I conceived that they would suck the riches and treasures of the nation, and in the end carry it away to other countries: I instanced the Jews that would never incorporate with us . . .'. (*Pap. Mem.*, 71.)

[87] N.D.T., pp. [xxxix–xl], 140–41.

[88] N.D.T., 106–8.

no more or less liable to export bullion than the merchants who belonged to trading companies.[89]

No doubt Child opposed certain mercantilist restrictions, as many other mercantilists did, but he did not oppose them in principle. He objected to those restrictions which embarrassed the branches of industry that concerned him and consistently advocated restrictions that fostered those branches. His position was exactly analogous with that of a textile manufacturer, for instance, who opposes import restrictions or protective duties on the fibres he buys while insisting that heavy duties be placed on foreign finished goods that compete with those he sells; and such a manufacturer might, as Child did, use the phraseology of free-trade when he attacks that variety of protection which is damaging to his interests.

It is for this reason that Child's resounding maxims are so contradictory in effect. They seem to paraphrase 'Laissez-faire!': 'All restrictions of trade are naught.' 'Advantage of trade would have all freedom laid open.'[90] But what they mean is that all freedom should be laid open to some people. The man who advocated above all that interest rates be reduced by law did not mean that *all* restrictions on trade were naught. His objective may be obscured but cannot be altered by the slogans he used. He might borrow Petty's liberal maxim, 'Nature must and will have its course', but instead of using it to show that some restrictive regulation was futile, he turned it to a more congenial purpose: 'the matter in England is prepared for an abatement of interest, and it cannot long be obstructed.'[91] The intellectual foundation of his policies is much better represented by a maxim he pronounced before the Lords' Committee, 'All trade [is] a kind of warfare'.[92]

Child's words belie their appearance not because he spoke the language of free-trade with the faltering tongue of one first discovering it, but rather in the ambiguous terms of one who speaks it only when a superior principle dictates

[89] N.D.T., 108.
[90] N.D.T., 103; M.B., f. 4.
[91] B.O., 17.
[92] M.B., f. 6.

that it is appropriate. Thus he wrote: 'If we would engage other nations to trade with us, we must receive from them the fruits and commodities of their countries as well as send them ours', a sentiment whose apparent meaning is altered by the hasty and emphatic qualification, 'but it's our interest by example and other means (not distasteful) above all kinds of commodities to prevent, as much as may be, the importation of foreign manufactures'. In further discussion of this policy Child revealed his thorough mercantilism, endorsing its methods as well as its objective of maintaining a favourable balance of trade—'gold and silver being taken for the measure and standard of riches'. His exposition of this doctrine in one concrete case, for instance, is as follows:

> The trade for Canary wines I take to be a most pernicious trade to England, because those Islands consume very little of our manufactures, fish, or other English commodities; neither do they furnish us with any commodities to be further manufactured here or re-exported; the wines we bring from thence being for the most part purchased with ready money; so that, to my apprehension, something is necessary to be done to compel those Islanders to spend more of our English commodities, and to sell their wines cheaper (which every year they advance in price) or else to lessen the consumption of them in England.[93]

'Example and other means (not distasteful)' gave way to 'compel'; the commerce was judged 'pernicious' according to the doctrine of particular balance of trade; the export of bullion was treated as more damaging than the export of goods; and altogether the passage brilliantly vindicates Smith's description of mercantilist thought. Indeed, in this, and in the general spirit of his thought, Child was not an intellectual ancestor of Smith, but as nearly as anyone can be the perfect example of the chief antagonists whom Smith attacked.

How easily the seventeenth-century merchant's demand for the removal of burdensome regulation can be con-

[93] N.D.T., 175–77, 153, Chap. IX.

founded with the principle that all regulation is burdensome is shown by Ashley's inclusion of Child among the
Tory free-traders.[94] Ashley's example turns out to be even
more unfortunate when it is remembered that the *New Discourse* though published after 1690, was composed about
1670, at which time Child was a notable 'Whig'. Far from
being a Tory free-trader, Child was, in so far as the terms
have any distinct meaning, a Whig mercantilist.

If, from the standpoint of economic policy, Child has little
claim to be considered a great innovator, what can be said
of his contribution to abstract economic theory? Was Child
one of those merchants who, as Schumpeter would have it,
enlarged the growing body of economic theory with bits of
insight garnered from his great commercial experience?[95]
There is but little in Child's writing to justify this opinion.
Most of it cannot by any stretch of the imagination be called
economic theory, or be said to rest on implicit economic
theory. Most of it consists of facts that are supposed to prove
the value of a policy or disprove the validity of objections to
the policy. On some rare occasions Child made general statements, but these were more often *clichés* than theoretical
principles. The statement, for example, that great population makes a country rich, was old by Child's time, and
though it may have been true then, it was merely an accidental truth, a prejudice that happened to conform to
reality.[96] It could have been elevated to a theoretical statement only by showing the mechanism whereby population
affects wealth, by analysing the causal relation between
them, but this Child failed to do.

Only at two or three points in the whole of the *New
Discourse* did Child produce a bit of theoretical analysis

[94] W. J. Ashley, 'Tory Origin of Free Trade Policy', in *Surveys,
Historic and Economic* (1900), 268.

[95] J. A. Schumpeter, *Economic Doctrine and Method* (Aris trans.,
1954), 24–26. He speaks of Child's works, with King's, Gee's and
others, 'as examples of a primitive economic theory and of the way in
which it grew into a scientific system of economics'.

[96] Schumpeter's analysis of *why* it was true in that time is based on
modern economic theory and there is no reason to suppose that Child
knew why. J. A. Schumpeter, *History of Economic Analysis* (1954),
251 ff.

properly speaking. The most powerful of these occurs in the course of defending his proposition that the colonies did not depopulate England, when, after invoking a great deal of his usual factual evidence, he maintained that if too many Englishmen emigrated the situation would naturally correct itself: 'for much want of people would procure greater wages, and greater wages . . . would procure us a supply of people . . .'[97] This analysis, simple as it is, transforms what would otherwise be a mere dogmatic assertion into a bit of theory; but it is exactly this sort of analysis that Child very nearly always omitted.

Whether Child understood his subject well enough so that he could have supplied such analyses on request cannot be known. Schumpeter credited him with a general awareness that all economic phenomena respond to the same laws and result from a single system of causes.[98] The awareness can at best have been only a very uneven one; to assert that labourers will be attracted by high wages while denying that capital will be attracted by high interest rates does not demonstrate a vivid sense that economic phenomena are uniform in character. However, our uncertainty as to the condition of Child's inner mind cannot be resolved. What remains is the fact that Child never set down any systematic analysis of economic relations,[99] and his influence on the development of scientific economics, if any, must therefore have been quite mystical.

To say that Child's work lacks system is not to maintain that he was irrational or that he merely threw together a mass of random reflections. The defect was caused not by

[97] N.D.T., 187.

[98] Schumpeter, op. cit. n. 96, p. 49 above, 196, 242, 290–91, 362–64. Schumpeter's admiration of Child seems to rest heavily on a statement by Philopatris to the effect that precious metals are commodities and that it is therefore of no greater importance to the nation that they be imported or exported than that any other commodity be; Philopatris (op. cit. n. 68, p. 37 above), 4. But Child did not write the Philopatris pamphlet; see Appendix I below, pp. 253 ff. Moreover, the New Discourse clearly takes the older view, associated with Mun, that bullion ought to be exported freely whenever it appears that the effect of its exportation will be a net import of bullion, but not otherwise: N.D.T., 73.

[99] As Schumpeter concedes: ibid., 242.

deficiencies of mind but of method. The method was not even very satisfactory as a polemic device. All the good reasons in the world cannot obliterate the possibility that there are good reasons, better reasons, against a policy. All the objections refuted are but a reminder that more forceful objections may not have been refuted. But ineffective as it may have been in point of rhetoric, Child's method was of no use at all in theoretical work, and his economic writing did nothing to advance economics.

Child is of great interest in the history of economic thought precisely because, however one classifies him, whether as a mercantilist, liberal or something between, and whatever one makes of his personal motives, he is the example *par excellence* of the economic writer working in the old style just as it was being superseded by the first scientific economists. Such contemporaries of Child as William Petty and Dudley North faced the same problems as he did. They too were anything but detached; whether merchants or civil servants, practical men or not, all were partisans, fighting for particular policies; they aimed at persuading their fellows to act in certain ways rather than at teaching them new truths. Yet, despite their practical intention, or rather as the most effective means of realizing it, they based their polemics on distinctly scientific theories of economics which they devised for the purpose. Their science was inspired by the needs of rhetoric, and men who were no more interested than Child in promoting objectivity created in this uncommon way an objective theory.

Chapter 2

NICHOLAS BARBON: PROJECTOR

I

In 1690, at almost the same moment that Josiah Child's old treatise reappeared as *A Discourse about Trade*, a very similar document, composed by Nicholas Barbon, was published under the title *A Discourse of Trade*. Similarities between the authors there were not a few: Barbon, like Child, was something of a buccaneer, though much more blatantly so, at once more outrageous and less sinister than the sombre mogul of the East India Company. Both of them, businessmen in every moment of living, took to the pen to write tracts that merit their reputation as among the better early works on economics. And the works share the same major defects: despite all the bits of wisdom accumulated by the authors, men exceptionally gifted and long engaged in active affairs—bits that lie scattered in odd corners of the tracts—their works taken as wholes are neither disinterested nor systematic. To put it more exactly, Barbon, like Child, indulges in special pleading so transparent as to be comic, and a willingness to meander from one thing to the barely connected next that is more commonly met in family letters than in scientific papers. Barbon, like Child, is an example, no mean example, of the Old Style economic writer.

As Child's life is an epitome of the Restoration mercantile magnate, so Barbon's is the type of the late seventeenth-century 'projector'. His heritage suited him to boldness in his profession, for his father was that Barbon whose name has been immortalized in 'Barebone's Parliament', the house that sat during the last years of the Interregnum and enjoyed the displeasure of all parties. The elder Barbon—of whom it was said that he was blessed with the Christian name, 'Unless-Jesus-Christ-Had-Died-For-Thee-Thou-Hadst-Been-Damned', but who passed in society under the handier, if not less pious, name of Praisegod—was by religion a Paedo-baptist fanatic and by trade a leather merchant of London. Into such surroundings Nicholas was born in 1637.[1]

His education would seem of little relevance to his career were it not that two other of the principal economic writers of the period, Petty and Locke, also studied medicine, as did still other contemporaries prominently involved in economic policy, such as Benjamin Worsley and Hugh Chamberlen. Perhaps medicine, especially as it was then taught in the Lowlands, was one of the few academic disciplines that could appeal to energetic young men interested in the modern learning rather than the ancient, and ambitious ones, who wanted an education that could be put to work. Whatever may have been the reasons, Barbon studied at Leyden, and at Utrecht, where he took the degree of MD in 1661. He was admitted an Honorary Fellow of the College of Physicians at London in 1664; yet, although he was referred to as Dr Barbon to the end of his life, he does not seem to have practiced medicine for long.[2]

He became instead a builder, soon the most prominent London builder of his age. His talents in bargaining and raising capital, if not in architecture, were considerable, and fortune obliged him by arranging the Great Fire just before he was starting. Another fire in 1678 procured him a commission to rebuild much of the Middle Temple, in the course of which work he became acquainted with Roger North —a bencher of the Temple and brother of Sir Dudley North —to whom we owe most of the facts, if facts they are, about Barbon's business practices.

North tells, not without a certain cynical delight, how

[1] PRAISEGOD BARBON: North, *Autobiography* (1887), 53. DNB. Wheatley, *London Past and Present*, II, 62. BIRTHDATE: On registering at Leyden in 1661, he gave his age as 24; cf. *Album Studiosorum, Acad. Lug. Bat.* (1875), 490.

[2] *Album Stud.* (*op. cit.* n. 1 above). *Album Promotorum Acad. Rheno-Trajectina* 17. Munk, *Roll of the Roy. Coll. of Physicians* (1878), I, 345. Luttrell, IV, 409.

badly Barbon built—'He had like to have lost his trade by slight building in Mincing Lane, where all the vaults for want of strength fell in, and houses came down most scandalously'; how he financed his operations by never paying bills until his creditors won judgments in the highest courts (his will directs the executor to pay none of his outstanding debts); and how he browbeat and disregarded anyone who stood in his way. Roger North reports that he once asked Barbon

how he did to take off opposition when he was upon a design that concerned many, whom it would be very chargeable to buy off directly, as when a hundred or more old houses were to be pulled down to accommodate a building design.

To which Barbon replied:

He never bought off all, but only some few of the leaders and most angry of them. . . . He appointed a meeting. They would certainly be early at the place, and confirm and hearten one another to stand it out, for the Doctor must come to their terms. So they would walk about and pass their time expecting the Doctor, and inquiring if he were come. At last word was brought that he was come. Then they began to get towards the long table (in a tavern dining-room for the most part) for the Doctor was come! The Doctor was come! Then he would make his entry, as fine and as richly dressed as a lord of the bedchamber on a birthday. And I must own I have often seen him so dressed, not knowing his design, and thought him a coxcomb for so doing. Then these hard-headed fellows that had prepared to give him all the affronts and opposition that their brutal way suggested, truly seeing such a brave man, pulled off their hats, and knew not what to think of it. And the Doctor also being (forsooth) much of a gentleman, then with a mountebank speech to these gentlemen he proposed his terms, which, as I said, were ever plausible, and terminated in their interest. Perhaps they were, at this, all converted in a moment, or perhaps a sour clown or two did not understand his tricks, or would not trust him, or would take counsel, or some blundering opposition they gave; while the rest gaped and stared, he was all honey, and a real friend; which not doing he quarrelled, or bought off, as I said, and then at the next meeting some came over, and the rest followed. It mattered not a litigous knave or two, if any such did stand out, for the first thing he did was to pull down their houses about their ears, and build upon their ground, and stand it out at law till their hearts ached, and at last they would truckle and take any terms for peace and a quiet life.[3]

Given his peculiar talents he could operate on a large scale, as he intended. For, as he told Roger North, 'It was not worth his while to deal little. That a bricklayer could do. The gain he expected was out of great undertakings, which would rise lustily in the whole.' Whether the gains materialized we cannot be certain, but the great undertakings certainly did. About 1675 he built up the Essex House estate, on a site stretching from the Strand to the river; and about the same time York Buildings, the Duke of Buckingham's estate near the west end of the Strand. Indeed almost all of his developments were placed along the western edges of the City of London, as it then was, to take advantage of the spread of population in that direction. Perhaps the biggest of these projects was the building of Red Lion Square during the middle of the 1680s, a work which so offended his neighbours at Gray's Inn that they charged into unarmed but victorious battle against his labourers, and used their distinguished legal skills to procure warrants 'for the suppression of Dr Barbon and his men from committing any insolence in their late riotous meeting in Red Lyon Fields and to prevent them from annoying his Majesty's subjects'. But neither this nor other attacks in the courts stopped Barbon, and he continued until the end of his life in 1698 to build throughout the chosen area, and to negotiate in his characteristic style. Many ended by refusing to deal with him further, but there were others, who knew him perhaps

[3] Roger North, *Autob.*, 56–57.

only by his works, that had a contrary impression; even so sober a lawyer and elevated a minister as Sir John Lowther said that 'Dr Bairbones has, in this Town, not laid out less than £200,000 [in speculative development], for which, in my opinion, he deserves more of the public than any subject in England'. If the sum mentioned is at all near the truth, then Barbon deserves at least the reputation of a great mobilizer of capital, for £200,000 was about as much as a tycoon on the scale of Josiah Child accumulated during his whole life, or as much as the Bank of England held as vault cash during its first years.[4]

Speculative building was not Barbon's only enterprise. He also pioneered, with characteristic imagination and rashness, in two of the great financial innovations that transformed the English economy toward the end of the seventeenth century, insurance and banking.

Insurance, like building, was much encouraged by the Great Fire, but being an art whose principles were as yet little known, it took some time coming into being. A series of proposals for fire insurance, the most important being that of the merchant, Augustine Newbold, were put forward during the 1670s, considered, but allowed to languish. To Barbon belongs the honour of establishing the first operative scheme. His company, the 'Insurance Office for Houses', was heralded in a prospectus, issued in 1680, which explained that Barbon and his eleven associates would insure up to 5,000 houses in London, for terms up to thirty-one years, and that ground-rents in London worth £2,100 annually had been settled on trustees as a reserve fund, a fund that would increase with the number of houses insured.

Almost immediately competitors entered the field. First the City of London proposed to take action it had been considering since 1670, offering to do so at rates lower than Barbon's. A pamphlet war, of the sort traditional in the seventeenth century and on a scale befitting so small a matter, ensued. Barbon said it might appear 'that the gentle-

---

[4] John Summerson, *Georgian London* (1945), 22–35. N. G. Brett-James, *Growth of Stuart London* (1935), 324–49. Sir John Lowther to William Gilpin (19 Feb. 1697), quoted in Nathanial Lloyd, *History of the English House* (1949 ed.), 143.

men of the [City] Committee did not well understand the design they were about; for which they are not to be blamed; for it is not reasonable to expect that they should so well (on a sudden) understand a design as the inventor of it, who had spent much time and study in the contrivance'. The Corporation, not to be outdone, answered that they could manage an insurance company better than a 'foreigner'—Barbon had presumably not been admitted a Freeman of London— 'whose chamber door daily suffers an assault and battery from a whole posse of bricklayers, carpenters, masons, etc., and who, if one may judge by the several actions of debt that every term are brought against him, is in a fair way to retire for refuge into one of his own chambers, which he hath built in the Temple'. But the City shortly found itself engaged in the great charter struggle, in which Papillon and Dudley North played such notable parts and the Court Party emerged victorious; it was too hard pressed trying to preserve its old established powers to think of undertaking new functions.[5]

Another competitor appeared in the City's place. William Hale and Henry Spelman established in 1684 The Friendly Society, a mutual insurance company, which within a year had insured 1,000 houses. Although Barbon's company by now was supposed to be insuring 4,000,

[5] P. G. M. Dickson, *The Sun Insurance Office, 1710–1960* (1960), 5–16; Horsefield, 106–7. The City's decision was apparently announced in Mayor Moore, *At a Common Council . . . 16 Nov. 1681 . . . Upon reading of proposals . . . presented . . . for Insuring of Houses in Cases of Fire.* BM 816 m. 10 (70); Horsefield No. 38. The Insurance Office published two answers in short order, which may have been written by Barbon, though there is nothing to establish this: *An Enquiry, Whether it be the interest of the City to insure houses from fire . . .* [1681], Kress 1533; and *Observations on the proposals of the City to insure houses in cases of fire* (1681), Kress, Supp. 625. But the literature of the controversy was more extensive than this, including at least the sources of the passages quoted by Dickson (pp. 8–9) and above. Evidence that the City actively engaged in fire insurance, contrary to the suggestion in Dickson (p. 9), is offered by a contract in the Kress Library, dated 5 May 1682, in which the City insures William Stephens' house, for an amount of £100, at a premium of £3 8s. 6d. for fifteen years; and endorsed '10 Feb. 1684/Recd. the contents of the within policy / . . . Wm. Stephens'. Luttrell, I, 135.

he nevertheless found the rivalry uncomfortable enough to warrant an assault by pamphlet, which of course evoked a counterblast. Both companies surviving this engagement, Barbon turned to his great ally, the law, and in 1687 petitioned the Privy Council for a monopoly of fire insurance in London. James II, after hearing both parties and on the advice of ministers, ordered a grant of letters patent for a monopoly to Barbon's rivals; which judgment, however, Barbon succeeded in persuading the King to annul. That episode left no permanent mark on either the contestants or the industry, which slowly expanded and soon became a commonplace among economic institutions. The Insurance Office, renamed the Phenix Office, outlived Barbon by a generation.[6]

Barbon's other big financial venture was in banking. In 1695, shortly after the Government's pressing need for funds had induced it to accede to the formation of the Bank of England, Barbon and John Asgill opened another sort of bank. It was a land bank, following somewhat the models proposed by Hugh Chamberlen and John Briscoe, but whereas the paper money (or interest-bearing bills of credit) that their banks proposed to issue would be secured solely on landed property, the issues of the Barbon-Asgill bank were to be secured on capital subscribed mainly in the form of cash and only in small proportion in the form of titles to land. All three land banks were similar—as have been their numerous successors among farm banks and building societies—in proposing to invest largely or exclusively in mortgages. The notion was an attractive one, for it promised landowners a new ease in raising capital, but it was strange and suspect, for it seemed a magical way of manufacturing money out of mere paper.

For one moment it seemed that the land bank might win a status as official and secure as that of the Bank of England.

6 Dickson, *op. cit.* n. 5, p. 57 above, *ibid.* N[icholas] B[arbon], *A letter to a Gentleman in the Country, Giving an Account of the Two Insurance Offices* . . . (London, Milbourn, 26 Jan. 1684 [85?]), BM 816 m. 10 (74). H[enry] S[pelman], *An Answer to a Letter to a Gentleman in the Country* . . . (London, Horton, 1684 [85]). On the dispute before the Privy Council, see H.M.C. 75, *Downshire I*, 282, 287.

In 1696, when the Government's current deficit was peculiarly large, Barbon and Briscoe merged their concerns into the Land Bank United, which offered to lend the Government £2,000,000, in return for which Parliament would settle on the Bank an annual income of £140,000, secured on revenues from the salt duty. A coalition in the House of Commons, led by Paul Foley, the Speaker, and Edward Harley, passed a Bill authorizing the acceptance of these terms, provided that one-half of the total loan had been subscribed to the Bank by August of 1696. This time was, however, the worst that could have been chosen for opening a subscription, since England's stock of money had just been run down to a bare minimum by the beginning of the Great Recoinage. In the end only three subscribers appeared, offering a total of £2,100, and the 'Government' Land Bank ended in a fiasco. The merger was dissolved, the Barbon-Asgill Bank limped along on its own for only two years longer, and was wound up soon after Barbon died.[7]

Barbon's inventiveness as an entrepreneur, though considerable, was not eccentric, for fire insurance and mortgage banking were obvious ancillaries to his chief occupation. So were a few other undertakings that he is known to have initiated, such as a scheme for a new pump to bring water up to the development sites.[8] Only when Barbon was writing his economic pamphlets does his mind seem to have strayed from his immediate commercial concerns. But it remains to be seen how far those writings stemmed from an abstract interest in knowledge or a disinterested desire to promote better public policies.

II

Of Barbon's writings, a number are of no importance as economic theory. His pamphlets and broadsheets on fire in-

[7] Horsefield, Chap. 16.

[8] Brett-James, 346 and *passim*. Barbon procured a patent for the new pump in 1694, and shortly thereafter offered to sell contracts for water delivery together with fire insurance policies. [Barbon], *An Advertisement, being a proposal by Dr Barbon and partners* . . . (1694, br.), Kress Supp. 778.

surance and the land bank[9] are straightforward pieces of advertising, sometimes distributed gratis by the managers. Another pamphlet, *Apology for the Builder*, although by no means a work of pure speculation, transcends advertising. It was, to be sure, a by-product of Barbon's development at Red Lion Square and the battle that it provoked between his workmen and the members of Gray's Inn. In July of 1684, the Justices of Middlesex County reported to the Privy Council that a Grand Jury had protested against the continued building in the County, especially by Barbon; and the Justices expressed their 'sense of the many great inconveniences occasioned by the late increase of buildings . . .', thus harping on a theme that had accounted for repeated, futile efforts, since the time of Elizabeth, to restrict London's growth, and for repeated allusions to the danger, in Hobbes' famous metaphor, of London becoming 'too large a head for England's body'. Barbon defended himself at law against the Justices' attack, but the more interesting defensive manoeuvre was *The Apology*, published anonymously during 1685, in which he maintained that increased building had for its cause the 'natural increase of mankind' and for its effects a host of benefits to London, country and Crown.[10]

But it is the *Discourse of Trade* on which Barbon's considerable reputation in economics depends,[11] and it is here,

[9] See works cited at nn., pp. 57–58 above. *An account of the Land-Bank, showing the design and manner of the settlement . . .* [1695], BM 816 m. 10 (7). Horsefield, Nos. 125, 189, 229, 601.

[10] [Nicholas Barbon], *An Apology for the builder: or a discourse showing the cause and effects of the increase of building* (1685), Kress 1608; and (1689), Kress 1683. JUSTICES OF MIDDLESEX: Brett-James, 330–31. LONDON: Hobbes, *Leviathan*, II, xxix. Other samples are the remarks of the famous London goldsmith, Thomas Violet, in *A Petition against the Jewes . . .* (1661), Kress 1078, p. 11: 'London to the Kingdom looks like a man in a deep dropsie, all belly and no legs or other limbs but weak and withered'; and of Sir Thomas Roe: 'In my opinion it is no good state of a body to have a fat head, thin guts, and lean members,' in 'Touching decay of trade . . .' (1662?); MS. in PRO 30/24 Bundle 40, #43.

[11] N[icholas] B[arbon], M.D., *A Discourse of Trade* (1690); Kress 1720, Hollander Reprint (1905). REPUTATION: Douglas Vickers, *Studies in the Theory of Money 1690–1776* (1959), Chap. 5 and works cited there. Stephan Bauer, 'Nicholas Barbon . . .', 21 Conrad's *Jahrbücher f. Nationalökonomie* (1890), 6 Heft, 561–90.

if anywhere, that one must look for an organized general treatment of the theoretical fragments that appear as hints in his earlier writings. The *Discourse* rewards these expectations by an appearance of orderliness in the table of contents. The nature of trade is to be discussed first; then quantity, quality, value and price of goods; and finally the effects of trade, and the causes that promote or hinder trade. Within this basic pattern are to be discussed a number of what have come to be considered the canonical questions of economics. The plan is excellent, it is only the execution that is wanting.

The first shortcoming, which becomes apparent at once, is that like so many pre-scientific writers in all branches of science, Barbon depends heavily on that natural but empty substitute for analysis: definition and classification. Faced with a complex and puzzling whole, a watch or a beetle, the child's instinct is to pull it apart, believing that he will thereby come to understand it better. And Adam, it will be remembered, is supposed to have refined his knowledge about animals when he gave each different kind of animal its own name; but either he must already have understood the differences between animals and assigned names merely in recognition of this knowledge, or else naming was a merely arbitrary act that committed him to a certain language but could not have taught him anything about the outside world. So it is with Barbon, who begins by giving definitions, but either these faithfully followed previous usage or else they merely assigned new names to well-known things.

The *Discourse* opens with an array of preliminaries:

Trade is the making, and selling of one sort of goods for another.

The making is called handicraft trade, and the maker an artificer.

The selling is called merchandizing, and the seller a merchant.

The artificer is called by several names, from the sort of goods he makes, as a clothier, silk-weaver, shoe-maker, or hatter. . . .

And the merchant is distinguished by the names of the country he deals to, and is called Dutch, French, Spanish or Turkey merchant.

Now these distinctions, neat though they be, are fruitless, because they have no theoretical content. Had Barbon argued, for instance, that all trade consists of making and exchanging something or other, so that what the artificer does is in principle the same as what the merchant does—the one changing the form of goods as the other changes the location of goods—then the effect would have been altogether different. He would have mentioned the distinctions only in order to show that they were irrelevant to his purpose. He would, in short, have been abstracting, that is, demonstrating that things ordinarily thought different are fundamentally the same, in the light of economic theory.

The stages in the development of a science, indeed, can be represented by the broadening of abstractions. Physics, for instance, jumped ahead when it was shown that an apple falling from a tree and a planet travelling in its orbit both move according to the same laws, or that magnets and lightning operate according to the same principle. In economics, the process of increasingly powerful abstraction led to recognition, for instance, that capital in the form of land responds to the same laws as capital in the form of tools, or buildings, or taught skills. But Barbon, in using distinctions, often, almost always, insists on the conventional differences rather than searching beneath that veil for the fundamental similarities. Intent on cataloguing the species of artificers and traders, Barbon denies himself the opportunity to say, as Adam Smith did later, 'Every man thus lives by exchanging, or becomes in some measure a merchant. . . .'[12]

A second and equally striking defect in the *Discourse* is the logical incoherence of its parts. After distinguishing the variety of traders, Barbon goes on to distinguish the 'stock' or 'wares' of trade into 'native staples' and 'foreign staples', the former being the goods that 'each country doth naturally and best produce', the latter 'any foreign commodity which a country acquires by the sole trade to a foreign

[12] Smith, *Wealth of Nations*, I, IV; Cannan, I, 24.

place or sole possession of a particular art, as spices are the staple of Holland, and the making of glass and paper were the staple of Venice'. From this Barbon instantly proceeds to a surprising conclusion. The native staple of each country is perpetual, he asserts, for the plants and animals naturally increase 'and the minerals of the earth are inexhaustible'; and from this it follows that Thomas Mun was mistaken in arguing that parsimony makes a nation rich 'for what is infinite can neither receive addition by parsimony nor suffer diminution by prodigality'.[13]

What matters most in recognizing the flavour of Barbon's work is not the unreasonableness of his assertion that the mineral content of the finite earth can itself be infinite, nor the cavalier dismissal of Mun's argument for parsimony (which rests on a comparison of consumption with *production*, not with the total stock of raw materials), but rather the fact that Barbon's conclusion is in no way based upon or drawn from the material that precedes it in the *Discourse*. He might just as well have put this 'demonstration'—as the supply of raw materials is infinite, Mr Mun is mistaken . . . —at the beginning of the book or slipped it into any other page. No science, to be sure, is so simple that it permits of only a unique order of deduction and demonstration—not even in Euclid is the order of the propositions absolutely inescapable; but no work in which the sequence of the parts is variable at will can be presenting a proper scientific theory.

System is not incompatible with digression, but in the *Discourse* digression is so frequent and lengthy that little system is left. Thus when Barbon turns to his second subject, the quantity and quality of wares, he announces, to begin, that 'the quantity of all wares are known by weight or measure', and proceeds to unfold the statement in this manner:

> The reason of gravity is not understood, neither is it material to this purpose. Whether it proceeds from the elasticity of the air, or weight of the utmost sphere, or

13 Barbon, *Discourse*, 3–6. Thomas Mun, *England's Treasure by Forraign Trade* (1664), Chap. II; Kress 1139.

from what other causes, it is sufficient that the ways of
trying the weights of bodies are perfectly discovered by
the balance.

This passage, in the best manner of a Virtuoso, is typical of
the irrelevant learned meanders through which the book
runs its course. 'Whether the Goths were part of the Ten
Tribes . . .', 'Whether, since the invention of guns and gunpowder, so many men are not slain in the wars as formerly?'
—these and other equally fascinating speculations are grist
for Barbon's mill.[14]

But if all the formalities and vagaries are overlooked, what
solid matter is left in the *Discourse?* The material most
pushed on the reader's attention are certain conclusions as
to public policy, conclusions at which the *Discourse,* a work
of advocacy rather than of speculation, aims; and which are
brought forward in the closing chapters, 'Of the chief causes
that promote trade' and 'Of the chief causes of the decay of
trade'. The first of these conclusions is that

> Building is the chiefest promoter of trade. It employs
> a greater number of trades and people than feeding or
> clothing: the artificers that belong to building, such as
> bricklayers, carpenters, plasterers, etc. employ many
> hands; those that make the materials for building, such
> as bricks, lime, tile, etc. employ more; and with those
> that furnish the houses, such as upholsterers, pewterers,
> etc. they are almost innumerable.

The assumption, that those trades which employ the most
labour are the most beneficial, served as an axiom of policy.[15]
   The second conclusion, for which Barbon earned the ac-
claim of classical economists like McCulloch, who commended with the greatest warmth any right-thinking predecessor of his school, is that international trade should be left
free. Barbon's argument on this score is cogent far beyond
any other he gives, and is carried out with a delicacy unusual to his time, as when, for instance, he maintains that

[14] Barbon, *Discourse,* 9, 49, 43.
[15] Barbon, *Discourse,* 68, and cf. 39. See Vickers, *op. cit.,* n. 11,
p. 60 above, *passim,* sub 'Employment'.

there is no point in prohibiting the import of foreign goods that appear to compete directly with native products. 'A person may have English lace, gloves or silk as much as he wants and will buy no more such, and yet lay out his money on a *point* of Venice, Jessamine gloves, or French silks. He may desire to eat Westphalia bacon when he will not English. So that the prohibition of foreign wares does not necessarily cause a greater consumption of the like sort of English.' It is only curious that having argued so well for free trade he takes back in his summary much of what he has given before.

> To conclude, if the bringing in of foreign goods should hinder the making and consuming of the native (which will very seldom happen), this disadvantage is not to be remedied by a prohibition of these goods but by laying so great duties upon them that they may be always dearer than those of our country['s] make. . . .

This rule and Barbon's comments on it make him appear after all to be something less than a perfect free-trader. Phrases such as 'the freer the trade is, the better the nation will thrive' can be found at crucial points in his writings, but these are the liberal cant of his time, and like all cant, their express meaning is understandable only when one has gathered exactly what the author means by the key terms. By 'free' Barbon meant no more than the absence of import prohibitions and *prohibitive* duties; but protective duties he did not regard as an abrogation of commercial 'freedom'.[16]

The last conclusion at which Barbon arrives is that the interest rate should be reduced by law. The arguments he advances are quite like those presented by Child; the occasion for his work, as for Child's, may well have been the attempt in 1690 to have Parliament—to which Barbon had just been elected—pass a law reducing interest to 4 per cent,[17] and he had plenty of reasons of his own to desire a law that could hardly fail, as he thought, to ease the lot of a perpetual debtor. Barbon's policy conclusions, in short—es-

[16] Barbon, *Discourse,* 73, 78. *Concerning coining,* 59.
[17] Cf. n. 79, p. 42 above.

pecially as two of them run so close to unsupported special pleading—are of little consequence in the long-run development of economic theory.

His contributions to pure theory are more interesting. Of some of them, to be sure, too much has been made, especially of his discussion of value and price. Value, Barbon says, arises from use, that is, from the capacity of goods to satisfy men's needs and desires. The price of a good approximates its value, being determined not only by use but also by the cost of production; and as demand (deriving from use) and supply are co-ordinated in the market, 'the market is the best judge of value'.[18] Barbon thus refers implicitly to the distinction between value in use and value in exchange, but far from offering any way of resolving that famous paradox—an oversight that is not, of course, blameable—he does not even sharply realize that the paradox is there.

For another piece of pure theory, Barbon has lately been much lauded by Schumpeter. The passage concerned is a fairly short one in which Barbon states his theory of interest.

> Interest is the rent of stock, and is the same as the rent of land. The first is the rent of the wrought or artificial stock; the latter of the unwrought or natural stock.
> Interest is commonly reckoned for money, because the money borrowed at interest is to be repaid in money. But this is a mistake, for the interest is paid for stock; for the money borrowed is laid out to buy goods or pay for them before bought. No man takes up money at interest to lay it by him and lose the interest of it.[19]

The salient arguments are (1) that interest is *really* a payment for the use of goods though *apparently* for the loan of money, and (2) that interest is in this respect like rent, which is also a payment for the use of goods, although a different sort of goods. These are strong arguments, although it was becoming fairly common to recognize that the fees paid for hire of land and for hire of money were similar, a similarity suggested by the fact that both fees, in French,

18 Barbon, *Discourse*, 13–20.
19 Barbon, *Discourse*, 31.

bore the same name, *rent*.[20] But Schumpeter elevates Barbon's comment into the first explicit statement of the doctrine that prevailed throughout the nineteenth century, that interest is identical with the net yield of capital goods. He interprets the passage in Barbon as saying that 'interest is the return on "wrought stock"—produced means of production—exactly as rent is the return on "unwrought stock" —natural agents of production . . .'. Unfortunately, however, the explanatory phrases that Schumpeter inserts cannot fairly be read into the text. 'Wrought or artificial stock' —Barbon's words—may sound as though they meant 'produced means of production', but Barbon did not mean them that way. Among his opening definitions and distinctions occurs this:

> The stock and wares of all trade are the animals, vegetables and minerals of the whole universe, whatsoever the land or sea produces. These wares may be divided into natural and artificial. Natural wares are those which are sold as nature produces them, as flesh, fish and fruits, etc. Artificial wares are those which by art are changed into another form than nature gave them, as cloth, calicoes and wrought silks, etc., which are made of wool, flax, cotton and raw silks.[21]

'Wrought or artificial stock', in other words, means a supply of processed commodities, 'unwrought stock', of raw materials. What Barbon meant by the interest passage is something vastly more primitive than what Schumpeter read into it.

Barbon had in mind a simple picture. On the one side stood a merchant, who must have goods if he is to go about his business of selling. A 'merchant' was not, as now, anyone who buys and sells but peculiarly a *foreign* trader (thus, 'the merchant is distinguished by the names of the country he deals to . . .'); hence, he generally traded in

[20] Cf. Petty, *Treatise of Taxes* (1662), in Hull, I, 42: 'But before we talk too much of rents, we should endeavour to explain the mysterious nature of them, with reference as well to money, the rent of which we call usury, as to that of lands and houses. . . .'

[21] Schumpeter, *History Econ. Anal.*, 647, 330; and cf. 720, 924, 1,119. Barbon, *Discourse*, 3.

processed goods. Therefore, if he borrowed money in order to have something to sell, he was really borrowing the processed goods that he generally sold. In the other panel of Barbon's picture stands the farmer, who rents land. Land contains a 'natural stock', natural because the goods 'are sold as *nature produces* them'. The farmer rents the land in order to extract from it (not produce with the aid of it) the 'flesh, fish and fruits, etc.' that it is his business to sell; so that when he pays rent, apparently for the land, he is really paying for the goods he will sell. It is no more than this that Barbon means, certainly nothing so abstract or sophisticated as the notion that interest is the net return to real capital goods. In recognizing, as Barbon did, that merchant and farmer carry on somewhat similar economic activities, he was helping to forward economic theory, but the scale of the advance can easily be exaggerated.[22]

As to two other points of doctrine, there seems to be firmer ground for assurance that Barbon made advances. He was one of the first writers clearly to see that 'prodigality' or a taste for luxury, however much it might run counter to established rules of State, Church or good morals, might easily benefit the economy. To make such a distinction between moral and economic consequences took a certain cynicism or wit; it might have drawn fuel from Barbon's own 'foppishness', as Roger North put it; in any event, when writing on luxury, Barbon suddenly turns from schoolmaster into poet.

> Fashion, or the alteration of dress, is a great promoter of trade because it occasions the expense of cloths before the old ones are worn out. It is the spirit and life of trade; it makes a circulation, and gives a value, by turns, to all sorts of commodities; keeps the great body of trade in motion. It is an invention to dress a man as if he lived in a perpetual Spring; he never sees the Autumn of his clothes . . .[23]

The like of this was not again seen in economic literature until Mandeville; it is good company for any seventeenth-century writer to have kept.

[22] Cf. North, p. 217 below.
[23] Barbon, *Discourse*, 65.

Praise has been bestowed on Barbon, finally, for being free—as but few in his time were free—of the bullion illusion. He did not consider gold and silver so especially valuable that the state's economic policy ought to be directed to accumulating them in great quantities. On the contrary, he stated clearly that the value of gold and silver, as of any other commodities, is determined by supply and demand; and insisted that though gold and silver might enjoy certain advantages as materials for coin, they were by no means irreplaceable. Indeed, paper money or checks were much more convenient, 'by preventing the continual trouble of telling over [coins]'. The bullion illusion was fast becoming *passé*, as any number of economic pamphlets of this time can show, and Barbon's critique is as decisively put and well-founded as any:

> If there could be an account taken of the balance of trade, I can't see where the advantage of it could be. For the reason that's given for it—that the overplus is paid in bullion and the nation grows so much the richer . . . —is altogether a mistake. For gold and silver are but commodities, and one sort of commodity is as good as another, so be it of the same value.[24]

This principle of monetary theory—that the precious metals are commodities whereas 'money is a value made by a law'—Barbon elaborated later, in his pamphlet on the recoinage of 1696. But in order to follow the course of this, the best of Barbon's work on economics, we must pause to consider the coinage problem of the 1690s.

III

The central fact of the coinage problem was that at a certain point the English public lost all confidence in silver coins. Many refused to accept those coins at face value, weighing them instead and giving for them only as much as the silver they contained was worth. Ordinary trade became an elab-

24 Barbon, *Coining*, 40.

orate ritual requiring sensitive scales and long computations. Finally this disorder forced the Government to action, and during the Recoinage of 1696 it recalled to the Mint all the silver coins that had naturally or artificially gone bad, and eventually transformed them into new ones.[25]

But why did the silver coins deteriorate so badly in the first place? The fundamental reason, though not the whole of the explanation, is this: coins are perishable. In the course of being handled, they slowly wear down, losing a bit of their weight at each transfer, until they end as hardly recognizable shadows of themselves. Some are lost altogether: burned or drowned, or buried by a hoarder who forgets them as a dog may forget a buried bone. And still others are deliberately defaced or mutilated. Yet as the spirit is stronger than the body, a stock of old and dilapidated coin may serve a trusting or sophisticated community as well as a shinier stock, and sometimes, curiously enough, better, for the fact that a coin is or appears to be old is sometimes interpreted as evidence that it is genuine.

But there are limits to this toleration. Just as the ageing leader of a wolf-pack, who continues to rule by prestige after his power has waned, will be destroyed by the pack as soon as he refuses a challenge or is defeated by a rival, so a coinage (or indeed any money supply) will be set upon by a people who have hitherto honoured it, as soon as it is shown up as 'bad'. The willingness to pretend that a disc of metal is money depends on an act of faith, and secular faith can survive some disagreeable facts but not very many.

The coinage of England before 1663, judged by later standards, was peculiarly subject to wear. To make it, a bar of silver was rolled to the proper thickness, discs of required weight were stamped out, and the discs were imprinted by being hammered between two dies. The result was crude, since the wafer was not of the same thickness throughout; the discs therefore varied considerably in weight, and the imprint was seldom if ever perfectly centred on the disc.

[25] The following account of the Recoinage is drawn largely from Horsefield, although the analysis of why the crisis started is my own; for certain other amendments to Horsefield's analysis, see Appendix III, p. 260.

Although the Crown imposed certain requirements of regularity on the Mint, the private interests of the officers of the Mint—whose incomes rose with the output—and the state of technology set limits to the regularity that could be demanded or produced. Coins, when issued, differed markedly in weight, deviated noticeably from perfect circles, and showed a crescent or border of unstamped silver depending on how nearly concentric were the disc and die-stamped design.

A host of enterprising subjects set themselves to correcting these imperfections. They culled out the coins that were heavier than standard—that is, whose silver content was worth more than their face value; these made especially valuable hoards, and if need be, they could be melted and the bullion returned to the Mint at a profit. Besides those who were thus narrowing the variations in weight another group were hard at work reducing the coins to a more perfect circularity. These, the 'clippers', rounded off the redundant edges of silver around the design, though sometimes, in the enthusiasm of cutting and filing, they intruded on the design itself; the reward for their labours was the bits of silver they salvaged, and which they could melt down into bullion, without much difficulty, in an ordinary charcoal fire. And still others made other amendments to the coinage, not least among them the counterfeiters, some of whom to their credit worked in sterling silver.

All of these activities, in addition to innocent wear, constantly lowered the weight of coins in circulation. Because much of the coin being used in 1663 was fairly old, it must have been, in comparison with the standard weight prescribed by law, quite surprisingly light. In fact, of the entire stock of silver coin, which may have amounted to £12,000,000, about four-fifths was thirty years old on the average and the remaining fifth over fifty years old. Yet by dint of faith—which extended even to workmanlike counterfeits—this old worn coin continued to circulate at face value.

So the matter stood in 1663 and so it might have continued indefinitely, the coins wearing, the oldest wearing out, and the losses being made good by an unremarkable flow of fresh coins from the Mint. But in 1663 an innovation took place that changed all that. The Mint introduced an altogether new technique that turned out much more uniform —though by no means perfectly uniform—coins. Above all, the new mills and presses made it possible to produce a coin with raised and grooved rims and whose faces stood in higher relief. These changes made it almost impossible for the clippers' work to go unnoticed, and indeed the 'milled' coins, unlike the old 'hammered' ones, succeeded in escaping the clippers' attention. Moreover the milled coins not only avoided artificial wearing, but also wear of the usual sort, for being 'heavy' they would be preferred for hoarding, and must therefore have had less than their share of handling.

As the stock of milled coins increased—and by 1690 about £4,000,000 of new silver had been issued—it must have become a standard of invidious comparison, against which the old hammered and clipped coins looked increasingly 'bad'. And sooner or later, this impression must have become just striking enough to destroy the common faith in hammered coins. That moment seems to have come about 1690. From that time on, the statement that the old coins were clipped ceased to be a casual observation, as it had been throughout the century, and turned into a mounting clamour for reform; the change can be traced in the activity of pamphleteers, who had little if anything to say about the deterioration of the coinage before 1690, but burst out in that year and the following five in a huge crescendo of complaints and recommendations.

As is often the case, destruction of faith destroyed the foundations of faith. After sober and respectable men had sufficiently explained how bad the old money was, the rest of the community went to work to make it worse. The more the coin was clipped, the less could suspicion fall on anyone who passed coin that had recently been clipped; the more clippers there were, the less likely that the penalty of death would be imposed on anyone caught doing what everyone else was doing; and the more likely that coin would soon pass only by weight, the greater the hurry to clip it while it might still pass at face value.

The loss by deterioration can be estimated. About 500

bags of silver coin weighed at the Exchequer in 1695 contained hardly more than half the weight of bullion they should have done; and when the recoinage finally came, clipped coins at face value of almost £10,000,000 did not contain enough silver to make up £7,000,000 of new fullweight coins. Of course it was only the poorest of the coins that returned to the Mint, the better exemplars being held in hoard; but it seems likely that by 1695 all the hammered silver coins had lost, on the average, about one-fourth to onethird of their weight, not less than half of which loss must have been due to theft in the various forms of clipping and counterfeiting. The amateurs of these arts may thus have earned commissions of more than £1,500,000. But the heavier cost to the community was the collapse of a large part of its monetary system; the scales went to work, the expenses of doing business jumped, and the costly and troublesome recoinage had to be undertaken. And the proximate cause of all this disorganization was the introduction of an improvement into a poor but passable system.

By the beginning of 1695 it was certain that the hammered silver coin would have to be demonetized and reminted; during spring the House of Commons went so far as to resolve on a recoinage, though nothing further was done before Parliament prorogued for the summer. It was not at all clear, however, on what terms recoinage would take place. In fact, since 1690 the experts and pamphleteers had been conducting a great debate about devaluation and costs of recoinage: should the new coins contain the same amount of silver as before, or less; and should the Treasury absorb the difference in value between the face of old coins and their actual silver content at the moment they were demonetized, or should the bearer; or should the costs be divided between the two? If the Treasury were to take the full loss, then it must accept at face value all hammered silver coins, no matter how badly worn or clipped. If, on the other hand, the public were to take the full loss, then all the hammered coins, no matter how good or bad they appeared, would be accepted at the Mint—once they were demonetized—only by weight.

In such a state of uncertainty, a flight from the hammered silver coins was sure to start. Nobody could be pleased to hold coins whose value tomorrow was so doubtful, whose value, in fact, could not possibly rise but might very easily fall. Two things must have happened very quickly.

In the first place, the clippers must have gone to work even more vigorously than before, though there was by now less raw material to work on. Any coin that was not already pared to the bone became a tempting subject, for the clipper could reason that the coin might still pass at face value after enduring one last delicate trim, and so afford him a profit; but that if it did not, he could not lose much, as he still could get a good price for the bullion.

But more important was the effect of the uncertainty on hoarders. Those who had stored away hammered silver coins must now have scrutinized them closely, weighing them with the greatest care to be quite certain that they contained full weight of bullion. The coins that met the test were safe to keep, for nothing in the proposals for recoinage suggested that silver bullion would be worth less than before: the currency might very possibly be devalued, but nobody ever suggested the opposite. All those hammered coins that had been kept in hoard because they were 'heavy' —heavy enough to have been sure to pass at face value in the ordinary way—yet which showed any deficiency in weight, however minute, when now weighed anxiously and scrupulously—all those coins were taken out of hoard, and rushed off to market to be spent on safer stores of value.

The goods most fit for hoarding, in these circumstances, were silver and gold in bullion. The prices of these accordingly soared, silver bullion rising by almost a fifth and gold bullion by over a third during the first half of 1695. As the value of gold bullion rose, so did that of gold guineas, so that by June they were exchanging not as usually for twenty-one or twenty-two silver shillings but for twenty-nine to thirty. Although gold and silver were the best matter of which to build hoards, any commodity that was fairly imperishable would serve almost as well. Cloths of various sorts accordingly rose in price by about one-fifth during 1695, and the price of wool at Reading almost doubled between the summers of 1695 and 1696.

In the meanwhile, all prices were being sharply bid up. This was due partly to the mere fact that the supply of money in circulation had sharply increased when a large fraction of the hammered silver coin was dishoarded and when the exchange value of the guinea rose; partly perhaps also because in a rapid inflation everyone tried to buy goods needed for consumption or production as soon as possible, before prices rose still further. Cash balances, to put it in other terms, were converted into inventories of goods as quickly as possible, and prices accordingly spiraled upward. They rose throughout 1695, slowly during the first half of the year, faster after the summer, until by the spring of 1696 they had reached a peak about 20 per cent above the starting-point.

Finally, prices of English goods may have risen partly due to an increase in exports. This apparently paradoxical effect —for normally a price increase would tend to reduce the demand for exports—is due to the fact that the price of gold in England had risen by more than the price of either silver bullion or goods. It therefore became profitable to bring gold into England and carry out silver, but as the laws made this somewhat difficult (the would-be exporter had to produce evidence that the bullion had not been 'produced' by melting down English silver coin), goods were carried out instead. And this, of course, made a peculiarly effective contribution to inflation, for not only did it help swell the supply of money but at the same time it diminished the supply of goods. An inflation, proceeding from such causes and at so rapid a rate, might have become a calamity, had not the recoinage stopped it.

Early in 1696 the recoinage was decided on and the terms announced. Clipped coins or condoned counterfeits would be accepted at face value if paid into the Treasury for taxes before 4 May, or for subscriptions to Government loans before 24 June. All other such coins would be demonetized in stages, beginning on 22 February, after which they would be accepted at the Mint only by weight. In the end, some

£10,000,000 in face value of clipped silver coins were retrieved by the Mint, about half coming in at face value and
the rest by weight; the loss of recoinage was thus divided
between the Treasury and the public in more or less equal
proportion, albeit not equally among the public.

Within a few months, therefore, about one-third of the
total stock of money was withdrawn into the Mint, from
which it reissued in the form of new milled coin. It came
forth slowly; by the end of 1696 only about £3,000,000 of
it had emerged. The effect of this great and sudden con-
traction in the supply of money might have been an equally
great and sudden deflation, entailing considerable losses to
merchants, much misery among debtors, widespread unemployment and all the other lugubrious effects of such an
event. But nothing quite as startling as this happened. Prices
fell, the Bank of England suspended specie payments, creditors were obliged to extend the duration of loans and to put
off pressing for payment; and yet nothing warrants belief
that the situation was as disastrous as some had predicted.

The impact was so light because substantial sums of coin
were still being held in hoard at the moment the recoinage
began; and these could be and were brought into circulation
when there were no other means with which to carry on
business. It may well be that the shrinkage in money supply
reduced the stocks in hoards as well as in circulation, just
as the great increase in money supply during 1695 increased
both of these stocks.

During 1697 the Mint in London, as well as a set of tem-
porary provincial mints, worked full force to complete the
recoinage, and by the end of that year money and prices
were pretty much as they had been in 1694, except that the
old hammered silver coins had been superseded by the new
milled silver coins, some additional gold coins, and an increased supply of banknotes. The recoinage was over, and
might be little remembered, except as one of the recurring
crises in the history of English currency. What has made
the Great Recoinage memorable, however, is two facts connected with it, but connected almost coincidentally.

Banking began in England at this time. Although there
had been earlier beginnings, the Bank of England was not

created until 1694, and during the next few years a host of experiments in banking were attempted—among which the most interesting in many ways were the Land Banks —attempted at this moment partly because of the difficulties that the recoinage produced or was expected to produce.

Economic analysis after a modern fashion was also beginning in England at this time, for reasons that had little or nothing to do with the recoinage. But the crisis in coin and the problem of how to deal with it was a subject to which economic analysts, the best of that time as well as many of the most awkward and absurd, devoted much attention.

Houblon, Paterson, Godfrey, and Lowndes, Locke, North and Barbon are names that have, by association, made the recoinage seem a much more central episode of English history than in itself it was.

IV

During the coinage crisis the Government turned hungrily to experts for advice, and heard a great deal more than it either invited or took. The one adviser on whom it relied most heavily was John Locke. How Locke came to be an expert on economic questions, why his judgment more than anyone else's governed the Government's policy, and what were the details of his analysis—these questions will be dealt with later. For the moment it is enough to say that in his two principal pieces on the coinage problem, published in 1691 and 1695 and reissued in 1696, Locke insisted that silver coin must be restored to the previous standard of the Mint. A nation could no more be made richer by calling an ounce of silver seven shillings instead of five, so he and supporters of his view reiterated, than a man could be made taller by dividing a foot into fifteen inches instead of twelve.

The opposing body of commentators, devaluationists, maintained that the new coins should contain less silver than the Mint standard had previously prescribed. In order to justify their position they were bound to deny Locke's first premise, that silver has an inherent and intrinsic value which Government cannot alter, declare or do what it might. In the whole camp of devaluationists, nobody was better equipped by his characteristic mental style than Barbon to deny Locke's premise.

As the *Discourse of Trade* shows over and again, Barbon had a remarkable talent for detecting the subjective and conventional aspects of economic value. Or perhaps it was temperament rather than talent that led him to emphasize what some historians have described as the 'nominalist' view of economics; yet be that as it may, expressions of that attitude abound. According to Barbon, for instance, there is no 'natural' system of weights and measures, all existing systems being arbitrary, usable only because they are 'made certain by the custom or laws of the place'. Qualities of goods are just as difficult to assess in any objective way, for 'those organs that are the proper judges of those differences do very much disagree . . . and every man having a good opinion of his own faculties, it is hard to find a judge to determine which is best'. The difficulty is greatest as to apparel, for 'it is the fancy and approbation of the buyer that brings it into use'. Neither are there, in the long run, anything like standard, fixed, real or inherent values or prices of goods. Not only do accidents of supply affect value, but 'besides, the use of most things being to supply the wants of the mind and not the necessities of the body—and those wants, most of them proceeding from imagination, the mind changes—the things grow out of use and so lose their value'.[26]

But nowhere in the *Discourse of Trade* is this dominant tone clearer than in the terse pronouncement that opens the discussion of money: 'Money is a value made by a law.' And this maxim, so much part of the bent of his mind, Barbon took as the keystone of his treatise, *A Discourse Concerning Coining the New Money Lighter, In Answer to Mr Lock's Considerations about raising the value of money*.[27] By way of introduction he contrasted Locke's axioms against his own. Locke had said (the words, however, are Barbon's) that:

[26] Barbon, *Discourse*, 10, 11, 13, 18–19.
[27] (1696.) Horsefield, No. 283.

NICHOLAS BARBON: PROJECTOR 79

Silver is the instrument and measure of commerce by its intrinsic value. The intrinsic value of silver is the estimate which common consent has placed on it. . . . Money differs from uncoined silver only in this, that the quantity of silver in each piece is ascertained by its stamp, which is set there to be a public voucher for its weight and fineness.

Barbon replied:

There is no intrinsic value in silver or any fixed or certain estimate that common consent has placed on it, but that it is a commodity and rises and falls as other commodities do.

Money is the instrument and measure of commerce and not silver. It is the instrument of commerce from the authority of that government where it is coined, and that by the stamp and size of each piece the value is known.

Locke, in short, maintained that for the Government to put a shilling mark on a bit of silver worth less than a shilling was deception, wilful but futile. Barbon held, on the contrary, that there was no such thing, in the abstract, as a real shilling's worth; the price of anything could only be known after the Government specified some unit of money as the measure.

The rights and wrongs of this argument, in all its implications, are not easy to sort out. On the one hand, Barbon's theory alone is capable of explaining a completely fiduciary currency, one in which the money, say paper, neither has any intrinsic value in itself nor is redeemable for goods with intrinsic value, such as gold, yet is readily accepted in exchange. On the other hand, Locke was certainly right in implying that currency could not be made to pass at its face value simply by fiat—the fact that the old silver coins had been passing only by weight proved that he was right. The dilemma that made each of them both right and wrong could be resolved only by recognizing that the acceptability of a currency depends completely on the public's faith in it. For any group of people who had begun to doubt that a piece of money could really buy goods worth the face value of the piece, Locke's analysis would apply; whereas for any group of people who remained firm in the belief that money was and would be worth its face value, Barbon's axiom would correspond to the facts.

In some respects Barbon had the better of his opponent. Against Locke's argument that silver had *an* intrinsic value, it was too strong to assert that 'there is *no* intrinsic value in silver', but certainly correct to maintain that 'intrinsic' could not possibly mean the same as 'fixed', for, as Barbon showed, the Mint price of silver in terms of shillings per ounce had varied often and greatly.[28]

And as to the practical effects of their policies also, Barbon was quite possibly on sounder ground, since a recoinage that merely recognized the depreciation which had already taken place would have been economically neutral. The recoinage as it took place, on Locke's terms, introduced deflationary pressures that could hardly be welcome, especially in the course of a large-scale foreign war conducted by a government that had already strained, almost to the utmost, its powers to tax and borrow and was not yet aware of the fiscal utility of printing presses. As it is not clear, however, that Barbon understood the deflationary consequences to be expected, he should not perhaps be assigned special merit for having happened to be correct on this point.

But whatever the merits of his case in fact, there can be no doubt that the treatise on coinage was Barbon's finest exercise in economic reasoning. It is a work in the domain of concrete analysis rather than theory building, and the shadow of special pleading was still there to worry Barbon,[29] but it is by far the best he did. Written as a brief for a debate, it is too contentious to be systematic, for instead of building one long chain of argument, Barbon makes every debating point that he can, crushing Locke in the most elephantine manner when the matter is most trivial. On the other hand, it shows a degree of economic sophistication that is memorable for its time, and exhibits a definite, con-

[28] Barbon, *Coining*, 75–84.
[29] See below, p. 101 f.

sistent, intellectual style. But style is not system, and though it may be said of Barbon that he carried the old style of economic reasoning to its limit, in doing so he showed what its limitations were.

PART II

The New Style

Chapter 3

SCIENCE AND OBJECTIVITY IN THE
SEVENTEENTH CENTURY

I

RECOINAGE WAS NOT new in 1696, having often in the past
been the recourse of poor kings who, by issuing a new, de-
based currency, could for a short while ease their finances.
It was regarded as a sort of magic; for by making up the
new pieces lighter than before, the royal treasury profited
at the same time that every subject received just as many
pieces as he had surrendered. The new pieces, of course,
contained less silver.

At no time in modern English history was this fiscal
stratagem employed with more vigour than during the last
years of Henry VIII and the first few of Edward VI. It happened in 1549 that the great preacher and perennial heretic,
Hugh Latimer, giving a sermon before Edward VI, remarked, by way of parable, on the new coins:

> We have now a pretty little shilling, indeed a very
> pretty one. I have but one, I think, in my purse, and
> the last days I had put it away almost for an old groat,
> and so I trust some will take them. The fineness of the
> silver I cannot see. But therein is printed a fine sen-
> tence: . . . the fear of the Lord is the fountain of
> life or wisdom. I would God this sentence were always
> printed in the heart of the King. . . .

Not all the listeners were charmed by this homily, and one
of them, perhaps a Minister of Finance to the twelve-year-
old King, called Latimer a seditious fellow.

At his next sermon, Latimer replied to the aspersion:

I have now gotten one fellow more, a companion of sedition, and wot you who is my fellow? Esai the prophet. I spoke but of a little pretty shilling. But he spoke to Jerusalem after another sort, and was so bold as to meddle with their coin. Thou proud, thou covetous, thou haughty city of Jerusalem. . . . Thy silver is turned into dross. Ah seditious wretch, what had he to do with the mint? Why should not he have left that matter to some master of policy to reprove?

Thy silver is dross, it is not fine, it is counterfeit, thy silver is turned, thou hadst good silver. What pertained that to Esai? Mary, he espied a piece of divinity in that policy, he threatened them God's vengeance for it. He went to the root of the matter, which was covetousness, which became him to reprove; or else that it tended to the hurt of the poor people, for the naughtiness of the silver was the occasion of dearth of all things in the realm. He imputed it to them as a great crime. He may be called a master of sedition indeed. Was not this a seditious harlot to tell them to their beards, to their face?[1]

This was perhaps the last time that the Church, in England, spoke on matters of economic policy in that tone. The tone is prophetic, the appeal is to authority; Latimer invokes Scripture against masters of policy; he speaks *ex cathedra*. Sin is his text, and his vestments are his credentials. But the fire that Latimer lit helped destroy the power of the English Church to speak with such authority again.

A century and more later, another churchman spoke out about another coinage crisis. William Fleetwood, chaplain to William III though not yet bishop, preached a sermon before the Mayor and Aldermen of London, on clipping. He demonstrated at length that though the clipper might not be injuring any certain neighbours, there was no doubt that he was injuring them all, as clipping raised prices at home and turned foreign exchange rates against England. He adduced evidence from the old laws to show that the

---

[1] Latimer, *Seven Sermons* (ed. Arber, 1869), 34-35, 82, 84-86; reprinted in *Tudor Econ. Docts.*, II, 180-81.

death penalty recently decreed was far from cruel; Anglo-Saxon kings had chopped off clippers' hands or submitted them to ordeals by comparison with which simple hanging was almost compassionate. Only in the last paragraph of the sermon did Christianity creep in, as Fleetwood ended on the theologically feeble, or comfortable, note that 'an honest man and a good Christian will never be two distinct things in a Christian kingdom'.[2]

The voice of the Church had changed with its position. It was now an arm of the State, engaged in the State's business, and although it might retain some considerable independence of judgment, Fleetwood would have been thought maddened by illusions of grandeur had he said, as Latimer did, 'Yet I comfort myself with that, that Christ himself was noted to be a stirrer up of the people against the Emperor and was contented to be called seditious'. The national Church could no longer claim supremacy over the State in matters, such as economics, that had come to be defined as Caesar's, and the Church accordingly lost its power to speak authoritatively on matters of social policy. Its authority was weakened further by the rise of powerful dissenting churches, the spread of Latitudinarianism and the doctrine of toleration; if churches and ecclesiastics were accorded no less respect, they had lost all claims to universal obedience and absolute trust. By 1668 it was easily possible for Pepys to say of the *Life* of Archbishop Laud that it was 'worth reading, as informing a man plainly in the posture of the Church, and how the things of it were managed with the same self-interest and design that every other thing is . . .'.[3] If the primate could be accused of acting for the special interests of the Church, then his words and its would no longer be heard as the words of God's appointed ministers.

The final outcome of the decline in the authoritativeness of theological pronouncements on economic matters was the emergence of economics as an inquiry independent of religious and ethical considerations. That decline can in fact be traced, stage by stage, through the literature on usury.

[2] Fleetwood, *A Sermon Against Clipping* (1694), Kress, 1843.
[3] Pepys, *Diary*, 29 Nov. 1668.

Throughout the Middle Ages, the discussion of usury had been a staple, indeed a high point, of casuistry. And even into the seventeenth century, the late Scholastics of Spain were still engaged in spelling out the cases in which interest could and could not be taken in good conscience. In England the divide had been reached a bit earlier. Until about 1640, there is a continuous literature of the medieval sort, one of the latest examples being John Blaxton's book of 1634, *The English Usurer, or usury condemned by the most learned and famous divines of the Church of England.* . . . After 1640, and especially after 1660, such works cease, and although much is written on 'interest', the word 'usury' almost disappears; the moral aspect of the question has been superseded by the economic one. Even as early as 1621, the transition was clearly visible in Sir Thomas Culpepper's *Tract Against Usurie,* which opens, 'To leave the proofs of the unlawfulness of usury to divines, wherein a number, as well Protestants as Papists, have learnedly written, here is only to set down some arguments to show how great the hurt is it does to this Kingdom. . . .' The title bears the old name usury; but the matter is the newer subject, the economic effects of a high rate of interest; and the moral argument is left behind, to divines. After 1660 what the divines had to say about money was hardly mentioned even in passing, and the Church took to saying little at all about economic questions of any sort.[4]

Nor could any man other than a cleric speak on economic affairs after 1660 in confidence that his words would be accepted as authoritative because of the office he held, his class, rank or profession. Neither was any man widely regarded as so wise and disinterested that sheer personal merit would give his utterances oracular weight. Kings had been supposed, in some dim past, to rule on behalf of the realm, to provide disinterested justice, to seek no private advantages and do no harm to their subjects; but the subjects of Charles

<hr/>

[4] Blaxton, Kress 492; cf. Kress 124, 159, 259, 318, 422, 492, 523, 551, 574 for other treatises on usury. Culpepper, Kress 380. See Bernard Dempsey, *Interest and Usury* (1948); Thomas F. Divine, *Interest* (1959); and R. H. Tawney's introduction to his edition (1925) of Thomas Wilson's *Discourse upon Usury* (1572).

II and his brother or nieces must have been very blind to imagine that their sovereign corresponded to that ideal image. Ministers of the Crown were so far from faithful servants that even the King could not unquestioningly trust them to be other than venal, and however broad the group with which their self-interest allied them, it was generally a very incomplete sample of the whole nation.

Moreover, even had there remained an olympian voice, its task would have been vastly more difficult after the Restoration than before. To say that England was becoming more democratic, or less oligarchic—it does not matter which —is to say that politics was becoming more impersonal, and the rhetoric of authority is more difficult to carry off when the audience is not familiar with the speaker. How was the writer of a pamphlet to persuade his readers of what might be true and well-known to his intimate friends, that he was indeed an honest, generous, and public-spirited man? If that was his chief claim to belief, if he must rest his case finally on the assertion, 'As I am honest so you may trust me', then his associates and neighbours might trust him, and so might a master who had long experience of his devoted service, but why should a shrewd squire trust him who had never seen him and knew him only for a foreigner, or why should a London merchant who had prospered by never trusting a stranger? The more that political decisions were taken out of the hands of a small clique of cronies at Court, the more great matters of State were influenced not to say decided by burgesses of provincial towns and obscure county landowners, the less was it possible for a writer on political questions to claim the deference that might or might not be due to his opinions. The spread of representative government, like the decline of religion, put unwonted obstacles between advocates of policy and the makers of policy.

One group alone in Restoration England, the academics, might have been trusted, because of their remoteness from the practical world, and believed, because of their scholarly competence. But they were not inclined to meddle with questions of economic policy nor for that matter with economics in any guise. Among the many good and new things that have come from the universities, economic science is not one. Of the seventeenth century Englishmen who were the founders of the discipline, most had not attended the universities and none thought of economics as a scholarly study. But considering the goals that were set for the British universities during the seventeenth century, and the attitude of learned men towards economic questions, it is not surprising that the science of economics was born outside of the universities and without their blessing.

By the middle of the seventeenth century, the English universities had recovered from a period of degeneration; they were once more sufficiently serious to undertake discovery and invention. For the greater part of the previous hundred years, critics had bewailed what they called the 'obscure and neglected condition' of academic learning, and had complained that tutors and students alike were turning the colleges into drinking societies—if not worse. To such charges of laziness the Tudor scholar replied: 'You know we labor with our minds . . . as ye may perceive by the complexions, how wan the colour is, how faint and sickly be our bodies. . . .' If this was the ultimate test of the dedication of the learned, then they must have been in worse health after 1636, when Bishop Laud imposed on Oxford the statutes that made for a more severe regimen than had been known there for several centuries. Though complaints against the universities were not less frequent afterward, it was neither frivolity nor laziness which was complained of, but the conception of learning that Laud's statutes encouraged.[5]

Laud was conservative, to put it mildly, and so was his programme for the higher education. According to his system, 'the importance of dialectics and the authority of Aristotle were to be strenuously inculcated, it being especially enjoined that . . . [the] Regent should deliver an address expressly designed to vindicate [them]. . . . In the Bachelor of Arts course the subjects were to include grammar, rhetoric [logic, geometry, and Greek], Aristotle's ethics, politics, and economics.'[6]

[5] [John Hales], *Discourse of the Common Weal* . . . (Lamond ed., 1929), 157, 21.
[6] Cf. Mullinger, *Cambridge*, III, 135.

Although Aristotle's *Ethics* is still ethics, and his *Politics* still politics, the modern study of economics does not stem from Aristotle's *Economica*. In that short work, whose text and author are almost equally uncertain, Aristotle, or some-one who followed or imitated him, undertakes to bridge the gap between the *Ethics*, which is concerned mainly with the individual, and the *Politics*, which deals with the community as a whole. The *Economica* concerns itself with the nature and governance of the household; it 'precedes the *Politics*, because its subject is anterior: the household is part of the city'. The *Economica* takes up, very briefly, the way to earn the family's living—agriculture is the best way—the differ-ence between the sexes, and the reciprocal care of parents for children and later, of children for parents; the proper conduct of the husband towards his goods, his slaves, and his wife, and the proper attitude of the wife towards the husband—she should obey, tolerate, respect, and remain faithful in his absence. There is a so-called Book II of the *Economica*, its origin even more dubious than that of Book I, which rehearses stratagems that rulers have used to raise money from their subjects; but that goes beyond the proper matter of the work.

At least some of the seventeenth century Englishmen who heard lectures on the *Economica* did not consider it a dead letter. As late as 1669 a Cavalier Baron published a long tract, *Observations and Advices Oeconomical*,[7] which as-sumes that the family, though small, is 'an aggregation ca-pable of Government', defines 'Oeconomy' as 'the art of well governing a man's private house and fortunes', and offers such wisdom as that a man ought to pick for his spouse a lady who 'may be no less useful in the day than agreeable at night'. But the subject, thus limited, had no great future —perhaps all that could be said about it had been said—and other students of the *Economica* were not inclined to bridge the gap between the economics of the family and the eco-nomics of the nation.

The dons and Professors of Oxford and Cambridge were not likely to extend Aristotle's *Economica* into a modern

[7] Dudley, 4th Baron North (Sir Dudley North's father). Kress 1245.

economic treatise; to study trade was not respectable. The universities conceived it one of their main tasks to educate gentlemen, and if they did not speak of a 'liberal education', much the same thing was intended by the phrase, 'liberal arts'—'liberal', because they are the arts of the free man, not 'servile' or 'menial', as befit a slave or a mechanic. Now the conduct of trade, the mercantile profession, was not yet considered the business of a gentleman, although Restoration England was beginning to honour the trader, and some of the minor nobility were not ashamed that their younger sons should become merchants and many were positively happy to have their younger daughters marry merchants. But no gentleman, and especially no self-respecting scholar, would study the profession if he were not forced to. Since the nation's trade, wealth, poverty, population, manufactures, and all those subjects which are treated by economics seemed to seventeenth century scholars to be intimately connected with the profession of Merchandise, they seemed to pertain to the 'illiberal arts', and therefore to be outside the proper scope of learning.

During the 1620s, when John Wallis was being educated at Cambridge, even mathematics (other than geometry) was considered beneath the dignity of learning. 'For mathematics, at that time with us, were scarcely looked on as academic studies, but rather mechanical—as the business of traders, merchants, seamen, carpenters, surveyors of lands, and the like.'[8] That this attitude, like so many others, had radically altered by 1660, no other evidence is needed than Wallis' own appointment as Savilian Professor of Geometry at Oxford in 1649. The universities after 1660 were no longer just as Laud had left them; but universities have in them something that retards change, wanted and unwanted alike, and it took them more than a century longer before economics followed its illiberal cousin, algebra, into the common rooms and lecture halls.

The amateur scholars of Gresham College and the Royal Society had no such qualms, and as we will see, they did set to work on economic questions, some of them with the

[8] Wallis, quoted by G. N. Clark, *Science and Social Welfare* (1949), 88–89.

utmost enthusiasm. But their amateur standing in scholarship, together with the reputations that many of them had in the world of affairs, kept them from speaking as authoritatively as the more professional and more cloistered scholars might have done, and indeed have done, since the time of Adam Smith.

No group in Restoration society that might interest itself in economic questions could escape the imputation of mercenary motives. A universal cynicism had become dominant. So Henry Coventry, Secretary of State, complains in 1666 that although a policy he favours is supported by 'arguments of public concern in great plenty . . . [the argument] of particular interest may dispose men to understand them not so exactly as perhaps else they would'. And among his contemporaries, many referred casually to 'men's ordinary self-interestedness' or took it as a matter of course that 'shopkeepers are, *like all other men*, led by their profit'. And as it happened, the group that could least avoid this charge was the group that supplied most of the economic literature of the time.[9]

II

Authority disallowed, detached reason is the only means of persuasion left for an advocate who does not wish to make an unsupported appeal to emotion and prejudice. All that the appeal from detached reason requires of the audience is the willingness to consider an argument purely on its intellectual merits; it is much less than the willing suspension of disbelief that the novelist requires; yet it is no little thing. Readers will especially refuse detached attention to writers whose motives they systematically suspect. And the group best suited by both experience and inclination to write on economic questions in seventeenth century England, businessmen, were the group most open to the suspicion of special pleading.

[9] BM Carte Mss., 49, f. 365, quoted in Louise F. Brown, *First Earl of Shaftesbury* (1933), 135. Roger North, *Lives*, II, 299. Child, *N.D.T.*, 107 (italics added).

Medieval philosophy conventionally identified the merchant with the sin of covetousness; even the pure act of trading, *negotium*, was considered essentially vicious. Though in the sixteenth century, as the moral power of religion faded the social utility of commerce was more readily recognized, still merchants were not highly esteemed. They could be described as 'even utter enemies to the weal public', who cared for enriching themselves alone whatever the consequences might be for anyone else. The customs officer, Thomas Milles, wrote in 1604 that 'though Kings wear crowns and seem absolutely to reign, particular bankers, private societies of merchants, and covetous persons, whose end is private gain, are able to suspend their counsels and control their policies'. In the presence of this attitude, any economic proposal made by a merchant would be considered more suspect than if it had been advanced by anyone else.[10]

The suspicion was used, and in use undoubtedly enhanced, by the merchant-pamphleteers themselves. In the furor of the Recoinage, for instance, the proponent of a scheme to reduce the high price of guineas wrote: 'there may be five hundred or one thousand men that have above five hundred or one thousand guineas each, which are the men that may or will make the most noise against' the proposal. Replied an adversary, using the conventional form of a letter to a friend, 'I have perused the paper you sent me . . . and I believe it was writ by one whose private interest it is' to have guineas priced lower.[11]

Accusation and cross-accusation had become the most constant feature of economic writing. Extolling Doctor Hugh Chamberlen's Land Bank, a writer who signs himself 'A friend to so good an undertaking' but was probably Chamberlen himself, produces the following catechism:

Q. Do other banks, namely Doctor Barebone's, the Orphans', etc., do so well as [Doctor Chamberlen's]?
A. No; they are purely contrivances for profit to themselves. . . .

---

[10] *Tudor Econ. Docts.*, III, 135. Thomas Milles, *Customers Replie* (1604), Kress, S. 106, p. 33.
[11] *Guineas at 21s. 6d. Will Make Money Plenty* (20 Mar. 1696), br., BM 816 m. 10 (29); Horsefield 366. *A Letter for Settling Guineas* (1696), br., BM 816 m. 10 (33); Horsefield 305.

And John Briscoe uses similar tactics in answering a pamphlet attacking his land bank: 'Our usurer (for such a one I am credibly informed he is, and therefore I hope he will not be offended for calling him by that name, especially since he thinks fit to conceal his own) tells us . . .'; Briscoe answers in turn each of the arguments stated by 'our usurer' or 'Mr Usurer', as the unfortunate opponent is repeatedly described.[12]

Writers were perfectly sensitive to the problem, sometimes almost pathetically so. One Richard Haines, in proposing a system for coupling indoor poor relief with promotion of linen-weaving, laments:

> Now for the better effecting a design so profitable and honourable to the Kingdom, I have improved my small genius to the utmost, notwithstanding I, above all projectors, have been most discouraged. And I know whoever will attempt anything for public benefit may expect these three things. The first is necessary, the second customary, and the third diabolical; viz., to be the object of wise men's censure, other men's laughter, and if advantageous to himself, Envy's implacable displeasure.[13]

How was the economic pamphleteer to answer such vilification? Granted that he had no hope of proving to a large, remote and suspicious audience that he was a man of guaranteed righteousness, how could he go about persuading them, at least, that he was not altogether base, a mere fraud or hypocrite, a mercenary liar, to be disbelieved at sight?

III

There are many ways in which writers might try to prove that they are disinterested, and after they have been at it for a while, they will turn fairly cunning. They are fishermen,

12 [Chamberlen], *A Bank-Dialogue, or Doctor Chamberlen's Land-Bank explained* . . . (1695), Horsefield 135, [p. 3]. John Briscoe, *An Answer to a Late Pamphlet, intituled Reasons Offered* . . . (1695), Horsefield 132, [p. 1].

13 R[ichard] H[aines], *Proposals for Building in every county a working-almshouse* . . . (1677), 4.

who turn to ingenious and sparkling lures as soon as the
quarry shows a jaded indifference to worms and minnows.
But these fish were far from innocent in the beginning, and
even if they had thought of biting they would have been
turned off by the fishermen themselves, each of them shrilly
warning that the others were deceitful. With that much
notice only the very least shrewd stood much danger of being caught, while the catchers, not hopeful, went on doing
the best they knew how.

As it is difficult to indict a man if you do not know his
name, anonymity was the most obvious way to avoid the
charge of special pleading. An unknown author cannot easily be convicted of favouring the Levant Company, let us
say, merely because he is a member. Anonymity, to be sure,
has other uses; it is an obvious way also to avoid charges of
seditious libel, but this cannot have been the reason why so
many writers on economic subjects chose to be anonymous,
for after 1660 the Star Chamber was no longer on the scene
and prerogative proceedings against writers became fairly
rare; besides, few economic problems had roots deep enough
to involve them with sensitive constitutional issues, and no
writer appears to have been prosecuted for anything he said
about economics.

Yet despite the immunity from official interference, economic writers preferred to leave their writings unacknowl-
edged. Of some hundred and more pamphlets on money
issued during 1695, for instance, almost two out of every
three appeared without the author's name.[14]

Neither diffidence nor modesty can explain this remarkable penchant. Some other causes may explain part of it.
Anonymity may sometimes have been assumed in order to
simulate unanimity. A prolific writer dashes off a heap of
thin pamphlets and broadsheets all favouring the same proposal, in order to make it appear that the proposal has wide
support; he is stuffing the ballot-box of opinion. In a hand-
ful of cases, anonymity may have been intended to shield a
lampooner or parodist from reprisal in the law courts or

[14] Cf. Horsefield, pp. 289 ff., which gives a very voluminous list
of publications.

outside. But the chief cause of anonymity appears to have been the author's fear that if anything were injured by revealing his name it would be the force of his argument.

Not that anonymity insured belief; pretending not to be there does not make a man a smaller target. Briscoe's adversary who thought 'fit to conceal' his proper name was labelled 'Our usurer' for his pains. Chamberlen, in replying to 'a Late Nameless and Scurrilous Libel', made the most of his assailant's reticence. 'It seems the author himself is conscious he is in the wrong, he takes such care to conceal not only his own name but also the printer's.' It would be pleasant to know whether readers refused Chamberlen a hearing because while thus rebuking the other he too took care to conceal his name.[15]

As plain anonymity was obviously not good enough, some more enterprising spirits took to embellishing it. One of them, known only by his initials, J.S., slipped in such views as he cared to propound among passages from Sir Walter Raleigh, publishing the unholy mixture under the modest title, *Select Observations of the Incomparable Sir Walter Raleigh . . . as it was presented to King James. . . .* He was then able to tout the work as follows:

> The name of the author stamps [this book] standard proof against all the efforts and false allays of counterfeits, who slily, under the mask of public service, have insinuated their gilded notions, and essayed to make their sophistical positions pass for current reason. Tis for this cause that now this incomparable author interposes, whom the world knows to have been free from partiality and self-interest.

J.S. was frank enough to declare that he added some things referring to present circumstances—his readers could hardly have forgotten that Raleigh and James I were a half-century

---

[15] Briscoe, see p. 95 above. Chamberlen, *Some Remarks upon a late nameless and scurrilous libel entitled, A Bank Dialogue between Dr H. C. and a country gentleman* . . . (1696), Horsefield 374; the original is Horsefield 134.

dead—but he did not take the trouble to say just where his amendments begin and end.[16]

A somewhat similar technique, that coupled anonymity with lies about the author's occupation and deceptive remarks about the direction of his private interest, was used by Josiah Child in his *Discourse about Trade*.[17] Indeed the wonder is that anonymous writers did not often take to lying about their own standing; it is surely a tribute to man's instinctive honesty.

To face the presumption of self-interest head on and assert that one is free of it may not be a much more subtle device than anonymity, but its boldness may have made some rhetorical appeal. Edward Misselden[18] made his disclosure and disavowal in these terms: 'It is true I am a brother, though unworthy, of that worthy Society [of Merchant Adventurers], and so I am of other companies also; and so also I am a member, though one of the least, of that great commonwealth of this Kingdom; wherein I have learned to prefer that public, to all these particular obligations.' Conceding that his private interest and the public good might clash, Misselden asserted that he would always prefer the public good. And so perhaps he did; but perhaps others wondered whether saying so made it so. Nor would it be much more satisfying to hear from the author of a tract on the Africa trade this solemn avowal: 'I can easily foresee that some people may be apt to mistake me for some person concerned in the Royal African Company, but I solemnly profess, upon my veracity and as I would be believed in the greatest of truths, that I have no particular or immediate concern in either the stock of that Company or any of the separate traders to Africa; and may therefore reasonably hope to be the least suspected of partiality in what I write. . . .'[19]

[16] J.S., *Select Observations* . . . (1696), Horsefield 362; cf. W. A. Shaw, *Select Tracts and Documents* . . . (1896), 108, 121–30.
[17] See p. 43 f. above.
[18] [Edward Misselden], *The Circle of Commerce* (1623), 65.
[19] *Reflections upon the Constitution and Management of the Trade to Africa* . . . (1709), BM 712 m. 1 (19), [p. ii].

Perhaps this device is met with rarely because the writers recognized that it would not meet the purpose.

A more radical method of solving the problem is to assert that public good and private good cannot ordinarily conflict. Proof of an assertion so contrary to ordinary presumptions would require a very subtle structure, and it is therefore worth looking closely at an example to see just how the doctrine was buttressed. Thomas Mun set up such a proof in his famous treatise, *England's Treasure by Foreign Trade*. In the first place, he said, the King must gain by foreign trade, because of his income from customs. And the nation might gain even though the merchant lost; for instance, if the East India Company exported £100,000 of goods and imported £300,000, and lost money in the process because its total expenses were £350,000, still the nation would gain by the import surplus of £200,000.

And as for the really difficult case, where the merchant profits by a transaction which harms the nation by making the balance of trade unfavourable, still there is no necessary discrepancy between his private interests and the public interest—for in this case the fault lies not with the merchant but with a 'disorder in the people, when through pride and other excess they do consume [an excess] of foreign wares', or with the King who may be so intent on increasing the revenue of the customs that he ignores the balance of trade.

Mun concludes that in a properly regulated State, where the King restrains his own and his people's excessive appetites, the merchant must always contribute to the good of the realm and of the King. He is always a beneficial member of the community, always by his 'laudable endeavours' enriching the State, improving its arts, supplying its wants, employing its labourers, developing its lands, nursing its mariners, and protecting it against enemies. Mun ends with the admonition that any reasonable government will protect the merchants, because 'it is a principle in reason of State to maintain and defend that which doth support them and their estates'. The reader is supposed to draw the further conclusion that economic proposals made by the trader should not be gainsaid, since the traders' interests always concur with the best interest of the State. And it would follow on Mun's theory that once a writer identified himself as a merchant, he established a claim to authority.[20]

Somewhat after Mun's day, Adam Smith remarked: 'I have never known much good done by those who affected to trade for the public good. It is an affectation, indeed, not very common among merchants, and very few words need be employed in dissuading them from it.' In the seventeenth century, however, it was an affectation usual with merchants, who had not yet forgotten the medieval injunction that all economic activity must be for the common good, and who accepted the mercantilist dogma that England's treasure must be earned by foreign trade. But if an argument like Mun's convinced some readers, it could not convince those who noticed that Mun was only one of many traders, each advocating his own special plan for producing public benefits. A great deluge of economic writings descended on England after the middle of the seventeenth century, most of it produced by merchants, most of whom disagreed. The mere assertion, that merchants were almost bound to act in the public interest, was not enough when different merchants urged patently contradictory policies.

What militated still further against Mun's attempt to establish the merchant's disinterest was the evident fact that merchants differed by trades, each proposing what was in the interests of his own trade. A contemporary wrote that no matter how much traders invoked the public good, they used it only as a camouflage for their own private colours.

. . . There are many, who to gain a little in their own trades, care not how much others suffer; and each man strives, that all others may be forced, in their dealings, to act subserviently for his profit. . . .

So clothiers would have men forced to buy their manufacture; and I may mention such as sell wool, they would have men forced to buy of them at a high price, though the clothier loseth. The tinners would have their tin dear, though the merchant profits little. And in general, all those who are lazy, and do not, or are not active enough, and cannot look out to vent the

[20] Mun, chap. vii, pp. 26, 88.

product of their estates, or to trade with it themselves, would have all traders forced by laws, to bring home to them sufficient prices, whether they gain or lose by it.[21]

In view of the evident self-seeking of merchants, as well as of all other men, no single merchant's proposals could be taken as a fair statement of the nation's interests.

Might one allay suspicion by going a step further than Mun, and demonstrating that the proposal one favoured ran absolutely contrary to one's private interests? So gallant and sportsmanlike a gesture was made by Nicholas Barbon. He opened his treatise on coinage by emphasizing the divergence of interests. 'That which seems to be the greatest difficulty in clearing this controversy is that, if being a matter where profit accompanies the decision of it, gentlemen are jealous of the arguments, lest they should be biased by private interest and so run contrary to the truth. . . .' And then Barbon enters the evidence that his arguments merit faith.[22]

Anyone who invested in a bank, Barbon explained, might gain whether the recoinage took place at the old standard or at a devalued standard. If the new coins were made lighter, as he himself advocated, then a bank holding a large stock of old money would profit; it would receive more new shilling pieces than it turned in of the old. If, on the other hand, the new coins were at the heavy standard, the banks would profit anyway by melting down the new coins—for as Barbon and many others realized, the silver content of a full-weight coin made on the old standard was worth slightly more as bullion, at least for the time being, than it was worth as money, a difference that could be pocketed by anyone who melted down such coins and sold the bullion in the open market. Moreover, Barbon continued, banks would be better off in another respect under these circumstances, for heavy coins must mean fewer coins, and 'nothing can be of greater advantage to banks than scarcity of money, when

[21] Sir Dudley North, *Discourse* [p. vii].
[22] Barbon, *Concerning coining*, at sig. 'A3' ff.

men will be glad to take a bank note for want of it'. All of
which led Barbon, the banker, to his desired conclusion:

> So that if I were to consider my private interest, I
> ought to be of the contrary opinion to that I argue for.
> And therefore I hope I shall be believed when I de-
> clare that I have no other design in writing this dis-
> course than the service of my country.

It is not perhaps setting too much stock in mere accuracy
to point out that this argument is specious. Barbon wins his
way through by showing that the single reason why it would
be in his self-interest to have the new money lighter is out-
weighed by two reasons why it would not. This may be a
good calculus for debaters, but has nothing to do with economics. For while it is true that the arguments against out-
number their opposite, the only thing that really matters is
whether the profit one way would be greater or less than the
other, no matter how many separate sources it came from.
And that question nobody could answer in advance, for it
depended on how large the circulation of bank-notes was,
how great the bank's profit on each, the market price of
bullion and any number of similar details. There is no way
of telling, therefore, whether Barbon's proposal would or
would not have enriched Barbon the banker. But it is easy
enough to tell how it would have affected the fortunes of
Barbon the man. He was, after all, less of a banker than a
builder, as a builder he was a heavy debtor, and as a debtor
he could not fail to gain by a devaluation. So that his whole
argument, considered on its merits, collapses.

It collapsed also in the eyes of his contemporaries. One of
them, after reflecting how much devaluation would have
been worth 'to Dr Barbon, as to his expected Bank—by
which means the sum subscribed would have been ¼
more . . .', seizes the weak link:

> And here I remember what the Doctor says in answer
> to this, in his Epistle: that he could have got more by
> melting down the new coin of the present standard than
> he could propose to do by a new coinage [that raised
> the face value of a given weight of silver from 5 shil-

lings] to 6 shillings and 3 pence. But this he should talk
to children or such projectors as himself, for I would
fain know whether it is safer and more for advantage to
gain 15 pence in a crown legally, or to gain but one
penny . . . in a crown, and incur thereby the penalty
of the law against such melting down.[23]

But even had this fatal flaw not been present, even had
the argument been utterly sincere, the demonstration of al-
truism was altogether too good to swallow. Of course there
are people who lean over backward, but anyone who announces that he is doing so raises the doubt that he is assuming a pose rather than a position. The English public
after 1660 was just as apt as Adam Smith to suspect most
that merchant who most professes public spirit. It may not
be a generous attitude, but it was the common one.

IV

As the customary writers on economic matters could not
hope to assume the mantle of personal authority and were
obliged instead to defend themselves constantly against personal disqualification, to find a form of argument as impersonal as possible was their best hope. Such a form was
discovered—or rather adapted, more or less independently, to
economic argumentation—by Sir Dudley North. There is no
particular reason to believe that he chose his method deliberately or instinctively, but choose it he did; and his brother,
Roger, in the preface he wrote to Dudley's *Discourses upon
Trade*, described the way out, a means of proving, so far as
can ever be proved, the objectivity of any policy statement.[24]

Roger North realized as well as any that private motives could interfere with the clarity of thought about economic matters. He listed many instances in which it had
happened, and conceded that Dudley might have done the

[23] E.H., *Decus & Tutamen* . . . (1696), 2–3.
[24] Sir Dudley North, *Discourses upon trade* (1691); for Roger
North's authorship of preface, see Appendix IV, p. 271.

same: 'He is liable to the same suspicion which attends those of a different judgment, that is, partiality to his own interest.' In showing why Dudley's conclusions might nevertheless avoid suspicion, Roger outlined the requirements of an objective argument. It is all very simple. The demonstration must be 'built upon clear and evident truths', the premises must be 'principles indisputably true'. The 'course of the argument' must be 'limpid and intelligible'. The conclusions will then inevitably be correct.

It will seem to others, less optimistic than Roger North, that it is asking very much of any premises that they be indisputably true. But a confirmed believer in Descartes, such as Roger North was, accepted as an article of faith that no solid knowledge can come from doubtful premises, that is, from premises which can be doubted. 'Clear and evident', as Roger North used the terms, was a Cartesian slogan meaning nothing more than 'true beyond question'. But even a non-Cartesian might agree that the more nearly self-evident the premise of an argument, the more certain will be the conclusions drawn from it. Every argument, in fact, seems objective just so far as it derives from indisputable premises. But if Roger North was convinced that Sir Dudley had prepared a perfectly objective treatment of trade, still his appraisal included that last reservation which is the final defence of an objective argument. Sir Dudley's work, Roger wrote, might not be perfect, but 'he hath given his judgment with his reasons, which everyone is free to canvass; and there is no other means whereby a wise and honest person can justify his opinions in public concerns'.

Roger North's prescription for objectivity, in short, is a taut deductive system that infers its conclusions from a set of simple principles. This is the method of 'demonstration', as that term was understood in classical logic; it is precisely the method of Euclid's proofs, and as Roger North suggested, nobody would accuse Euclid of maintaining any of his theorems because they suited his self-interest. The only relevant critique is that the premises are false or inadequate or the chain of reasoning imperfect; failing this, the conclusions are binding, no matter what may be the character of the author.

But this method for guaranteeing objectivity is also the method *par excellence* of scientific theory. The theory consists of a deductive system linking a few fundamental principles with a set of conclusions, as modern price theory, for instance, links fundamental propositions about utility and costs of production to conclusions about equilibrium conditions of an economy; and here too the only pertinent questions are whether the premises are correct and adequate and the chain of reasoning flawless.

In the search for a way of dispelling the problem of special pleading, a scientific method was hit on. The needs of rhetoric brought forth the method of economic theory.

This happy concurrence was not altogether accidental. North learned Descartes' doctrine from his *Discourse on Method*, a work expressly intended to lay a foundation for science, a work connected with the great interest that seventeenth-century Europeans took in scientific discovery.

Another method of science was being propounded at the same time. The inductive empiricism advocated by Francis Bacon, and adopted as official dogma by the Royal Society, also had its impact on the development of economics. How it did so, and to what effect, is evident in the work of John Collins and Sir William Petty.

And there is one further strand in the development of scientific economics. It traces back, surprisingly enough, to the long tradition of moral and political philosophy, in which economic thought was long embedded, and from which it was only slowly and never perfectly detached. The influence of the philosophic tradition on the development of modern economics can nowhere better be studied than in the works of John Locke.

Petty, Locke, North, each in his own way shows the direction in which economic theory developed after their time.

Chapter 4

JOHN COLLINS: MATHEMATICS
AND ECONOMICS

THE SCIENTIFIC REVOLUTION that accompanied the Restoration of Charles II owed much of its vigour to faith. One
of the chief elements of this faith was the simple belief that
many things in nature, as yet mysterious, could and should
be measured precisely. Men suddenly persuaded themselves
that dimensions which had always been matters of conjecture could be counted or weighed or somehow stated in
precise numbers. Hand in hand with this revolutionary ideal
went a devout but misplaced notion that to measure and to
understand were one and the same. Restoration scientists
believed that to cast a mathematical mantle over a problem
was tantamount to solving it.

The scientists united themselves in the Royal Society and
set off on an absolute orgy of measurement. Some of their
work was eventually fruitful, producing at the best Boyle's
law of gases or Newton's laws of motion. But most fellows of
the Royal Society failed to see that what explained these
successes was not the mere acts of measuring the volumes of
gases or recording the locations of stars. As they over-valued
observation and calculation, so they ignored the imagination
and luck that enabled some men to make theoretical inventions. Failing to see this, the virtuosi continued, endlessly
and pointlessly, to record, catalogue and count. The best
minds of England squandered their talents in minutely recording temperature, wind and the look of the skies hour by
hour, in various corners of the land. Their efforts produced
nothing more than the unusable records.

This impassioned energy was turned also to the measurement of economic and social dimensions of various sorts. Fellows and affiliates of the Royal Society set about establishing

more precisely some of the facts that makers of economic policy needed to know but could only guess at. In undertaking this perfectly worthy task, the early economic statisticians could not rid themselves of their 'scientific' optimism; they assumed that correct information would automatically transform itself into the best possible policy. The search for number, weight and measure was conducted in the happy belief that good numbers would inevitably make for good policy.

Nowhere can the operation of this frame of mind better be seen than in the life and work of John Collins. He is a simpler, less successful version of Sir William Petty, but it is precisely because he is less ostentatious and more tentative that the aims of Political Arithmetic stand out more clearly in his work than in Petty's.

I

His was such a wild, wandering youth as was shared by many of the men whose normal careers were interrupted by the Interregnum. His father was a 'poor minister' in Wood Eaton, a village near Oxford, where John Collins was born in 1625. He was sent to the local grammar school, but both parents dying, he stayed there only long enough to learn so much Latin 'as an ordinary schoolboy' and no Greek. He then went out apprentice to a bookseller in Oxford, who however failed. This was the first appearance of two characteristic features of his whole life: a passion for the publication and sale of books, and an unhappy tendency to find employment with institutions that shortly thereafter perished.[1]

---

[1] Some minor details of Collins' life are uncertain, chiefly because facts of time, place, and date fluctuate slightly in his various autobiographical accounts; in selecting from among the ample sources I have generally preferred a contemporary to a later account and an intimate letter to an official or public statement. BIRTH: *Correspondence of Isaac Newton* (H. W. Turnbull, ed., 1959), I, 5. SCHOOL: *James Gregory Tercentenary Memorial Volume* (H. W. Turnbull, ed., 1939), 16; Collins to John Wallis, Feb. 1667, in S. P. Rigaud, *Correspondence of Scientific Men of the 17th Century* (1841), II, 481–82. BOOKSELLER: *Gregory*, 16.

Another of the chief facets of his life shows up in his next job, which was as a clerk in the royal kitchen or wine-cellar. How he came by the position is not clear, but he spent the years from 1639 to 1642 working under John Marr, Clerk of the Kitchen to the then Prince of Wales, later Charles II. Marr was also by way of being an expert on sundials, and laid out several dials in the gardens of Whitehall Palace; in this science he instructed Collins, who, though he was forgetting what Latin he knew, was making 'no small progress' in mathematics. A basis was thus laid, before he reached seventeen, for the chief intellectual interest of his life. The Civil War now broke out; Charles I began to retrench his expenses, especially 'his household's diets'; and so Collins went on elsewhere again.[2]

According to various of Collins' accounts, he spent the next seven years, his seventeenth to twenty-fourth, at sea, on an English ship, which for much of the period was engaged in the Venetian service. The Venetians were involved in a prolonged, intermittent war with the Turks, and were recruiting mercenaries, some of them English; the fighting became most intense when the Turks in 1644 attacked Crete, the last outpost of the Venetians in the Eastern Mediterranean. Collins participated in the naval defence of Crete, though he left the Venetian service, happily, before Crete fell. He seems to have been purser of the ship, perhaps because of his mathematical bent, which he continued to follow during this service; 'having leisure, I applied part of my studies to mathematics and merchants' accounts'.[3]

When he returned to London in 1649, at the age of twenty-four, he set up as a teacher of writing, mathematics, and accounting. In 1652 he wrote a brief textbook called *An Introduction to Merchants Accounts*, which had the

[2] *Gregory*, 16. Collins, 'Proposals delivered to some Eminent persons in November 1667', PRO 30/24 4/160. Collins, *Introduction to Merchants' Accompts* (1675 ed.), published in Malynes *Consuetudo* (1686), 'To the reader . . .'. RETRENCHING OF EXPENSES: *C.S.P.D. 1641–43*, 201, 263.

[3] Collins, *Merchants Accompts* (*op. cit.* n. 2 above). PURSER: Collins, 'Proposals' (*op. cit.* n. 2 above) [p. 2]. MERCENARIES: see, e.g., *C.S.P.D. 1648–49*, 115. CRETE: Musatti, *Storia di Venezia* (1936 ed.), chap. XXV.

good fortune to be published as an appendix to Malynes' *Consuetudo*, the most popular merchants' handbook of its time. The *Introduction* was well-liked; Collins was soon sent for by the Treasurer of the Excise Office, who offered him a position as accountant in the office. His work, in fact, was that of an auditor, it being his responsibility to review the reports of the subcommissioners and farmers of the excise. Collins proudly reported that 'he suddenly raised the debts' (that is, the accounts receivable) of his office from £8,000 to £40,000, and indeed the Committee for Regulating the Excise very soon commended him as an 'able officer' who should be rewarded by a rise in salary—though it is not recorded that the rise was ever confirmed. So began Collins' long, honourable, and underpaid career with the Civil Service.[4]

At the Restoration he found himself in the same precarious position as other servants of the Commonwealth, and like others, petitioned the King for reinstatement in his office. His petition, presented by Sir Robert Moray, was embellished with a summary that Collins had drawn up of all the Excise accounts, and reinforced with a record of royal associations: he had been a clerk at Court and had later married Bellona, daughter of William Austin, one of the King's master cooks. Charles II directed Southampton, the Lord Treasurer, to continue Collins in his appointment, and there he continued at a salary of £100 for the next eight years. In the meanwhile he had kept up his amateur work in mathematics, on the strength of which he was elected a fellow of the Royal Society in 1667, and entered on a voluminous correspondence with all the great mathematicians of the age, an activity to which he owes his minor fame.[5]

But his career in the Civil Service did not flourish. In 1667, by then past forty, he was still at his post in the Excise Office. He had not advanced; on the contrary he was 'appre-

---

[4] TEACHER: Collins, *Merchants Accompts* (*op. cit.* n. 2, p. 108 above). EXCISE: Collins, 'Proposals' (*op. cit.* n. 2, p. 108 above), [p. 3]. ABLE OFFICER: *C.S.P.D.* 1652–53, 240.

[5] Collins, 'Narrative' (ca. 1674), in H.M.C. *Montagu*, 177–78; a similar paper is in *C.S.P.D. Mar. 1677–Feb. 1678*, 542. *Cal. Treas. Bks.* 1660–67, 5, 241.

hending a period to that employment to draw near'. He now began to broadcast among the highest officers of the crown, ministers and privy councillors by the dozens, schemes to assure him public employment as an auditor-accountant-statistician-economist-bibliographer. The petitions did not take effect; but the Excise Office, as he feared, was dismantled, its functions being taken over by the London Farmers of the Excise, who did the work gratis, though, Collins darkly hints, 'notwithstanding, the King's charge was increased'. But luckily, Collins had made good his escape. The help was afforded by a mathematical friend. Just as in 1660, his petition to Charles had been presented by Sir Robert Moray, the Royal Society's first president, so now his new employment was offered by Lord Brereton, another virtuoso and patron of scientists.[6]

At the end of 1667, shortly after the Second Dutch War, the parliamentary opposition seized an opportunity to embarrass the King by questioning the financial administration of the war. A Commission of Accounts was appointed to investigate, Lord Brereton was chosen its chairman, and he appointed Collins the chief accountant of the Commission. The new work began early in 1668; prudently and in the delightfully proprietary manner of seventeenth century office-holders, Collins left a friend to substitute in his place at the Excise Office while he set to work, in person, at the Commission's offices at Brook House. But the appointment with the Brook House Commissioners soon proved to be less than ideal, for 'not liking their methods and urging things too far, as some thought, to the King's advantage, he became a sufferer thereby', that is, he was paid less than had been promised. Moreover, although the Farmers of the Irish excise—and especially Sir James Shaen, one of Petty's great enemies—asked him to go to Dublin as their chief accountant, the Commissioners would not let him. By 1670 the Commissioners had prepared a report very unfavourable to the War government, which Collins later said he had *not*

[6] Collins, 'Proposals' (*op. cit.* n. 2, p. 108 above). PETITIONS: *Cal. Treas. Bks.* 1667–68, 137, 340. LONDON FARMERS: *Cal. Treas. Bks.* sub 24 June 1668; Collins, 'Narrative' (*op. cit.* n. 5, p. 109 above).

helped to draft. Quite the contrary, Charles II, on seeing the report, gave it to Sir Philip Warwick for criticism; Warwick referred it to Collins, who pointed out its defects, which so pleased Warwick that he asked Sir John Trevor, Secretary of State, to get Collins an appointment worth £200 a year. But this was not done.[7]

In the summer of 1670 a new job turned up. As part of the growing apparatus for central, expert economic administration, a Council for Plantations—parallel to the Council for Trade—was established on a permanent basis, with ten paid members under the Chairmanship of Lord Sandwich. Among the members was Henry Slingsby, Master of the Mint, who served as Secretary to the Council, and who appointed Collins as one of the two clerks. The work was not all of it inspiring: in March 1671, on the Council being enlarged by the addition of seven dignitaries, Collins was too busy to maintain his scientific correspondence because it fell to his 'lot to transcribe copies of the [lengthy] Commissions and Instructions for their use'. Moreover, as the Council met in the afternoons, Collins was prevented from attending the meetings of the Royal Society. The pay should have been some compensation, since the salary was supposed to have been £150 a year, the highest Collins had yet earned. But as these were the years preceding the Third Dutch War, during which Charles' finances were more strained than ever, Collins' handsome salary simply was not paid—in his two years with the Council he was paid 'little more than a tithe' of it. Worse than that, a half-pay pension awarded him for the loss of his place in the Excise Office had stopped altogether in 1671, as also his 'wife's pay as laundress of the table linen to the Queen'. He survived, apparently, by doing some accounting work on the side, among others for the Alum Farmers, that is, the contractors who farmed the royal alum monopoly. He economized by living in his father-in-law's house, but with a numerous family—

---

[7] SUBSTITUTE AT EXCISE OFFICE: Collins to Pell (6 Feb. 1668), in BM Slo. MSS. 4278, f. 331. COMMISSION OF ACCOUNTS: W. A. Shaw, Introduction to Cal. Treas. Bks. 1667–68, l–lxxxvi. COLLINS' DIFFICULTIES: Collins, 'Narrative' (op. cit. n. 5, p. 109 above).

which by 1677 included seven children—he could not continue as he was.[8]

His patron, Henry Slingsby, helpfully led him into his next employment, a position in the Farthing Office. A new attempt was at this time being made to solve the perpetual but now especially marked shortage of small coin by producing at least £15,000 worth of copper farthings. Slingsby, as Master of the Mint, installed Collins as distributor of the farthings—'to deliver out all that are coined, on Tuesdays, Thursdays, and Saturday, in the mornings, in crown-papers ready tied up'. As there were subordinates to tell out the coins and one known as the 'tier-up-in-paper' to prepare the rolls, Collins thought it would be almost a sinecure, and that he might concurrently set up as a stationer and eventually perhaps a publisher as well. This latter dream he did not realize, but he stayed on in the Farthing Office as long as he could, which was three and one-half years. But then it was proposed that copper farthings should go out, perhaps because the copper had to be imported. Collins was identified as one of the copper party—he spent a fortnight in August 1676 'engaged in transcribing etc. many papers and arguments against tin farthings, in which argument being shipwrecked, and the matter determined for tin and against copper farthings, my employment at the farthing office . . . is ceased'. That was the end of his public service.[9]

The last stage of his professional career now began. Just as he was leaving the Farthing Office he had written to a

[8] SLINGSBY: Collins, 'Narrative' (op. cit. n. 5, p. 109 above). TRANSCRIBING: Collins to Gregory (25 Mar. 1671), in Rigaud, II, 217. ROYAL SOCIETY: Collins to Vernon (4 Apr. 1671), in Rigaud, I, 161. PAY: Collins to Beale (20 Aug. 1672), in Rigaud, I, 200–1. PENSION: Collins to Beale, ibid. Collins' complaint is borne out by Cal. Treas. Bks. 1669–72 (et seq.), which shows the pension being paid for the last time in June 1671; pp. 103, 255, 875, and passim. ALUM FARMERS: Collins to Vernon (7 Feb. 1671), in Rigaud, I, 141. FAMILY: Collins to Thomas Baker (23 May 1677), in Rigaud, II, 23 ff.

[9] COPPER FARTHINGS: Cal. Treas. Bks. 1672–75, 611; Craig, The Mint, 174–76, 178–79. COLLINS' APPOINTMENT: Collins to Beale (20 Aug. 1672), in Rigaud, I, 200–1; Cal. Treas. Bks. 1672–75, 124–25. END OF COPPER: Collins to Baker (19 Aug. 1676), in Rigaud, II, 4; Cal. Treas. Bks. 1676–79, 1267, 1297.

friend, 'I begin to enter into a small employment, as to part
of my time, under the Company of the Royal Fishery, yet in
its infancy. . . .' It was a curious infancy, without a future,
an attempt to revive a fishing monopoly that had never been
more than a paper scheme and never came to much more.
This latest effort at revival was launched in 1676 by a group
of projectors, headed by the Earls of Suffolk, Scarsdale and
Carlisle. The heart of the scheme was to have been an
arrangement to pay over great public subsidies to the Company and require victuallers to buy its products. The corresponding public benefit was to be that the need to buy from
the Dutch fishermen, whose exports to England were calculated at £300,000 a year, would be reduced or eliminated.
But the Dutch had developed the industry to a peak of
efficiency, and the English adventurers suffered not only
from this entrenched competition, and from the Crown's
refusal to grant a subsidy, but also from the fact that most of
their ships were captured by the French during 1676.[10]

Collins, therefore, almost as soon as he became the Royal
Fishery Company's accountant, had to reveal that it was
virtually moribund. He proved to them 'that they had lost
£9,000 of £11,000 stock and were near ruin'. In 1680, the
proprietors were forced to sell their remaining vessels and
stores to Benjamin Watson, a merchant, and several associates, who tried to raise the needed capital by a public
subscription, and 'yet the affair would have fainted away
again' if Sir James Shaen had not put up more money. Collins continued accountant to this limping concern almost to
his death. He died in 1683 of a disorder contracted, it is
said, 'by drinking cider when he was too warm'.[11]

Thus, so far as the public records can reveal, Collins was
a minor technician, impecunious and importunate. Schemes

[10] INFANCY: Collins to Baker (23 May 1677), in Rigaud, II, 23 f.
APPLICATION FOR SUBSIDIES: C.S.P.D. Mar. 1676–Feb. 1677, 4,
154–55, 219, 574. SUBSIDY REFUSED: C.S.P.D. Mar. 1677–Feb.
1678, 54; C.S.P.D. 1682, 275. CAPTURE OF SHIPS: C.S.P.D. 1682,
275; Collins, A Plea [sig. A3].
[11] LOSS: Collins, 'An Abridgement of divers papers . . .', PRO
30/24 30/8 (2). WATSON AND SHAEN: Collins, Plea [at sig. A3];
Collins, Salt and Fishery, 'Dedication'. DEATH: Gregory (op. cit. n. 1,
p. 107 above), 16.

and proposals showered from him; occasional offers were held out to him, most of which turned out to lack substance; and he drudged on, taking occasionally a small employment as it offered. Some of these employments were hack writing —he lent his name, even, as presumed translator, to a broadsheet extolling the omnipotent restorative and curative powers of spirits of saffron, selling at half-crown the pint. He mentioned that Shaftesbury, while Chancellor, nominated him 'in divers references concerning suits depending in Chancery, about intricate Accounts, to assist in the stating thereof, which has not been without emolument to myself, and to the shortening of the charge of the parties concerned'. 'Not without emolument to myself' is probably the least modest way in which his earnings, taken all in all, could be described.[12]

II

But among the mathematicians of his time this minuscule bookkeeper figured as a giant. He was a friend of Newton, and for a long while his most constant correspondent. He was on similar terms with Gregory, among British mathematicians second only to Newton himself, and with Wallis, Pell, Vernon, Gregory, Beale, Strode, and Baker. Leibniz, writing to Henry Oldenburg, asked to be commended to only two men, 'the illustrious Boyle' and 'the learned Collins'.[13]

The learning that produced this praise and made Collins a coveted friend of so many great mathematicians of the time is, as the correspondence shows, of a particular sort. In the first place, Collins was the consumate bibliographer, bibliophile, and book-supplier. He was constantly informing the great mathematicians of each other's latest writings, of

[12] Collins, *The virtues and uses of the cordial spirit of saffron*, BM 1865. c. 20 (52). Collins, *Merchants' Accompts* (*op. cit.* n. 2, p. 108 above), 'To the reader . . .'.

[13] Leibniz to Oldenburg (18 Dec. 1675), in *Newton Corres.* (*op. cit.* n. 1, p. 107 above), I, 402. For Collins' mathematical correspondence, see the works cited in n. 1, p. 107 above, and BM Sloane MSS. 4278, *passim*.

the new and old books wherever published or to be had; and by virtue of his access to the London stationers, and access—via the Alum Farmers—to foreign exchange, was constantly buying and sending treatises throughout the learned world, and arranging to have them edited or published. A characteristic passage in his letters reads: 'Reinaldinus' folio volume of algebra is extant and Mr Allestree has some of them remaining, together with Borellus *de vi percussionis,* and a treatise of running waters, entitled *Direttione di fiumi.* Let not Mr Branker fear that I shall be instrumental or assenting to the printing of Kinckhuysen's Conics without your and his leave.' At any time between 1668 and 1680, Collins, it is quite safe to say, knew more about the frontiers of mathematical inquiry than any other man. He was supremely well-informed about the state of work in algebra, the calculus, infinite series, and the theory of equations.[14]

Yet, knowing all that was being done, at these frontiers he did nothing himself. His own published writings are applications, and mainly obvious applications, of what he learned from his great friends. His treatises on the geometrical laying-out of sundials, on rule-of-thumb navigation, on gauging, on the computation of discounts and interest-charges—none of these shows or is intended to show much mathematical sophistication. Indeed these productions are, on the whole, more of the hack work that Collins undertook 'not without remuneration'.[15]

In the correspondence, Collins' relation to these problems shows itself in still sharper light. He appears as a broker between practical and theoretical problems. When his friend and disciple, Michael Dary, a poor tobacco-cutter and teacher of gauging, posed a problem in gauging, Collins transformed the question into abstract form, forwarded it to Newton and Gregory, and retransformed their solutions into methods of approximating. The problem of

[14] FOREIGN EXCHANGE: Collins to Francis Vernon (7 Feb. 1671), in Rigaud, I, 141. REINALDINUS: Collins to Pell (6 Feb. 1668), BM Sloane MSS. 4278, f. 331.

[15] Collins: *Sector on a Quadrant* (1658); *Geometrical Dyalling* (1659); *The Mariner's Plain Scale new plain'd* (1659); *The Doctrine of decimal arithmetick . . .* (1685).

gauging was to measure, mainly for excise purposes, the capacity of the variously and oddly shaped vats, hogsheads, and barrels in which inn-keepers and vintners kept their wine. The old-fashioned method of measurement was empirical, the contents being emptied into containers of known capacity. But this method had many defects, not to mention its scientific inelegance. Dary, therefore, aimed to refine the process by determining the capacity from the linear measures of the vessel. The vessels often had parabolic, elliptical, or spherical cross-sections, and so the question Dary put, as Collins well understood, was how to determine the area under a parabola, or the volume enclosed by the rotation of a conic section. Newton and Gregory responded to Collins' queries by offering converging infinite series that enabled one to approximate the volume to any degree of accuracy required. Dary did the next stage of popularizing: he constructed detailed tables, from which ordinary gaugers could read off the answers. What is revealing in all this about Collins, is that Newton did not say to Collins: you need only integrate the following expression. He handed over the finished answer, but did not reproduce his reasoning, for it—so the tenor of the letter suggests—would have been beyond Collins' understanding.[16]

And Collins was nothing but modest about his own mathematical powers. He told John Wallis that his treatise on quadrants was 'despicable'—written at the instance of Sutton, who wanted an occasion to prepare plates by way of advertising his skill as a mathematical engraver; his book on navigation 'altogether unworthy the view of a geometer'; and said, in summary, 'nor am I at all conceited of anything I have done, nor would be sorry if they were all burned, being toys done in ignorance and haste'. He never pretended to keep great company, confessing himself a man of 'no estate', not too proud to frequent a mathematical club 'consisting of divers ingenious mechanics, gaugers, carpenters, shipwrights, some seamen, lightermen, etc., whose whole discourse is about equations'. One thing he coveted above all

16 See, for instance, the letters between Collins and Newton in *Newton Corres.* (*op. cit.* n. 1, p. 107 above), I, 27, 28, 29–30, 307–8, 344.

else, his 'correspondence with the learned'; and of one thing he was proud, 'being a member of the Royal Society (though but a mean person), admitted, as he believes, on opinion that he might be serviceable to the republic of literature'. Whenever he could, he signed himself 'John Collins, Fellow of the Royal Society, Philomath'. It was philomathia rather than mathematical skill that led him toward political arithmetic.[17]

III

One might have thought that Collins would make a mark on Economics, if he chose to deal with it at all. His long and peripatetic career in the Civil Service had acquainted him in detail with taxation and public expenditures, coinage, and trade, foreign and colonial; the variety and importance of the subjects allow one to guess that he knew more about the sheer facts of economic policy than any other man of his time. He was also well versed in economic opinion, having long been an avid collector of tracts on this subject, as on mathematics.[18] Moreover, his skill in mathematics, including accounting, was, if not of the highest, far greater than was needed for economics. It is a mistake to deduce from the conveniences that mathematics now provides for economists that mathematics played an essential part in the development of economic theory; but there is no doubt that a natural facility for mathematics, such as Collins obviously had, can be and perhaps must be an important facet of the economist's

[17] Collins to Wallis (28 Feb. 1666?; 1 Aug. 1666; Feb. 1667; 21 Mar. 1672), in Rigaud, II, 462, 463, 481–82, 525–26. CORRESPONDENCE WITH LEARNED: Collins to Thomas Baker (23 May 1677), in Rigaud, II, 23 ff. ROYAL SOCIETY: Collins, 'Narrative' (op. cit. n. 5, p. 109 above).

[18] Collins to Pell (11 Feb. 1668; 18 July 1668), BM Sloane 4278, ff. 332, 340; the latter suggests that Collins wanted for his own use 'Baker, of the Smyrna trade, Free ports stated, Cradock's book of trade, Lambe of trade, etc.' In 'Narrative' (op. cit. n. 5, p. 109 above) Collins writes that he has 'divers collections and all the printed books and papers about [trade] that he could by any means in above twenty years time obtain'.

mentality. Yet given Collins' unusual combination of knowledge, endowments, and interest, his finished economic writings are disappointing.

The first, *A plea for bringing in of Irish cattle and keeping
out of fish caught by foreigners*, published in 1680, tells
much of its story in the title. 'Keeping out of fish caught by
foreigners' was the beginning and end of policy for the
Royal Fishery Company, with which Collins had linked his
career three years earlier. The *Plea* is as much an advertising brochure as was his piece on saffron, with the difference
that here the range of the promoter's interest was somewhat
wider. Sir James Shaen, whose investment saved the Company's life in 1680, happened also to be Surveyor-General of
Ireland, chief Farmer of the Irish revenues, and probably
owner of a large Irish estate. He had also been Collins' patron for a long time. It is hard to believe that the strange
combination of proposals—to couple Irish cows with Dutch
fish is not very natural—is a pure coincidence, having nothing to do with the connection between Shaen and Collins. Even if, as Collins pointed out, the prohibition of foreign fish had been written into the same Act that prohibited
Irish cattle, it does not follow that while supporting the one
he was bound to criticize the other.

As a mercenary may be a fierce fighter for his paid cause,
and an advertisement may command intellectual assent, Collins' *Plea* might have been good economics. In fact it is hope-
less. Disorganized to the point of incoherence, it merely
reiterates mercantilist dogma at its rawest. The only principle that Collins can 'invoke is: 'Those provisions or wares
that England does or may afford enough, good, and to spare,
ought not for our own expense [i.e. not unless for re-export]
to be imported or admitted from abroad.' The reason for importing Irish cattle is that unless England imports and re-
exports them, they will be offered elsewhere at prices below
those for English cattle or by-products. The reason for not
importing foreign fish is that unless they are kept out, they
will 'blast in the bud' the Royal Fishery Company, which is
on a very precarious footing. The arguments are presented
with no more subtlety than that.[19]

19 Collins, *A Plea*, 2 [at sig. A3].

Collins' second effort was no more enlightening. The theme again is fish, this time to the accompaniment of salt. The relations between these two are more direct, and Collins, soon after joining the Fishery Company, had outlined them in one of those draft proposals that he habitually broadcast among high officials. The excise on salt produced a large revenue, having recently been farmed out for as much as £24,000 per year; the excise rate had once been higher and should again be raised; which being done, all the taxes collected on salt sold to fishermen should be handed over to the Royal Fishery Company 'for carrying on the fishery trade'. It was a neat little scheme, whereby the small commercial fishermen of England would pay higher taxes on the salt they used for curing their catch, in order that the Royal Fishery Company might be subsidized to compete with them.[20]

But, again, if the justice and wisdom of the policy advocated are overlooked, and only the quality of reasoning considered, Collins' second economic tract has still no value other than antiquarian or comic. It is a commonplace book more than anything else, as is shown by an abbreviated version of its title, which goes unusually far in the seventeenth-century tendency to merge title with table of contents. It reads:

Salt and fishery, a discourse thereof insisting on the following heads. 1. The several ways of making salt in England and foreign parts. 2. The character and qualities, good and bad, of these several sorts of salt. . . . 3. The catching and curing, or salting, of the most eminent or staple sorts of fish. . . . 4. The salting of fish. 5. The cookery of fish and flesh. 6. Extraordinary experiments in preserving butter, flesh, fish, fowl, fruit, and roots. . . .[21]

In fact it goes on so long in this vein that one might suppose

[20] Collins, 'Proposals for the advancement of his majesty's revenue and for the encouragement of the Royal Fishery Co.' [endorsed, Feb. 1677/8], among Pepys' papers, Bod. Lib., Rawlinson MSS., A191 f. 151 et seq.
[21] (1682).

Collins had become passionately, fanatically addicted to salt. But the last heading brings him back to his starting point—it is 'Proposals . . . for the advancement of the fishery, the woollen, tin, and divers other manufactures . . .'— which suggests that his advocacy of salt was calculated to increase the public's desire to buy a good, the excise on which might furnish a subsidy to his employer. The book is a recipe book, in which methods for cooking meat and advancing trade are detailed without any attempt to show by reasoning that his instructions for either art, cooking or politics, are good instructions.

Judged only by his published works on economic matters, Collins would not be worth mentioning in a history of economic thought. All the interest that he has for the subject rests on a scheme that he never carried out, but which in its conception, considered especially in relation to the whole of Collins' mentality, gives the clearest possible insight into the aims of that branch of economics which Petty named 'political arithmetic'.

That proposal is embodied in one of those everlasting papers, full of personal complaints and requests, with which Collins bombarded Ministers of State. In one such, which he sent to Shaftesbury in about 1670, he began by listing the projects he might have carried out had he 'merely had an easy employment, though but moderately beneficial', projects that would have enlarged his earlier books on accounting, gauging, making of sundials, and so on. He then turns to the future and outlines the plan that places him in the vanguard of political arithmeticians.

> And if the said Collins might obtain [official] employment, he humbly craves he might relate as a clerk to the Council of Trade, he having studied the argument and course thereof, being led thereunto by the stating and perusal of many accounts; and proposes that . . . a general account of trade may be stated so as thereby to manifest—if moderate encouragement be afforded—:
>   1. How much of each native commodity is yearly exported [and how much imported, etc.].

2. How we balance with each place or country where we have a trade.

3. A comparison between the English and Dutch charges upon imported goods, stated into a comparative account. . . .

4. Remarks upon the laws and impositions of several countries, with the alterations thereof from time to time observed.

5. All our English pamphlets and books about trade stated so, in a way of debitor and creditor, in an alphabetical manner on all heads, that whatsoever has been said on any head may stand on one side and what against it on the other.[22]

The schemes for drawing up accounts of the balance of trade, general as well as particular, were nothing novel; the air was full of them in the 1670s. But the scheme for a balance of doctrines was Collins' alone. Nobody before him had the boldness to imagine and to say that questions of economic policy could be resolved by referring to an account, drawn up 'debitor and creditor', in which all opinions were dressed in straight columns pro and con. Did Collins go so far as to believe that the truth lay in that column that had the most entries, or did he believe that the data was only a starting point for decision? He did not say. But if boldness was needed to believe that the balance would give its own answer, then Collins had sufficient boldness. Forwarding the scheme to Dr Beale, he wrote 'though I leave the Council, it does not follow but that I may be employed in stating the general balance of trade and heads of the proposals in the enclosed paper . . .'; and shortly after, commenting on a remark by Beale about religious controversy, he adds, 'I believe I have spent as much time to satisfy myself thoroughly in those controversies as I have done in the mathematics,

22 Collins, 'Proposals humbly tendered by John Collins to the King's most excellent majesty' [ca. 1670], PRO 30/24 30/8. This seems to be the manuscript that Collins refers to in his introduction to the 1675 edition of the *Introduction to Merchants' Accounts,* published in Malynes, *Consuetudo* (1686 ed.). The scheme for a 'Balance of opinion' is mentioned again in Collins, *A Plea,* 29.

and could wish all controversies stated in the method of the [enclosed?] proposal about trade.[23] It does seem that he believed a balance of opinions would help a man 'satisfy' himself about a controversy.

In due course, others took up the vision, though nobody has yet achieved those heights of moral and political science that Collins dreamed of. Hardly a generation later, Charles Davenant could speak calmly of such balancing and computing, almost as though men already were doing it. 'A great statesman—by consulting all sort of men, and by contemplating the universal posture of the nation, its power, strength, trade, wealth and revenues, in any counsel he is to offer—by summing up the difficulties on either side and computing upon the whole, shall be able to form a sound judgment and to give right advice; and this is what we mean by Political Arithmetic.'[24]

[23] Collins to Beale (20 Aug. 1672), in Rigaud, I, 200–1.
[24] Charles Davenant, *Discourses on the Publick Revenues* . . . (1698), Part I, 13.

Chapter 5

SIR WILLIAM PETTY: POLITICAL ARITHMETIC

REGULARLY DESCRIBED AS a genius, by discerning contemporaries, as well as admiring biographers, William Petty was a man of many varied talents and a few great accomplishments. Most renowned among his intellectual achievements has always been Political Arithmetic, a subject whose matter is usually identified with that of Statistics, and in the rôle of father of statistics he has been commended as one of the founders of modern economics. That laudable place he should continue to enjoy even after it is recognized that political arithmetic bore no important resemblance to statistical theory, that is, the mathematics of probability, and that whatever else it was, Petty did not so much invent it as give it a name. Petty deserves a higher, though different reputation, as an economic theorist of the first order, the best or equal to the best that existed before 1750. It does not matter that Petty himself would have balked at this assessment of his work, for his vociferous conviction that political arithmetic was the chief jewel of his diadem and one of the most luciferous works of Natural Philosophy merely illustrates the vanity of methodologizing.

I

Petty's life, so curiously parallel in part to Collins', shows the same pattern of disturbance produced by the prelude to the Civil War, and the same set of intellectual influences that affected men unusually curious and more or less worldly, who reached maturity during the War.

Petty was born in 1623, the son of a Hampshire cloth-worker, poor but decent. He attended a country school, where he was given the standard rote fare of the time; by twelve he 'had a competent smattering of Latin and was entered into the Greek'. And there his formal education might have closed, for at thirteen he went to sea as a cabin-boy on a cross-Channel ship. Like Collins and like many other ambitious sailors, he set himself to mastering the principles of navigation; and he might have been no more than an able seaman had he not broken his leg within a year of embarking. The captain, for some reason, decided to put him ashore in France; and Petty, for some equally obscure reason decided to stay there, and furthermore, to go back to school. He petitioned the Jesuit governors of a college at Caen to admit him, and they did, influenced perhaps by the fact that the petition was written in Latin. How long he stayed at Caen, what he studied and to what effect, is not known; we only know that Petty said—and we know also that neither modesty nor pedantry ever constrained him to undue exactness—that 'at the full age of fifteen years I had obtained the Latin, Greek and French tongues, the whole body of common arithmetic, the practical geometry and as-tronomy conducing to navigation, dialling, etc. with the knowledge of several mathematical trades . . .'. Some indi-cation of the rest of the curriculum at Caen, not unex-pected in a Jesuit school, is given by titles of papers he wrote in his fifteenth year, 'Cursus Rhetorices et Geograph-iae', and in his twenty-first, 'Collegium Logicum et Meta-physicum', as well as by his evident familiarity with classi-cal philosophy. He left Caen in about 1640, and may have spent the next three years in the Navy.[1]

By now, if not earlier, a taste for higher education seems to have been firmly implanted, and Petty went off to Hol-

[1] The evidence for Petty's biography is very conveniently and ably gathered in E. Strauss, Sir William Petty (1954), Parts I and II. In the present section I have cited other sources only insofar as they amend the evidence given by Strauss. It may be well to say at the outset, however, that I do not accept Strauss' interpretation, above all of Petty's economics, for reasons given in my review, 64 JPE 180 (1956).

land to study medicine. In those years, when parliamentary and royalist troops were making all England a battlefield, the best of English scholars—at least those whose interests and temperaments were non-political—had settled down to teach and study in Holland and France; and there Petty met them. He enrolled as a student in medicine, especially anatomy; but one of his earliest and apparently close acquaintances was Dr John Pell, then Professor of Mathematics at Amsterdam—later a retainer of Lord Brereton and as such one of Collins' regular correspondents. When Petty went off, in the peregrinating style of the day, to see what was being taught about anatomy in Paris, he carried Pell's introduction to Hobbes, with whom—if Aubrey is to be trusted—he stopped to 'read Vesalius'. For a short while he served Hobbes as a sort of informal secretary or research assistant, a relation that becomes more interesting if one accepts the tradition that Hobbes had in his time been secretary to Bacon; it is, for no good reason, easier to believe that one man's ideas influenced another if it is known that they met in the flesh, even at one remove. But at any event, Hobbes and Petty did meet. It seems likely that through Hobbes, Petty met also the scientific circle that met periodically in the cell of the friar, Morin Mersenne, the circle that included Descartes, Fermat, Pascal and Gassendi, and which met to discuss the latest theories and experiments in natural philosophy.[2]

From these beginnings Petty's acquaintance in the highest scientific circles grew quickly. Shortly after he returned to England in 1646, in order to study medicine at Oxford, Petty met—again probably by John Pell's introduction—Samuel Hartlib, then at the peak of his career as unofficial master of ceremonies to the new learning. Through Hartlib, Petty met Robert Boyle, one of the masters of the new movement, and this association, as well as those dating from Amsterdam and Paris, led him into the company of a group of men who, at the end of the Civil War, settled in Oxford to pursue peacefully their studies in science. The core of that group

[2] MERSENNE'S CIRCLE: Ornstein, *The Role of Scientific Societies in the Seventeenth Century* (1928), 140–43; Edmund Fitzmaurice, *Life of Sir William Petty* (1895), 7 ff.

was John Wilkins, Jonathan Goddard, John Wallis, Ralph Bathurst and Thomas Willis and a few others, most of them in holy orders, who abstained from the fierce sectarian struggles of the Protectorate, and took refuge in mathematics, medicine, or—such was the fashion of the time—in both. Their common interests in the new learning made possible an association that might otherwise have foundered on religious disagreement, for Wilkins, Goddard and Wallis had willingly served Parliament and Cromwell, whereas Bathurst and Willis remained royalists throughout, Willis' house being the scene of clandestine Episcopalian services. And despite the fact that their intellectual interests were, from the standpoint of the scholarly traditions of Oxford, sharply heterodox, the academic positions of their leaders put them above repression if not reproach. Wilkins was Warden of Wadham and Wallis Savilian Professor of Geometry; several of the others, like Bathurst and Goddard, were senior members of their colleges; and though they made few converts to the new learning, they could not be impeded in their own studies.[3]

Into this circle—the 'Invisible College' as it was known, which emerged in time as the Royal Society—Petty was immediately received. They adopted not only him but his residence, holding their meetings in his 'lodgings (in an apothecary's house) because of the convenience of inspecting drugs and the like'. And perhaps with their assistance, he flourished mightily in the University. He had hardly become a fellow of Brasenose before he was appointed Vice-Principal, and no sooner took his doctorate in medicine than he was elected Professor of Anatomy. The Invisible College seems also to have been involved in arranging his final academic accolade; for in 1649 Hartlib wrote to Boyle, 'My endeavours are now, how Mr Petty may be set apart or encouraged for the advancement of experimental and mechanical knowledge in Gresham College at London,' and shortly after Petty was appointed to Gresham as Professor of Music, a post which would probably have enabled him to teach applied mathematics. Not yet thirty, his education

[3] C. E. Mallet, *History of . . . Oxford*, II, 398–400 *et passim*.

finished and his intellect formed, he stood firmly planted a king of the academic heap.[4]

At this point, his career made, Petty threw it over. Within weeks of giving his first lecture, he took leave of absence from Oxford, for two years in the first instance, but in fact for the rest of his life. It may have been sheer restlessness that prevented him from staying to enjoy what had come so easily and quickly, or boredom, or merely the desire to make money, for he had now starved and spared for over ten years, and there was no hope of doing much better as long as he confined himself to his academic positions, all of which paid him only £120 per year. But if the cause of his departure is not clear, the occasion of his staying away

[4] LODGINGS: John Wallis, '. . . Account of some passages in his own life,' in C. R. Weld, *History of the Royal Society* (1848), I, 33. PROFESSOR OF ANATOMY: So Strauss, 40, following Fitzmaurice's biography. More precisely, Petty was deputy for the Regius Professor of Medicine (then Sir Thomas Clayton) and Tomlins Reader in Anatomy; H. M. Sinclair and A. H. T. Robb-Smith, *A Short History of Anatomical Teaching in Oxford* (1950), 71. The Reader was required, by conditions of the founding grant in 1624, to procure each spring 'a sound body of one of the executed persons', which after it was dissected by an assistant, he was to 'demonstrate' on several days; during the fall, in the absence of Assizes and hence of such bodies, he lectured on the skeleton. Cf. Mallet, II, 245, 322, and *Petty-Southwell Correspondence* (ed. Lansdowne, 1928), 222.

MUSIC: This appointment has been considered puzzling, as Petty was no great musician; and the name of the professorship may have been intended in the classical Greek sense, as arts and letters generally (*Petty Papers*, I, xxx); but Petty himself used 'music' in the ordinary present sense. He once placed it among the various branches of applied mathematics: 'their Statick and Hydrostatick, their Hydrolick, the Trocholick, Theroptick and Skenoptick, the Recowsticks and Musick, their Pnematicks and Ballesticks, and all other their mechanicks whatsoever . . .' (*Petty Papers*, II, 172); and this suggests that he may have taught music in its mathematical rather than aesthetic aspect, a possibility borne out by the fact that the Savilian Professor of Geometry at this time was required to deal with 'music' in his lectures; G. Ward, *Oxford University Statutes* (1845), I, 274. As to the Gresham professorship, its subject is indicated by the requirement that the 'professor of music and other the graduates in that science [!] are obliged at certain times to compose a song of 5, 6, or 8 parts, and with his lectures to intermix the harmony of voices and musical instruments . . .'; *An Account of . . . Gresham College* (1707), 36–37.

can be conjectured. Jonathan Goddard, an Oxford acquaintance, had gone off in 1649 as physician-in-chief to Cromwell's army in Ireland, and returned to Oxford in 1651 as Warden of Merton; in September of 1652, after Fleetwood had succeeded Ireton and Lambert in the Irish command, Petty landed in Waterford to follow Goddard as physician-in-chief. There he continued for a short while, but he had by no means come to rest.[5]

The opportunity to make his fortune arose from the fact that Parliament had pledged itself to the investors who financed the campaign against the Irish rebellion of 1641 and the soldiers who fought in it, to repay them with lands to be confiscated from the rebels. Now that Ireland was subjugated, and indeed decimated, the only impediment to carrying out the pledge was the need to determine the size and location of the forfeited lands, the need, in effect, to survey the larger part of Ireland. This responsibility was put in the hands of Benjamin Worsley—physician, fanatic, advocate of the Navigation Acts, friend of Hartlib and an acquaintance of Petty. Petty's later comment on Worsley, violently coloured though it is by the discomfort of their relations, reveals something of both men and shows what made Ireland inviting territory for these polite buccaneers. 'There went also into Ireland, at the same time, and on the same expedition, one Mr Worsley, who, having been often frustrated as to his many several great designs and undertakings in England, hoped to improve and repair himself upon a less knowing and more credulous people. To this purpose he exchanged some dangerous opinions in religion for others more merchantable in Ireland, and carried also some magnifying glasses, through which he showed, *aux esprits médiocres,* his skill in several arts, so at length to get credit to be employed in managing the geometrical survey of Ireland . . .'[6] But Worsley, as Surveyor General, was not moving quickly and Petty decided to intervene.

Petty boldly offered to carry out the whole survey in thirteen months, and with the help of Sir Hardress Waller, a parliamentary Major-General, who acted as Petty's public

[5] £120 PER YEAR: *Correspondence,* 222.
[6] Petty, *History of the Down Survey* [1659] (1851), 2.

relations man, persuaded the commissioners for land distribution to give him the job. It was no small undertaking, for it meant hiring and organizing hundreds of men, teaching most of them how to do their particular parts of the work, setting up workshops for making the various instruments, crude though they might be, and co-ordinating the multitude of narrow undertakings that the lack of skilled labour made it essential to divide the large one into. Worsley, convinced that Petty's plan was impracticable, kept making endless trouble. But despite such political troubles in Dublin; notwithstanding peculiar badness of the weather in the field; and although the fieldmen often had to fight off, if they could, bandits who marauded at will through the more remote and depopulated corners of the country; the Down Survey, as it was called, was finished promptly, as planned, on 1 March 1656.

Petty's profit on the undertaking was about £10,000 in cash, some part of which he spent in buying up debentures from needy soldiers. Other Irish lands he accumulated in lieu of cash payment for the Survey, and still more he bought outright, so that by 1660 he held estates amounting to perhaps 100,000 acres, which made him one of the greatest landlords in Ireland. Within five years he had turned himself from an impecunious scholar into a great magnate.[7]

His property was not, however, unencumbered. During the last years of the Interregnum he was repeatedly charged with having acquired much of his holdings by fraud and breach of trust. After the Restoration, and for the rest of his life, he had constantly to defend his estates against Royalists who tried to recover their former properties in the Court of Innocents or in the Court of Claims, attacks that entangled him in endless litigation, for he would neither surrender nor compromise. Moreover, his great estate in Kerry, barren, continually threatened by bandits, needing to be colonized and carefully developed if it were to yield a substantial income, demanded constant close attention. Of the rest of his life, Petty spent half of it in Ireland, chained to his posses-

[7] It has been estimated that at his death Petty owned about 270,-000 acres in South Kerry alone; Marquis of Lansdowne, *Glanerought and the Petty-Fitzmaurices* (1937), 7–8.

sions and his lawsuits, unwilling to buy ease at the cost of surrendering an inch of land.

Much of the time that was not filled with his Irish affairs Petty devoted to his two other chief interests, politics and science. He was ambitious for high office. He moved as a friend among the second level of officials, men who would now count as senior civil servants or junior ministers, Robert Southwell, John Evelyn, Samuel Pepys. He was well known to senior ministers, and received on friendly terms by Charles II and James II. Nevertheless, and although he never tired of submitting great projects for the reform of government and the perfection of economic policy, he did not attain to any office more substantial than a sinecure in the Admiralty Court at Dublin. Charles II gave him a knighthood, in recognition of nothing so much perhaps as the size of his Irish estates, and offered him a peerage, but political power he could not get, nor even political office.

It is easy enough to know why. He was the very opposite of tactful. To write, as he did, 'those states are free from foreign offensive wars . . . where the chief governor's revenue is but small . . .', could not endear him to Charles II, a chief governor constantly pressed for funds and generally faced by a parliament little disposed to grant them, as Petty must very well have known. A similar lapse of judgment helped alienate another patron. The story is told by Evelyn, in the course of commenting on Petty's gift of mimicry, especially his ability to imitate preachers of every different church and sect. The Duke of Ormond once persuaded Petty to give a demonstration, 'and was almost ravished with admiration; but by and by he fell upon a certain reprimand of the faults and miscarriages of some princes and governors, which, though he named none, did so sensibly touch the Duke, who was then Lieutenant of Ireland, that he began to be very uneasy, and wished the spirit laid which he had raised, for he was neither able to endure such truths, nor could he but be delighted. At last he melted his discourse to a ridiculous subject, and came down from the joint stool on which he had stood; but my Lord would not have him preach any more.' This capacity of Petty's for ridicule and scorn, much as it may attest to admirable qualities of mind, shows, by his willingness to use it, the insensitivity, indeed rashness, that would have been at the very least an obstacle to a political career, and in the case of a man who had no great family or connections to back him, an impassable obstacle.[8]

In another chief interest, science, he accomplished little more. Schemes, projects, prospectuses, sketches and outlines flowed from his pen by the ream; but remained in the form of words on paper. Only one of his inventions, the 'double bottom'—a twin-hulled ship—ever came to life. He built three or four versions of her, all of which sailed very fast but had an embarrassing tendency to break up in a storm, a defect in which Charles II took a certain amount of malicious glee. Despite this lack of real achievement in mathematics, medicine, or invention, Petty nevertheless continued to be honoured as a scientist, or in the term of the time, a virtuoso. His reputation depended partly on being identified with the Royal Society, of which he was a charter member and to which he continued to send communications, and also his rôle in founding its counterpart, the Dublin Society. The more substantial part of this reputation, however, depended on his famous works on political arithmetic, which seemed so perfect an expression of the philosophy of Bacon, the aspirations expressed by Hartlib, and the programme of the Royal Society.

II

The scientific method erected by Bacon rested on two main pillars: natural history, that is, the collection of all possible facts about nature, and induction, a careful logical movement from those facts of nature to the laws of nature. The proper exercise of these techniques, Bacon maintained, would dispel error, allow truth to reveal itself, and thus bring about the Great Instauration, that is, the total reconstruction of knowledge.

[8] 'THOSE STATES . . .': *Treatise of Taxes* (1662), in Hull, I, 22. John Evelyn, *Diary* (24 Mar. 1675), IV, 59.

The first principle of the new learning, which at times Bacon called 'natural philosophy', was to be a wilful subjection to Nature. Men who wanted to know her secrets must 'wait upon Nature instead of vainly affecting to overrule her'; they should dwell 'purely and constantly among the facts of nature'. To apprehend those facts was the work of the senses; all imaginary mental notions about nature—fables, superstition and folly—were to be exorcised. But this programme was not without its difficulties for, as Bacon recognized, the senses are not immune to error, and their impressions would need to be supplemented and rectified. The most excellent device for the purpose was experimentation. 'I contrive,' he wrote, 'that the office of the sense shall be only to judge of the experiment, and that the experiment itself shall judge of the thing.' Of the three forms of natural history therefore, dealing with 'nature in course', 'nature erring or varying', and 'nature altered or wrought', the last was the most important, since it dealt with nature deliberately manipulated, as in experiments. Unfortunately, Bacon felt, little work had yet been done on this part of natural history. A bit had been written about the history of trades, 'some collections made of agriculture, and likewise of manual arts; but commonly with a rejection of experiments familiar and vulgar. For it is esteemed a kind of dishonour unto learning to descend to inquiry or meditation upon matters mechanical'.[9]

'But if my judgment be of any weight,' Bacon continued, 'the use of History Mechanical is of all others the most radical and fundamental towards natural philosophy, such natural philosophy as shall not vanish in the fume of subtle, sublime, or delectable speculation, but such as shall be operative to the endowment and benefit of man's life. . . . For like as a man's disposition is never well known till he be crossed, nor Proteus ever changed shapes till he was straitened and held fast, so the passages and variations of na-

[9] 'WAIT UPON NATURE': Bacon, *Instauratio Magno*, in *Works* (ed. Spedding, Ellis, and Heath, 1857–59), IV, 7, 19. 'I CONTRIVE': *ibid.*, IV, 26. NATURAL HISTORIES: *The Advancement of Learning*, in *ibid.*, III, 330–33. See Walter J. Houghton, Jr., 'The History of Trades', 2 *Jrnl. Hist. of Ideas*, 33 (1941).

ture cannot appear so fully in the liberty of nature as in the trials and vexations of art.' In accordance with the importance he attached to this branch of natural history, he listed some forty particular trades that should be studied, to which catalogue he appended this note: 'Among the particular arts those are to be preferred which exhibit, alter, and prepare natural bodies and materials of things; such as agriculture, cookery, chemistry, dyeing; the manufacture of glass, enamel, sugar, gunpowder, artificial fires, paper, and the like. Those which consist principally in the subtle motion of the hands or instruments are of less use; such as weaving, carpentry, architecture, manufacture of mills, clocks, and the like; although these too are by no means to be neglected.'[10] To this great project, Hartlib, the Royal Society, and Petty, it will be seen, dedicated themselves, and not only to its spirit but to the letter.

Induction, the other chief foundation of Baconian methodology, aimed to reinforce the fallible intellect just as experiment and history of trades aimed to correct the imperfect senses. The innate weakness of the human mind, which accounted for the 'idols and phantoms' it credited, could be overcome by a proper logic. Traditional logic, Bacon maintained, jumped at once from particular sense-impressions to propositions of the highest generality. The rule for correct, inductive reasoning was to rise *gradually* from specific cases, so that the general principles arrived at by Philosophy would remain 'cogent to nature'. Methodical generalization would thus replace sudden abstraction; 'anticipation of the mind' would be superseded by an unprejudiced 'interpretation of nature'.[11]

Induction, though as important in Bacon's creed as natural history, was less easily described and vastly more difficult, or rather impossible to follow in practice. Indeed, though it was adopted as an article of faith by the Baconians, as well as by any number of scientific methodologists thereafter, even the admiring Thomas Sprat, first historian of the Royal Society, was forced to admit that Bacon had not had any

[10] Bacon, *Works*, IV, 25–26.
[11] See Karl R. Popper, 'On the Sources of Knowledge and of Ignorance', 46 *Proceedings of the British Academy* (1960), 39.

great success in applying the method of induction, and to admit, by silence, that the fellows of the Royal Society had done no better with it. Induction remained part of the Royal Society's official creed, but a good deal more emphasis fell, at least until 1700, on the much more practicable injunction to collect histories of trade.[12]

One of the most fervent disciples of Bacon was Samuel Hartlib, a half-Polish half-English publicist and amateur man of learning, who came to England in 1628 at the invitation of that wing of Parliament, which, opposed to clerical control of society as well as to royal control of the State, saw in him the instrument of a great Baconian reform in education.[13]

Hartlib, in the range of his own interests and activities, illustrated a complex of ideas and opinions that was characteristic among the second generation of Baconians. He was avidly eager to spread education, especially by spreading technical and 'experimental' information; he himself wrote a large number of didactic tracts on agriculture, the spirit of which can be gathered from one title, *Samuel Hartlib his legacie: or an enlargement of the Discourse of Husbandry used in Brabant and Flaunders; wherein are bequeathed to the commonwealth of England more outlandish and domestic experiments and secrets in reference to universal husbandry*. This and many related works were in effect, as Hartlib well knew, histories of trade following Bacon's edict; in fact they dealt with the 'particular art' that Bacon had put at the head of his list.

But in one respect Hartlib went somewhat further than Bacon, following the precepts of his friend and co-Baconian, the Moravian clergyman Comenius. According to Bacon, natural philosophy was desirable not solely for the sake of knowledge but also, and perhaps even more so, for its practical effects; 'light', beneficial as it might be, was less so than 'fruit'. Comenius went beyond Bacon so far as to insist that

[12] Thomas Sprat, *History of the Royal Society of London* (1667), 36.

[13] On the setting of the invitation, and the politics of the inviters, see H. R. Trevor-Roper, 'Three Foreigners', 14 *Encounter* (Feb. 1960), 3.

to seek light for the sake of fruit was a religious duty; he invented a religious system, Pansophism, which promised 'to simplify and shorten, by a kind of royal road to learning, all studies, arts, and sciences'. And to this combination of piety and technical education, good works and economic efficiency, Hartlib subscribed, advocating it one way or another throughout his voluminous writings.[14]

In still another respect Hartlib attempted to carry out in reality the abstract visions of Bacon. In the *New Atlantis*, a utopia, Bacon had conjured up Solomon's House, a scientific college devoted to experimentation and to natural history by way of manufactures, equipped with 'brew-houses, bake-houses, and kitchens' and shops of 'divers mechanical arts . . . papers, linen, silks, tissues . . . excellent dyes, and many others'. The history of trades was to be the main material of learning and teaching as well. Hartlib followed this model in constructing his own utopia, Macaria, and proceeded thereafter with the aim of bringing the vision to earth in England.[15]

He himself planned not a few colleges and societies. One was to be a College of Husbandry, in the prospectus for which he displayed his whole conception of the new learning and its functions. 'I find by experience that it is nothing but the narrowness of our spirits that makes us miserable; for if our hearts were enlarged beyond ourselves, and opened to lay hold of the advantages which God doth offer, whereby we may become jointly serviceable unto one another in public concernments, we could not be without luciferous employments for ourselves, nor unfruitful to our neighbours, as now for the most part we are.' And from these happy expectations, Hartlib deduced the desirability of his new academy. 'Why may we not conclude that in the science and trade of husbandry, which is the mother of all

---

[14] LEGACIE: (1651). 'TO SIMPLIFY': Henry Dircks, *Biographical Memoir of Samuel Hartlib* [1865], 52. HARTLIB AND COMENIUS: Trevor-Roper (*op. cit.* n. 13, p. 134 above).

[15] Bacon, *New Atlantis*, in *Works*, III, 159–61. Hartlib, *A description of the famous kingdom of Macaria . . .* (1641), reprinted in *Harleian Miscellany* (ed. 1808–11), IV, 382.

other trades and scientific industries, a collegial way of teaching the art thereof will be of infinite usefulness?'[16]

More important in the long run than Hartlib's own attempts of this sort were similar efforts that he inspired in others. The most famous of these was Milton's short tract *Of Education,* presented to Hartlib, who may however have found it little to his purpose; for Milton set forth a programme of strict literary education, one which would, to be sure, improve the morals and social purpose of his students, but which nevertheless made no use of experimental learning.[17]

Another person whom Hartlib constantly urged on towards sponsoring or contributing to academies was his very much junior but wealthy and noble friend Robert Boyle. In 1647, for instance, he wrote to Boyle to ask support for compiling a history of trades; the compiler would be 'one Petty, of twenty-four years of age . . . a most rare and exact anatomist, and excelling in all mathematical and mechanical learning'; Petty had submitted the scheme to Hartlib and would carry it out if—and here was the part for Boyle to play—he could be guaranteed a salary of at least £120 per annum. The guarantee was not forthcoming, but Hartlib never tired of addressing such suggestions to Boyle; and Petty, undiscouraged, placed a new scheme before Hartlib, in the form of his first printed work, *The Advice of W.P. to Mr Samuel Hartlib, for the advancement of some particular parts of learning.* . . . Petty advocated a new college to advance 'real learning'—learning whose flavour can be gathered from the recommendation 'that all children, though of the highest rank, be taught some genteel manufacture in their minority', such as making watches or musical instruments, 'navarchy, and making models for buildings and rigging for ships', or 'the confectioner's, perfumer's, or dyer's arts'. The core of the scheme was to be a *'gymnasium mechanicum* or a college of tradesmen': 'Here would be the best and most effectual opportunities and means for writing a

[16] Hartlib, *An Essay for advancement of husbandry-learning: or propositions for the erecting a college of husbandry* . . . (1651), quoted in Dircks, *Hartlib* (*op. cit.* n. 14, p. 135 above), 66–67.
[17] John Milton, *Of Education. To Master Samuel Hartlib* [1644].

history of trades in perfection and exactness; and what experiments and stuff would all those shops and operations afford to active and philosophical heads, out of which to extract that "interpretation of nature", whereof there is so little, and that so bad, as yet extant in the world?'[18]

Such projects—and Hartlib entertained many similar ones, from projectors as diverse as John Dury and John Evelyn—mingled with two existent societies, Gresham College and the Invisible College, to produce finally, in 1662, the realization of the dream in the Royal Society.

To the doctrines of Bacon as augmented by Hartlib, the Royal Society was a grateful heir. The great astronomer, Robert Hooke, the Society's first curator of experiments, wrote in 1663 that its functions were 'to improve the knowledge of natural things and all useful arts, manufactures, mechanic practices, engines' and to compile 'a complete system of solid philosophy for explicating all phenomena produced by nature or art'. Accordingly, the members—Petty among them—of one of eight committees appointed in 1664 to organize the Society's work were to devote themselves to histories of trade, and the Society proposed to gather a 'catalogue of all trades, works, and manufactures'. The virtuosi were often accused of wasting their time on fantastic inquiries, such as Swift satirized, not altogether unfairly, in the Academy of Lagoda, or as a nearer contemporary described less ironically and less justly: 'We prize ourselves in fruitless curiosities; we turn our lice and fleas into bulls and pigs by our magnifying glasses; we are searching for the world in the moon with our telescopes; we send to weigh the air on the top of Teneriffe, we invent Pacing Saddles and gimcracks of all sorts, which are voted ingenuities, whilst the notions of trade are turned into ridicule or much out of fashion.' But against this quite inaccurate accusation the

---

[18] Hartlib to Boyle (16 Nov. 1647), in Boyle, *Works* (1772), VI, 76–77. According to Hull (I, 118, n. 1), copies of Petty's notes for the history are in BM Sloane MSS 2903, ff. 63 *et seq.*; and the document in *Petty Papers*, I, 205, appears to be his own copy of the scheme. ADVICE: (1648), reprinted in *Harleian Miscellany* (ed. 1808–11), VI, 146.

Society could honestly answer that it did not disregard trade; and Petty—who, as inventor of the pacing saddle and other gimcracks, might have felt especially under attack— could answer that he certainly did not ridicule or ignore trade.[19]

Indeed, aside from the pacing saddle and the double-bottom ship, Petty's contributions to the Royal Society were exclusively concerned with trade. He presented one of the first histories of trade, in its time famous, 'An Apparatus to the history of the common practices of dyeing'; another on clothing, and a third on shipping.[20] And his chief 'scientific' works, the tracts on political arithmetic, were concerned with nothing if not trade. These, though not all written expressly for the Royal Society, were many of them presented to the Society, and conformed, if anything could, to its intellectual heritage. Whether they were scientific is another question.

III

It is anything but difficult to know what Petty intended political arithmetic to accomplish, for seldom can a writer have said so much about his method of work and still had time for the work itself. His voluminous papers, full as they are of declarations and devices, contain a huge abundance of statements about the technique and purpose of his new science; but perhaps the key passage occurs, as it naturally would, in his first great exercise in the genre, the *Political Arithmetick* that Petty began in 1671. This work, Petty says

[19] HOOKE: Ornstein (*op. cit.* n. 2, p. 125 above), 108–9. COMMITTEE: Weld (*op. cit.* n. 4, p. 127 above), I, 174 ff. CATALOGUE: Sprat (*op. cit.* n. 12, p. 134 above), 190. 'WE PRIZE OURSELVES': [Petyt], *Britannia Languens* (1680), reprinted in J. R. McCulloch, *Select Collection of Early English Tracts on Commerce* (1856), 357. PACING SADDLE: an adaptation of the calash, a two-wheeled carriage; for Petty's work on it, see *Petty Papers*, II, 149–51.

[20] For the histories of clothing, shipping and dyeing, presented in 1661 and 1662, see Thomas Birch, *History of the Royal Society* (1755–57), I, 55, 65, 83, and Sprat (*op. cit.* n. 12, p. 134 above), 284 ff.

in the preface, was intended to disprove the common complaints that England was suffering a decline of trade; he would show that England was in fact richer than ever before. And then he explained how he would go about proving it.[21]

'The method I take to do this is not yet very usual. For instead of using only comparative and superlative words, and intellectual arguments, I have taken the course (as a specimen of the *Political Arithmetick* I have long aimed at) to express myself in terms of number, weight or measure; to use only arguments of sense; and to consider only such causes as have visible foundations in nature, leaving those that depend on the mutable minds, opinions, appetites and passions of particular men to the consideration of others. . . .'[22]

Some of this is pure Bacon. 'Arguments of *sense*', that is, founded on sensation, or such as have 'visible foundations in nature', will elicit truth; whereas 'opinions' and all other mutable, accidental views are those 'idols of the mind' or 'intellectual arguments' that obscure truth. Petty's abhorrence of adjectives, 'comparative and superlative words', expresses the conviction, shared by his mentors Bacon and Hobbes, that words are prone to hide or distort the truth; a view that the Royal Society translated into constitutional rules against beauty, or at least embellishments. A statute stipulated that 'in all reports of experiments . . . the matter of fact shall be barely stated, without any preface, apologies, and rhetorical flourishes'. Thomas Sprat, belittling his own stylistic accomplishment, warned that 'of all the studies of men, nothing may be sooner obtained than this vicious abundance of phrase, this trick of metaphors, this volubility of tongue, which makes so great a noise in the world'. He announced with pleasure that the Royal Society 'have therefore been most vigorous in putting in execution the only remedy that can be found for this extravagance. And that has been a constant resolution to reject all the amplifications, digressions, and swellings of style; to return back to

---

[21] Petty. *Political Arithmetick* [1671] (1690); reprinted in Hull, I, 232 ff. For date of composition see *Petty Correspondence*, 60.
[22] Hull, I, 244.

the primitive purity and shortness, when men delivered so many things almost in an equal number of words. They have exacted from all their members a close, naked, natural way of speaking . . . bringing all things as near the mathematical plainness as they can. . . .'[23]

Petty, in his political arithmetic, considered that he had gone all the way to mathematical plainness, the core of his method being *Number, Weight and Measure*, a slogan that keeps reappearing as a symbolic refrain. 'You know,' he wrote to his intimate friend Southwell, 'my virtue and vanity lies in prating of numbers, weight, and measure . . .' And in a less modest vein, at the end of an essay on algebra, he wrote: 'Archimedes had algebra 1900 years ago, but concealed it. Diophantus had it in great perfection 1400 years since. Vieta, DesCartes, Roberval, Harriot, Pell, Oughtread, van Schoten and Dr Wallis have done much in this last age. It came out of Arabia by the Moors into Spain, and from thence hither, and W[illiam] P[etty] has applied it to other than purely mathematical matters, viz: to policy, by the name of Political Arithmetic, by reducing many terms of matter to terms of number, weight, and measure, in order to be handled mathematically.'[24]

Indeed the very choice of the phrase, number, weight and measure, was not altogether modest, for, coming from the *Wisdom of Solomon*, it describes how God made order; and from this source Petty quoted, when using it as the device of a mathematical paper that he submitted to the Royal Society: *Pondere, Mensura, & Numero Deus omnia fecit.* Since the phrase had been used during the Middle Ages as indicating the essence of unity implanted in the universe by God, it might have been thought the peak of pride for Petty to suggest that he was establishing order in the same way in his own realm, the realm of policy. But in fact the phrase had assumed by Petty's time a looser meaning, signifying justice, especially commercial probity. Thus Thomas Fuller said of the Good Merchant that 'he wrongs not the buyer in

[23] STATUTE: Weld (*op. cit.* n. 4, p. 127 above), II, 524 ff. Sprat (*op. cit.* n. 12, p. 134 above), 112–13.
[24] Petty to Southwell (19 Mar. 1678), in *Correspondence,* 51. *Petty Papers,* II, 14–15.

number, weight or measure. These are the landmarks of all
trading. . . . For God is the principal clerk of the market.
"All the weights of the bag are his work." (Proverbs, xvi.
11).' And by the time Abraham Liset, the author of a textbook on accounting, was writing in 1660, there was nothing
left but the flat factual statement, 'All trade is by number,
weight and measure.' How much of the magisterial and how
much of the commercial connotation Petty wanted to capture by using the phrase does not matter; being what he was,
he was probably happy to have both; what is important
was choosing a set of words that suggested a mathematical
way of dealing with a great subject that had not hitherto
been subdued by the method of the new learning.[25]

At first glance, Petty's actual exercises in political arithmetic
seem to contain many more words than numbers, and many
more 'intellectual' arguments than mathematical ones. But if
one looks more closely at a passage in which Petty considers
one of his favourite subjects, the comparative size of cities,
one finds that here at least he is abiding by his dictum,
eschewing 'comparative words', such as greater or smaller,
in favour of numbers. To see his method at close hand, one
can trace for instance the stages of the argument in a simple
yet typical example, the effort to establish, as Petty put it in
his dedicatory note to the King, that 'your city of London
seems more considerable than the two best cities of the
French monarchy', a conclusion between the lines of which
James II may have been intended to read that England,
having nothing to fear from France, should not ally herself
to her.[26]

Part of the evidence 'tending to prove', as Petty cautiously
put it, 'that London has more people and housing than the

---

[25] *Wisdom of Solomon*, 11:21. PONDERE: Petty, *Concerning the
use of duplicate proportion* . . . (1674). IN THE MIDDLE AGES: See
the sermon of Abbot Isaac, quoted by Otto Simson, *Gothic Cathedral*
(1956), p. 188; and Abbot Suger, *On the Abbey Church of St Denis*
(ed. Panofsky, 1946), 97. Thomas Fuller, *The Holy State* (1642),
114. Abraham Liset, *Amphithalmi* (1660), Part II, 15; bound up
with Malynes, *Consuetudo* (1656).

[26] Petty, *Two Essays in Political Arithmetick* . . . (1687), Hull,
II, 501 ff.

cities of Paris and Rouen put together and is also more considerable in several other respects', was the number of burials in each city. 'The medium [i.e. arithmetic mean] of the burials at London in the three last years, viz. 1683, 1684 and 1685 (wherein there was no extraordinary sickness . . .) was 22,337; and the like medium of burials for the last Paris Bills we could procure, viz. for the years 1682, 1683 and 1684 (whereof the last . . . appears . . . to have been very sickly) is 19,887.' Those facts are meant to imply that the population of London was greater in proportion as the number of deaths was greater, due allowance made for the difference in healthfulness; but Petty did not explicitly draw the conclusion, nor did he explicitly mention the necessary assumption, that the normal death rate was the same, or nearly the same in London as in Paris.

Neither did he say anything about the assumptions that underlay his use of the basic data. The figures on London burials came from the London Bills of Mortality, official weekly reports of the number of people dying in each parish and the causes of death; reports which Petty, and especially his close friend, John Graunt, had already made famous by their *Natural and Political Observations upon the Bills of Mortality* of 1662, a landmark of systematic demography.[27] The manner of collecting these statistics was described by John Graunt. 'When anyone dies, then either by tolling or ringing of a bell, or by bespeaking of a grave of the Sexton, the same is known to the Searchers corresponding with the same Sexton. The Searchers hereupon (who are ancient matrons, sworn to their office) repair to the place where the dead corpse lies, and by view of the same and by other enquiries they examine by what disease or casualty the corpse died. Hereupon they make their report to the Parish Clerk.' A reporting system conducted by braces of old women could not aspire to perfect precision; besides, deaths of Catholics

[27] How large a part Petty had in writing the *Observations* is a much disputed question, a bibliography of which is given by M. Greenwood, *Medical Statistics from Graunt to Farr* (1948), 36–39. It seems likely that Graunt was the principal author, but that Petty may have suggested the work and took some part in formulating the conclusions.

and Nonconformists were altogether omitted, as were those
also of Conformists buried elsewhere than in parish
churches or cemeteries. No doubt the Paris system of reporting had its own ways of deviating from the true state of
things, but they were different from those in London. It
might have been judicious, therefore, to wonder whether
the data based on sources as different as the London and
Paris bills would stand the direct comparison to which Petty
put them, but if he wondered, he said nothing about it.[28]

French savants having answered his arguments with
doubts and criticisms, Petty returned later in the year to expand and reinforce his argument. It is instructive to examine one short passage in this later work, *Five Essays in Political Arithmetick,* for another view of the spirit in which
Petty used the data. The problem was to estimate the population of London; of the three methods he used, one was
to deduce it from the number of houses in London; and the
first of three ways to determine the number of houses, he
said, was this. 'The number of houses which were burnt
Anno 1666, which by authentic report was 13,200; next,
what proportion the people who died out of those houses
bore to the whole, which I find . . . Anno 1666 to be almost 1/5, from whence I infer the whole housing of London
Anno 1666 to have been 66 thousand; then finding the burials Anno 1666 to be to those of 1686 as 3 to 4, I pitch upon
88 thousand to be the number of housing Anno 1686.'[29]

There was not much exact information to go on, apparently. What the 'authentic report' was that told him that
13,200 houses were consumed by the Great Fire he did not
say; perhaps it hardly matters that the same report had informed him, six months earlier, that 13,000 houses had
burned down. The next fact, that one-fifth of all the people
who died in London during 1666 had lived in those houses,
is somewhat conjectural, for the Bills of Mortality, apparently Petty's source for this information, gave deaths only

---

[28] 'WHEN ANYONE DIES': *Natural and Political Observations,* in
Hull, II, 346. ACCURACY OF BILLS: Hull, I, lxxxviii ff.

[29] Petty, 'The Third Essay,' in *Five Essays in Political Arithmetick*
(1687), in Hull, II, 533 ff.; for the controversial context, see Hull,
II, 522–23 and *passim.*

parish by parish, whereas the Fire did not confine itself
within neat parish boundaries. The final fact, summarized
in the passage, 'finding the burials Anno 1666 to be to those
of 1686 as 3 to 4', was also presumably drawn from the Bills
of Mortality; but if so, Petty drew it poorly, for the burials
recorded in the Bills were 10,740 for 1666 and 22,609 for
1686, a ratio of over 2 to 1, instead of 1.3 to 1, as Petty
would have it.[30]

These facts Petty combined by a calculation that is full of
hidden assumptions. If the houses that burned down in 1666
used to supply one-fifth of all corpses in London, then they
were one-fifth of all the houses; they numbered 13,200,
therefore the total number of houses in 1666 was 66,000.
But this conclusion would follow only if the average number of people living in the houses that burned was the same
as the average in all other London houses and if also the
normal death-rate in those houses was the same as in the
rest of London. The first at least of these assumptions is
doubtful, for the Fire burned mainly within the Walls of
London, in the heart of the city, where houses were notori-
ously more crowded than in the suburban parishes. Again,
according to Petty, the number of houses in 1686 stood in
the same ratio to houses in 1666 as burials in 1686 to burials
in 1666; but only on the assumption that the death rate had
not changed during the period, an assumption difficult to
maintain in view of the fact that 1686 was a healthy year,
whereas in 1666 the plague was still raging, even though
much diminished, so that unusually many people might
have been dying, if not of the plague directly then of other
diseases brought on by exposure to the plague or by the
hardships of life during the plague year. But none of these
assumptions is explored; all are blithely made and gaily
glossed over.

Indeed Petty's way with numbers, here as always, was ut-

[30] 13,000: Hull, II, 507. BURIALS 1666 AND 1686: *A Collection
of the yearly bills of mortality from 1657 to 1758 . . .* (1759), Kress
5773. The figure of 10,740 was for burials due to all causes but
plague; 1,998 additional Londoners died of plague in 1666, none in
1686. Even had Petty included these extraordinary deaths with the
1666 figure, a not very reasonable step for his purpose, the ratio of
burials 1686 to 1666 would still have been 1.8 to 1.

terly cavalier. The facts, whatever they were, always had a congenial way of upholding Petty's conclusions. Or rather, Petty's factual assertions did; for he was not averse to citing authorities mysterious, unknown, and even non-existent, when he needed their help. And all his conclusions, wherever they originated, had a wonderful sense of teamwork. An historian of statistics, noticing how nicely a series of independent calculations converged on a single figure, remarked, 'It is not I believe too cynical to say that any calculation Petty made would have produced war losses around 600,000.'[31]

For such fine adjustments as he made to his figures, Petty had already submitted a justification, included in his methodological credo. 'Now the observations or positions expressed by number, weight, and measure, upon which I bottom the ensuing discourses, are either true or not apparently false. . . . And if they are false, not so false as to destroy the argument they are brought for; but at worst are sufficient as suppositions to show the way to that knowledge I aim at.'[32] The justification in short is that the figures are merely illustrative; the important thing which they illustrate being the method of arriving at a certain kind of knowledge.

The original *Political Arithmetick*, composed in 1671, the most extended work in Petty's new medium, is the best stage on which to see this illustrative use of numbers displayed. The work as a whole was designed to refute the allegations, very widespread during the depression of the late 1660s, that England's economy was declining. Child, Papillon and many others had testified and written to this effect; but the particular authority that Petty chose to demolish was Roger Coke, a Tory publicist and not inconsiderable economic writer, who had just published *A Treatise wherein is demonstrated that the church and state of England are in equal danger with the trade of it*. Petty undertook to demonstrate ten theses contrary to Coke's position. One of these reads, in part, 'That a small country and few people, by its situation, trade, and policy, may be equivalent in wealth and strength

[31] SOURCES NON-EXISTENT: See, e.g., Hull's footnotes, II, 533–36. Greenwood (*op. cit.* n. 27, p. 142 above), 21.
[32] *Political Arithmetick* [1671], in Hull, I, 244–45.

to a far greater people and territory.' To establish this, Petty compared France and Holland, arriving at a conclusion which, while not exactly coinciding with his thesis, moved in that direction—he found that although France had thirteen times as many people and eighty times as much land as Holland, it was only three times as rich.[33]

A sample of the illustrative numbers that Petty used in making his case is this: 'The value of shipping of Europe, being about two millions of tons, I suppose the English have five hundred thousand, the Dutch nine hundred thousand, the French a hundred thousand . . . so as the shipping in our case of France to that of Holland and Zealand is about one to nine. . . .' That these numbers were merely illustrative is indicated by the admission, 'I suppose'; but what are they supposed then to illustrate? The principle implicit in them is that a nation's ships are part of its wealth, and that a small nation may be wealthier in this respect, as well as in all others, than a large nation. The notion is so obvious that one would have thought it could be stated directly, without needing illustration; if any honest doubter arose to question it, he would only be stilled by real evidence, not by hypothetical evidence; and it follows that the illustrative numbers, at least in this case, are perfectly redundant. Indeed in most instances where Petty used supposititious data, it served no more useful purpose than to give his beliefs an undeserved air of precision.

In one setting, however, and that an important one, the method of illustrative numbers was helpful in demonstrating a principle for which Petty contended. That was to establish that the people of England were worth more than all other forms of wealth; or, to restate it, that labour produced a larger fraction of the national income than did capital. This argument, which Petty reiterated many times, appeared earliest in *Verbum Sapienti* (1665). He began by computing consumption: the six million people of England each consumed $4\frac{1}{2}d$. worth of goods a day, which makes an annual national total of £40 million. The value of all capital

[33] CHILD, PAPILLON: See Chapter I, pp. 6–10 above, COKE: (1671). Petty, *Political Arithmetick*, in Hull, I, 249–51.

goods is £250 million, a figure arrived at by adding together the supposed values of land, buildings, ships, cattle, coin, and all commodities. These capital goods produce income at the average rate of 6 per cent, or £1.5 million per year. The difference remaining between total consumption, £40 million, and the income from capital goods, £1.5 million, Petty concluded, must be produced by 'the labour of the people . . . which may be done if but half of them, viz. 3 millions, earned but 8l. 6s. 8d. per annum, which is done at 7d. per diem, abating the 52 Sundays and half as many other days for accidents, as holy days, sickness, recreations &c.'[34]

The use of illustrative numbers in this instance would, if readers accepted the numbers as plausible, establish the plausibility of a proposition that could not easily have been demonstrated by an abstract argument. On what *a priori* grounds could one prove that labour produced a greater share of national income than did capital? It is not easy to imagine such grounds. But Petty could demonstrate its plausibility by using numbers that, while not pretending to be exact, were founded on common experience. The use of his method had certainly not led him to *discover* the principle that labour may produce most of the national income, for that had long been supposed, and indeed even the more radical view, that *all* economic values are aboriginally produced by labour, was already ancient by Petty's time. Still less did Petty's method enable him to *prove* such a proposition. What it did enable him to do was to persuade people that it might be true or was true. It was, in short, a rhetorical device, akin in spirit to North's. If the numbers Petty used could be accepted as 'obviously' correct, then they would serve the same function as North's 'clear and evident' introspective principles—a sure and impersonal foundation. And Petty's arithmetical manipulations of the numbers are precisely parallel to North's chain of deductive reasoning, for both represent an open and impersonal method of moving from premises to conclusions. In Petty's case, as in North's, therefore, the conclusions must be intellectually

[34] *Verbum Sapienti* [1665], in Hull, I, 103–8.

binding on anyone who accepted the premises and could find no flaw in the logic; and more than this no method of intellectual persuasion can hope for.

It is ironic however that in praising the method of political arithmetic, its rhetorical quality was furthest from Petty's mind. He thought of it, rather vaingloriously, as a contribution to algebra; though it was nothing of the sort. The mathematical devices he employed were most of them well within simple arithmetic. The only 'statistical' technique he used was the primitive one of averaging. But the notion of an average and the way of arriving at it were old before his time; he could use such phrases as 'at a medium' or 'one year with another', without needing to explain them. An economic survey drawn up a century earlier for the Landgrave of Hesse-Cassel had estimated the values of lands by averaging their incomes for three, six, or nine years; and the term 'average' itself was well known by that time; while 'medium' was being used in the same sense at least half-a-century before Petty. And as for the mathematical theory of statistics, that remained, untouched by Petty, for great eighteenth century mathematicians to explore. To pure science or pure mathematics, Political Arithmetic had nothing to offer.[35]

Petty lauded his invention also as a technique of politics. So in dedicating the *Political Arithmetick* to Charles II, he wrote: 'As few dare venture their discretions wholly to disparage arithmetic, so few do think much practice of it very necessary in matters of state, otherwise than in what concerns the revenue. I have, therefore, for the sake of several young noblemen who are now fitting themselves for your Majesty's service, adventured to show the use of common and easy computations in the ten political conclusions mentioned in this treatise; and do now humbly beg your Majesty's pardon for having presumed to practice a vulgar art

[35] LANDGRAVE: *Der ökonomische Staat Landgraf Wilhelms IV* (ed. L. Zimmerman, 1933–34), cited in G. N. Clark, *Science and Social Welfare* . . . (1949 ed.), 124–25. 'AVERAGE', 'MEDIUM': *New English Dictionary*. PROBABILITY THEORY: Helen M. Walker, *Studies in the History of Statistical Method* (1931), chap. II.

upon matters of so high a nature. . . .' It is allowable to
stretch a point in a dedicatory address; when it came to
more sober proposals for statistical surveys, Petty seemed to
recognize that good and precise information is only the raw
material of policy decisions rather than a completely auto-
matic system for making decisions. But he could never quite
get over the daydream of this childhood of social science,
that solutions lie hidden in the facts, impatient to reveal
themselves to anyone who will trouble to collect enough
facts and search out their deeper meanings. Petty should not
on this account be regarded as an antique comic. The dream
has not yet completely faded from the minds of social scientists.[36]

The last word on political arithmetic as an instrument of
social policy was spoken by Jonathan Swift. He took as his
text Petty's doctrine that human beings make up the greater
part of a nation's wealth, from which it followed that 'fewness of people is real poverty,' and more particularly that
'Ireland is underpeopled'. The corollary, for Petty, was that
the State should encourage procreation; and he spent no
little effort thinking how this might be done. One of the results of his ingenuity read as follows:

> The way of marriage is now such that of 100 capable
> women only 32 are married, and these 32 brought 11
> children per annum; whereas 100 teeming women may
> well bring 40 children per annum.
> Wherefore:
> (1) Let it be no sin or shame for a woman to bring a
> child.
> (2) Let there be places for women to lie down in.
> (3) For keeping the child.
> (4) Let there be a tax upon all men of between 18
> and 60 and upon all women of between 15 and 45 to
> defray the said charges of lying in and nursing; and the
> tax on the women but half that of the men.
> Over and above this general proposition: Let no

[36] 'AS FEW DARE': Hull, I, 239, n. 1. PROPOSALS: *Petty Papers*,
I, sect. VII.

woman, upon pain of being counted a whore, admit any man without an indenture of convenants concerning (1) the time of cohabitation, (2) the allowance to the woman, (3) the disposal of the children and the power of inheritance, portion[?], name, etc.[37]

Swift was apparently not convinced that such proposals should be commended for the humanity they display. He was not persuaded that Ireland was underpopulated; on the contrary it seemed overpopulated, for many of the Irish were without work, though Swift traced the unemployment to the English policy of restricting Irish exports. And he set himself to deal with both the method of political arithmetic and its conclusions. The result was that singular economic tract, *A Modest Proposal, for preventing the children of poor people in Ireland from being a burden to their parents or country, and for making them beneficial to the public,* published in 1729.

The *Modest Proposal* accordingly included all the paraphernalia that marked Petty's style. 'The number of souls in this Kingdom,' Swift wrote, 'being usually reckoned one million and a half, of these I calculate there may be about two hundred thousand couple whose wives are breeders; from which number I subtract thirty thousand couple who are able to maintain their own children . . . this being granted, there will remain a hundred and seventy thousand breeders. I again subtract fifty thousand, for those women who miscarry, or whose children die by accident or disease within the year. There only remain a hundred and twenty thousand children of poor parents annually born. The question therefore is, How this number shall be reared and provided for? which, as I have already said, under the present situation of affairs is utterly impossible by all the methods hitherto proposed. For we can neither employ them in handicraft or agriculture: we neither build houses (I mean in the country) nor cultivate land; they can very seldom pick up a livelihood by stealing, till they arrive at six years

[37] 'FEWNESS OF PEOPLE': *Treatise of Taxes,* Hull, I, 34. 'IRELAND UNDERPEOPLED': *Treatise,* Hull, I, 6. Petty, 'Concerning Marriages,' *Petty Papers,* II, 49–50.

old, except where they are of towardly parts; although I confess they learn the rudiments much earlier. . . .'[38]

His proposal in view of all this was modest, and simple, not 'liable to the least objection'. 'I have been assured by a very knowing American of my acquaintance in London, that a young healthy child, well nursed, is, at a year old, a most delicious, nourishing, and wholesome food, whether stewed, roasted, baked, or boiled; and I make no doubt that it will equally serve in a fricassee or a ragout.' The rest of the tract explores, in the best Pettyian manner, the economic advantages of selling off 100,000 children per annum.[39]

And finally, his exquisite ironic ear having caught the exact tone of an economic writer's declarations of good faith, Swift ends the *Modest Proposal* on this note. 'I profess, in the sincerity of my heart, that I have not the least personal interest in endeavouring to promote this necessary work, having no other motive than the public good of my country, by advancing our trade, providing for infants, relieving the poor, and giving some pleasure to the rich. I have no children by which I can propose to get a single penny, the youngest being nine years old, and my wife past child-bearing.'[40]

From quite another standpoint Adam Smith wrote, 'I have no great faith in political arithmetic . . . ,' meaning that he did not credit numbers arrived at by a process of guessing and fiddling.[41] Nothing more was said, because by the close of the eighteenth century, political arithmetic had quite faded from the scene.

IV

A man's best work is not always his favourite work. If he is as passionate and ambitious as Petty, he may choose to stake his reputation on his showy productions, underrating whatever cost him little effort, is restrained in manner, or has met

[38] Swift, *Modest Proposal*, in *Works* (Scott's 2nd ed., 1824), VII, 264.
[39] Swift, *Modest Proposal*, 265.
[40] Swift, *Modest Proposal*, 274.
[41] Smith, *Wealth of Nations* (Cannan's ed.), II, 36; cf. I, 439.

a cool reception. Some such reasons may be why Petty made so little of his finest piece of economic writing, *A Treatise of Taxes and Contributions*. Published in 1662, it was his first effort in economics, predating the works on political arithmetic.

Perhaps he deprecated the *Treatise* because he had been disappointed by its reception. This should not have mattered if he had continued to feel as he did at first, that the only motive for writing it was pure curiosity: 'I wrote these sheets but to rid my head of so many troublesome conceits. . . .' But obviously the work once finished, he looked upon it, saw it was good, and began to expect or hope that it would earn him some substantial reward. What he hoped for may have been the post of 'Surveyor General of the Lands, People, Trade, and . . . Revenue' of Ireland; for among the papers on which his rich dreams expressed themselves is a draft, drawn up by Petty, of a commission from Charles II creating such an officer and endowing him with great powers. It is certain that Petty had been using what little influence he had at Court, derived chiefly from the short-lived patronage of the Duke of Ormond, to get some similar appointment; and the *Treatise* opens with the most flattering praise of Ormond, who had just been appointed Lord Lieutenant of Ireland. But for all of that Petty waited in vain for office or thanks, and conscious of the great public service that the *Treatise* represented, he soured at the thought that its author's merit should go utterly unrewarded. The injustice of it was still irritating him almost a generation later, rankling as it might in a boy whose goodness is persistently overlooked by insensitive elders.[42]

When John Aubrey, in 1678, urged Petty to let the *Treatise* come out again, he answered petulantly, 'As for the reprinting the book of taxes, I will not meddle with it. I never had thanks for any public good I ever did, nor do I own any such book.' This anonymity was a pretence, for though he had kept his name off the title page, he had not kept his authorship secret, indeed Josiah Child had an-

42 'I WROTE': *Treatise of Taxes,* Hull, I, 5. SURVEYOR-GENERAL: *Petty Papers,* I, 98. INFLUENCE AT COURT: Petty to Ormond (1 Mar. 1660–61), in H.M.C. *Ormond* N.S., III, 11.

nounced it publicly in 1668. And he did not insist on keeping the book in the dark either. A few months later, when another friend, Sir Peter Pett, again urged him to authorize a reissue, he relented, though not without complaint. From Dublin he wrote to Robert Southwell asking him to look after the matter, adding his usual complaint. 'You know I have no luck with my politics. Slight court tricks have advanced many men, but the solid study of other men's peace and plenty ruins me. Wherefore let the stationer do what he pleases with the *Taxes*.' It obviously did not interest him much any longer.[43]

It is, nevertheless, in many ways a model work of its time. The quality most immediately apparent is the orderliness of its structure. The purely formal array is extremely simple. The chief types of public expenditure are quickly explained: they are defence, justice, church, schools, poor relief and public works. The second chief section considers methods for reducing the amount or inconvenience of taxes. The third section surveys all the types of taxes, considering each from the standpoint of efficiency and equity. The serviceability of this scheme was so obvious that Smith, when he came to write Book V of *The Wealth of Nations*, followed it extremely closely; though there is no evidence aside from the presence of Petty's works in his library that he took it over directly.

Yet neatness of form can be a substitute for instead of an attribute of systematic investigation. The excellence of the *Treatise of Taxes* arises from its internal unity, imposed by a few dominant theses. The chief of these is that any tax tending to reduce output should be avoided.

> . . . If there be too much money in a nation, it were good for the commonalty as well as the King, and no harm even to particular men, if the King had in his coffers all that is superfluous. . . .
>
> On the other side, if the largeness of a public exhibition should leave less money than is necessary to drive the nation's trade, then the mischief thereof would be

[43] Petty to Aubrey (29 May 1678), in E. Fitzmaurice (*op. cit.* n. 2, p. 125 above), 258. *B.O.,* 17. Petty to Southwell (5 Oct. 1678), *Correspondence,* 61.

the doing of less work, which is the same as lessening the people or their art and industry; for a hundred pounds passing a hundred hands for wages causes 10,000 l. worth of commodities to be produced, which hands would have been idle and useless had there not been this continual motive to their employment.[44]

Despite some overtones of mercantilist superstition in this statement, it is not too generous to read it as a roughly correct comment on the relation of taxes to inflation and deflation. It suggests the keynote of the *Treatise*, that an economically efficient tax policy would avoid all measures tending to reduce employment and output.

The unity of analysis in the *Treatise* qualifies it as a scientific work, even though the analytical principles themselves are, in the light of modern economic theory, partly erroneous. It is not the *ultimate correctness* of its principles that makes a work scientific—were that the test, only the very latest treatise in any scientific discipline could be called scientific, and it would retain that title only until a newer treatise appeared, containing some revision or extension of previous analysis. There would be no such thing as a growing corpus of any science, but only a growing number of pre-scientific works capped by a single piece of science proper, itself doomed shortly to join the ranks of the pre-scientific. It is not the correctness of its analysis, but the method of analysis that defines a work as scientific. One of the chief elements of the scientific method is a taste for economy in analysis, an abhorrence of *ad hoc* explanations, a determination to explain as wide as possible a range of phenomena in terms of a few simple principles. The *Treatise* meets this measure brilliantly, for the principles, such as the one already mentioned, are applied repeatedly throughout the work, sometimes with surprising results.

For instance, among the chapters dealing with particular taxes occurs one which appears at first sight to be an anomaly. It is titled 'Of Penalties', and opens, 'The usual penalties are death, mutilations, imprisonment, public disgrace, corporal transient pains, and great tortures, besides

44 *Treatise of Taxes*, in Hull, I, 36.

the pecuniary mulcts.' It is this last, slightly jarring phrase that leads to the real point, for Petty goes on to say that on monetary fines he will 'most insist, speaking of the others but in order to examine whether they may not be commuted for these'. This purpose, laudable as it would have been had unusual tenderness explained it, or amusing as an ultimate in the commercial instinct, turns out to be in fact a direct deduction from the governing principle. 'Here we are to remember in consequence of our opinion (that labour is the father and active principle of wealth, as lands are the mother) that the State by killing, mutilating, or imprisoning their members do withall punish themselves; wherefore such punishments ought (as much as possible) to be avoided and commuted for pecuniary mulcts, which will increase labour and public wealth.' And in the rest of the chapter Petty suggested how this might be done.[45]

The most important of such pervasive principles in the *Treatise of Taxes* is, as it happens, also the most important principle in the whole of Petty's economic work, and his greatest contribution to economic thought. It makes its first appearance by way of a digression, when in the course of considering the income of land as a source of taxation, Petty stops to explain the 'mysterious nature' of rents—adding, by the way, the striking comment—'with reference as well to money, the rent of which we call usury, as to that of lands and houses. . . .'[46]

The explanation begins with a definition as striking as the preamble: The 'natural and true rent' of a plot of land is the surplus of corn that would be left after a man cultivated the land and used as much of the crop as need be to pay for the expenses of cultivation, including the costs of his own subsistence. The definition, in short, applies a formidable theoretical invention—the notion of a 'real' economic magnitude—to a measure, rent, that had always been thought of as a money payment; and it comes very close to saying what again was remarkably original, that real rent is

[45] *Treatise on Taxes*, in Hull, I, 67 ff., and 68.
[46] *Treatise*, in Hull, I, 42–49. Cf. Barbon's views on interest and rents, pp. 66 ff. above.

a surplus, not merely—as it had always been considered, and long continued to be—a cost of production.

Faced with a few phrases that may imply a great theoretical advance, one is often at a loss to know whether the author was merely using an unconventional vocabulary—quite loosely and as a mere quirk introducing the word 'natural', for instance, instead of some more exact term which he would have had to spend time and effort groping for—or whether, on the other hand, he knew exactly what he was saying. In this instance Petty clearly meant it, for having defined the quantity that may be called 'real rent', he went on to ask the next question, what determines the money value of that rent? And in answering that question, he probed below the obvious, superficial answer, that rent in monetary terms is the real rent valued according to its current market price. He went instead to the underlying question, what establishes the value, in money, of any commodity? His answer was that the money value of the real rent of farming land is determined by the real rent of a silver mine. 'Let another man go travel into a country where is silver; there dig it, refine it, bring it to the same place where the other man planted his corn, coin it, etc.; the same person, all the while of his working for silver, gathering also food for his necessary livelihood, and procuring himself covering, etc.; I say the silver of the one must be esteemed of equal value with the corn of the other, the one being perhaps twenty ounces and the other twenty bushels, from whence it follows that the price of a bushel of this corn to be an ounce of silver.'[47]

Petty's solution is, of course, radically incomplete. He ignored, in the course of this passage though not elsewhere, the rôle of demand in determining prices. He ignored also the differences in productive qualities of each plot of farming or mining land: for the moment at least he was assuming that his farmer was working on a 'standard' piece of farmland and his miner on a 'standard' mine. He could not but have known that the amount of corn a farmer grows depends partly on the quality of the land; he certainly knew that

[47] *Treatise,* in Hull, I, 43.

mines vary in quality; but he did not incorporate this knowledge into his analysis of rent. Sometimes, indeed, when recognizing a difficulty of this order he boldly faced it, or to be more exact, faced it out—by averaging. He had, in the first stage of his analysis, assumed that the labour of a farmer and of a miner were of equivalent quality. He then removed the assumption. 'And forasmuch as possibly there may be more art and hazard in working about the silver than about the corn, yet all comes to the same pass. For let a hundred men work ten years upon corn, and the same number of men the same time upon silver, I say that the net proceed of the silver is the price of the whole net proceed of the corn . . . although not so many of those who wrought in silver learned the art of refining and coining or outlived the dangers and diseases of working in the mines.' This answer is not convincing unless one accepts Petty's special faith that a long-term average will tend toward the 'true and natural' figure; it is a mere article of faith, which cannot justify the common practice of supplying an analytic deficiency with a statistical trick. Petty did not or would not recognize that averaging the outcomes of a process does not explain the process.[48]

Despite, however, the many flaws that can be detected in the *Treatises of Taxes,* its basic structure must stand as a work of surpassing originality. The quality of its analysis makes it an unmistakable masterpiece of early economic science. It is a commentary on the general quality of economic thought at the time, that although Petty's work was immediately and very widely known—Child, Barbon and Collins were among the many writers who quoted him he was noticed and admired for political arithmetic rather than for his profound accomplishment in economic theory. And, so heavy is the hand of time, this tradition of interpretation has come down to our time. But there can be no doubt that although political arithmetic expressed perfectly the aspirations of those who considered numbers the answer to all mystery, it was in his least arithmetical work that Petty did most toward understanding economics.

[48] EFFECT OF DEMAND ON PRICES: e.g. *Treatise,* in Hull, I, 89–90. QUALITIES OF MINES: *Treatise,* in Hull, I, 50 f. 'AND FORASMUCH': *ibid,* 43.

Chapter 6

JOHN LOCKE: PHILOSOPHER
AS ECONOMIST

THE DISTINCTION BETWEEN moral and technical knowledge
is elusive. It is difficult to set out in precise theoretical terms,
and even more difficult, for most people, to keep in mind as
an unerring mental habit. So one must conclude from ob-
serving how reluctantly most people receive the proposition
that how to do a thing and whether the thing ought to be
done are questions that *can* be considered separately and for
the sake of clarity *should* be considered separately.

From the standpoint of any science the distinction is absolutely essential. A subject is not opened to scientific enquiry
until its technical aspect has been sundered from its moral
aspect. The operation is delicate, the Siamese twins do not
always survive, and no matter how successful the surgery,
many bystanders find it as appalling in recollection as they
did in prospect. How deep-seated is the natural antipathy to
this intellectual process can be seen by noticing that even
after many generations of being inculcated with the splendid
virtue of objectivity, men are still spontaneously offended by
The Prince, feeling that Machiavelli could not so coolly have
prescribed a technique without fully endorsing its ends. In
the same way, it is a rare economist who, after outlining the
theory of wages in a competitive economy, has not had to
defend himself against the accusation that he regards the
results of pure competition as perfectly just. Nevertheless
there can be no doubt that economic theory owes its present
development to the fact that some men, in thinking of economic phenomena, forcefully suspended all judgments of
theology, morality, and justice, were willing to consider the
economy as nothing more than an intricate mechanism, re-

fraining for the while from asking whether the mechanism worked for good or evil.

That separation was made during the seventeenth century. The signs of the change are obvious. Sir Thomas Culpepper did not hesitate 'to leave the proofs of the unlawfulness'—that is, the sinfulness—'of usury to divines'; as for himself, he only asked what were the economic effects of higher and lower rates of interest. Child followed him in this, and so did all subsequent economic writers, especially after Bentham finally cleared the air. Similarly Barbon extricated the subject of 'taste' from its moral context; he refused to consider under the aspect of gluttony the economic phenomenon of heavy consumption. His view, finding its boldest expression in Mandeville's doctrine that private vices might be public virtues, succeeded, as it still can, in outraging men of goodwill, just as Petty's manner of counting noses outraged Swift.[1]

The economist's view of the world, which the public cannot yet comfortably stomach, was introduced by a remarkable *tour de force*, an intellectual revolution brought off in the seventeenth century. It was difficult enough to make chemistry and physics into sciences; it is not comfortable to think of solid substance as an essentially empty space or to think of void as full of something called gas. It was more difficult to make a science of astronomy, which so nearly concerns Heaven. It was exceedingly difficult to treat economics in a scientific fashion, since every economic act, being the action of a human being, is necessarily also a moral act. If the magnitude of difficulty rather than the extent of the achievement be the measure, then the making of economics was the greatest scientific accomplishment of the seventeenth century.

But nothing could be more mistaken than to suppose that in separating positive from normative knowledge, the seventeenth century economists were totally isolating economics from its mother discipline, philosophy. How close the relation remained can be recognized by drawing up a list of the great British philosophers between 1660 and 1860: Locke, Berkeley, Hume, Bentham, and John Stuart Mill would cer-

[1] Culpepper, *A Tract against Usurie* . . . (1621).

tainly require places. Something more than coincidence must explain why each of these also wrote a good deal on economics, and why at least three of the five and possibly all five must be ranked as great economists. When one considers further that both Smith and Jevons were professors of philosophy, the contribution of philosophy to economics seems to be established beyond question. Indeed it has often been asserted. But the precise way that philosophy—either the philosopher's habit of mind or the substance of philosophic learning—contributed to the development of economics has not often been traced out. One important aspect of the connection can be made clear in the work of John Locke.

I

Locke was alone among the important economic writers of his time in having had a perfectly traditional education; although no more than they did he come from a family or class to which such learning was normal. His grandfathers were on one side a wealthy Somerset clothier, on the other, a tanner; they had acquired enough land to qualify them as minor gentry; and his father had risen so far as to be a country lawyer. One of his father's best clients, who became also his patron, was Alexander Popham, a neighbouring gentleman who served as a high parliamentary officer during the civil war and was MP for Bath in 1647. Westminster School having fallen under the control of the Long Parliament and John Locke having reached the age of fifteen, Popham nominated him for a place there; and so Locke's education, like that of so many of his contemporaries, was deeply influenced by the accidents and dislocations of the Civil War.[2]

At Westminster Locke came under the direction of a great master, Richard Busby, a conservative Royalist and strict Anglican, whose regime became so renowned as a model that Gladstone described him as 'the founder of the Public

2 My account of Locke's life is based on Maurice Cranston's excellent biography, *John Locke* (1957).

School system'. During the six years that Locke stayed at the School he spent six days a week, from dawn to dark, memorizing, reciting, and construing passages in Greek and Latin, composing prose and verse in both languages, translating from one into the other and from both into English. When he was older, Hebrew, Arabic, and a few other subjects were added to the diet. The school schedule under Busby is known from the remarks of a slightly older student:

> 5:15 a.m. called up by a monitor, and after Latin Prayers, wash.
>
> Between 6 and 8 repeat grammar—Lily for Latin, Camden for Greek—fourteen or fifteen being selected and called out to stand in a semi-circle before the Master.
>
> Between 8 and 9 we had time for a beaver [beverage], and recollection of selves and preparation of future exercises.
>
> Between 9 and 11 those exercises were read which had been enjoined us overnight (one day in prose; the next day in verse).
>
> At dinner and supper we read some portion of the Latin in a manuscript.
>
> Between 1 and 3 the [classical] author chosen by the Master for the day was gone through by construing and other grammatical ways.
>
> Betwixt 3 and 4 a little respite.
>
> Betwixt 4 and 5 we repeated a leaf or two out of some book of rhetorical figures and choice proverbs and sentences collected by the Master for that use. . . .
>
> After supper (in summer time) we were called to the Master's chamber and there instructed out of Hunter's *Cosmography*, and taught to describe and find out cities and counties in the maps.
>
> The Scholars were governed by several monitors (Two for the Hall, as many for the Church, the School, the Fields, the Cloister). The captain of the school was one of these, and therefore called *monitor monitorum*. These monitors kept strictly to the speaking of Latin in their commands, and with all they permitted their

complaints or accusations (as we called them) every Friday morning.[3]

Locke did well enough in these studies to be elected a King's Scholar at Westminster in 1650 and to win a scholarship to Christ Church, Oxford, in 1652. As the latter award was based not on merit alone, Locke and his father petitioned certain great men to intervene on his behalf, and so Locke was applying to Fleetwood for a place at Oxford just when Petty was taking up his place as physician to Fleetwood.

At Christ Church, when Locke entered in 1652 at the unusually advanced age of twenty, he found an academic programme pretty well in tune with what was already familiar. The substance of study was, as before, classical languages, rhetoric, grammar, and logic; these were enlarged by the addition of metaphysics, moral philosophy, natural philosophy (that is, the natural philosophy of Aristotle), and occasional lectures on history and Hebrew. The test of accomplishment was still the disputation, and candidates for the Bachelor's degree in Arts were required to attend the disputations, and each in turn to maintain a thesis against an adversary. The programme of learning, inherited largely intact from the Middle Ages and crystallized in the seventeenth century by the Laudian Statutes, had as yet been modified only in slight details. Formal education in the universities, at least in the Arts, still refused to recognize the new learning. It was in this tradition that Locke was trained.[4]

After the required six years, Locke qualified as Master of Arts and was elected a Senior Student of Christ Church, that is, an impermanent fellow. Two years later, in 1660, he was elected Lecturer in Greek, and in 1662, Lecturer in Rhetoric. In the latter post, the statute required him to lecture twice weekly to all first year students on Aristotle, Cicero, Quintilian or Hermogenes. In addition, as a tutor of his college, he taught and conducted disputations with the students. So he continued until 1665, by which time he had

[3] Fox Bourne, Life of John Locke (1876), I, 20–21. Cranston, 20–21.

[4] Mallet, Oxford, II, 319 ff. Cranston, 31 ff.

spent nearly twenty years of his life immersed in the matter and style of classics and classical philosophy.[5]

To say that he was immersed in it does not mean that he accepted it with unquestioning gratitude. But neither did he, for all his revolution in epistemology and heterodoxy in ethics, reject traditional philosophy as worthless. It is true enough that when he came to write his essay on education, he condemned the going system of schooling as inappropriate for gentlemen; it tried to pump into them a tasteless mass of dead and deadening matter. And Lady Masham reported that he 'never loved the trade of disputing in public in the schools but was always wont to declaim against it as being rather invented for wrangling or ostentation than to discover truth'. But he insisted, without qualification, that a scholar must be trained in that very tradition which had become his, for 'amongst the Grecians is to be found the original, as it were, and foundation of all that learning which we have in this part of the world'.[6]

As a young man, however, Locke himself was not satisfied to rest on this foundation, and like so many others who were somehow attracted by the new learning, he chose to explore medicine. Just what made for the special appeal of medicine is not altogether easy to tell. It had the great intellectual fascination at this time of any rapidly growing subject. William Harvey published his discovery of blood circulation just four years before Locke was born, and the excitement and hopes that this announcement stirred up had reached a peak just when Locke came to Oxford, having been brought to this pitch by the efforts of the Invisible Society. Like the other branches of the new learning, medicine too had the attraction of lying utterly outside the realms of political and theological controversy that continued but little abated after the Restoration; more important, it was a subject in which fanaticism and faction had little place, for the acolytes of the new philosophy were not so much given to abstaining from political controversy as they were to abhorring

[5] Mallet, II, 321 ff. Cranston, chap. 6.

[6] LADY MASHAM: Cranston, 38. Locke, *Thoughts concerning Education* (1693) [composed ca. 1685], secs. 94, 168, 195.

the intrusion of enthusiasts into it. And for some, the great attraction of medicine was that it coupled with its scientific glamour the promise of a rising social respectability and of extraordinary financial gain: the popular London physician whose riches were crowned by a Knighthood was beginning to be almost as common a figure as his counterpart, the great London merchant enriched by foreign trade.

For Locke, these considerations, especially the last, were perhaps less important than certain personal ones. He had among his closest friends a great source of information about medicine. Richard Lower was Thomas Willis' most distinguished pupil, had been a friend of Locke's at Westminster School and was now his contemporary at Christ Church; Locke's medical notebooks show how heavily he drew on Lower's training.

Moreover, medicine represented for Locke the most convenient avenue to academic tenure. His studentship at Christ Church could become permanent only if he took divine orders, and as late as 1663 he was still contemplating this step. But something kept him from going ahead toward ordainment. It may have been scruples of conscience, for although his works show signs of piety, they show no signs of dogmatically Anglican piety. It may, on the other hand, have been boredom with the subjects to which his teaching would have been confined had he continued as a don in philosophy. In any event, medicine was the way out, for the Christ Church statutes allowed two senior studentships in medicine, the holders of which need not be in orders.[7]

He began therefore to prepare himself for the MD, attending Willis' lectures, taking informal instruction from another great member of the Invisible College, Ralph Bathurst, and above all joining in the work and speculation that centred in the laboratory that Robert Boyle maintained in his High Street rooms, ending as one of Boyle's closest friends. In 1667, on returning to Oxford after an absence abroad, Locke set up a small chemistry laboratory with an Oxford doctor, David Thomas, where they experimented on pharmacology. He also met and became the friend of Thomas Sydenham, the most distinguished English physi-

7 LOWER: Cranston, 40. TENURE: Cranston, 74.

cian of his time and an important figure in the history of medical research. As a result of this interest and these connections, Locke was as early as 1666 considered a competent physician and considered himself such, for in the pleasantly loose fashion of the time, he set up as a physician, if not to the public, at least to family, friends, and a few chosen clients. In this guise he met Lord Ashley, later Shaftesbury, who instantly became his patron.[8]

This powerful patronage solved Locke's tenure problem in a rather roundabout way. The first effect was a letter that Clarendon, acting presumably at the suggestion of Ashley, wrote to the Vice-Chancellor in November 1666. 'I am very well assured that Mr John Locke . . . has employed his time in the study of physic [i.e. medicine] to so good purpose that he is in all respects qualified for the degree of Doctor in that faculty . . . but not having taken the degree of bachelor in physic, he had desired that he may be dispensed with to accumulate that degree, which appears to be a very modest and reasonable request, he professing himself ready to perform the exercises for both degrees. I therefore give my consent that a dispensation to that purpose be propounded for him.' The request, though coming from a man who was not only Chief Minister of the Crown but also Chancellor of the University, was nevertheless ignored.

A few weeks later another letter followed, which had the force of law. Addressed by Charles II to the Dean and Chapter of Christ Church, it read:

> Whereas we are informed that John Locke . . . is of such standing as by the custom of that college he is obliged to enter into holy orders or otherwise to leave his Student's place there; at his humble request that he may still have the further time to prosecute his studies without that obligation, we are graciously pleased to grant him our royal dispensation, and do accordingly hereby require you to suffer him, the said John Locke, to hold and enjoy his Student's place in Christ Church . . . without taking holy orders.

[8] Cranston, 74 ff., 88–95.

This command not only assured Locke a permanent position, but relieved him of the obligation to teach or even remain in residence; and in the spring of 1667, when Ashley invited Locke to join his household in London as personal physician, he went—much as Petty had earlier left Oxford to join Fleetwood.[9]

Locke continued throughout his life to prescribe for friends and acquaintances, and he kept up an interest in science, inside and outside of the Royal Society, to which he was elected in 1668. In science he acted as an intermediary, much as Collins and most other *virtuosi* did, collecting information and specimens, sending scientific materials about the learned world, keeping abreast of the work done by the serious scientists such as Newton, Boyle, and Sydenham, but himself doing nothing original or of consequence. The flavour of his own scientific studies, not untainted with the mystical attitude of a former day, can be seen from one of his earlier letters on pharmacological research, addressed to Boyle:

> . . . having from a passage in your writings taken the first notice of the time of gathering peony roots . . . that it must be in April, when Sol is in Aries and at a plenilunium before the rising of the sun, I rode to a place where was pretty good plenty of male peony, and on the 14th instant, between ten and eleven in the morning, had some roots dug up, and am promised others to be dug up on the 30th instant before sunrising. If there be any advantage in the time of gathering I owe the knowledge of it so much to you that I should be an unworthy reader of your writings if I should not return you my thanks and offer you some part of these roots. . . .

John Locke, riding out on horseback in the mists of dawn, his astrological eye cocked on the moon, searching the Oxfordshire fields for male peonies—it is a charming picture of what the new philosophy meant to the devoted amateurs.[10]

[9] Cranston, 96–104.
[10] Cranston, 116 ff. Locke to Boyle, 24 March 1667, quoted in Cranston, 91.

His interest in science left no discernible trace in Locke's economic writings; but his medical qualification, as it led to the association with Ashley, furnished the occasion for Locke's exceptionally broad familiarity with problems of economic policy. For from being Ashley's physician he rapidly became a sort of private secretary, counsellor, and political assistant, and, in time, the obligations of this post led him into political offices that were important albeit not honorific. It led Locke into the only workaday profession of his later life, that of a civil servant involved in the regulation of trade.

II

All of Locke's economic writings stem from a brief memorandum, that he wrote soon after joining Ashley's household, and expanded at various times during the ensuing thirty years, until at last it made up a set of quite sizeable pamphlets. The original seed was planted during 1668, when a great agitation about the state of business led to inquiries by the Council of Trade and by both houses of Parliament. One of the chief proposals before all of these bodies, it will be remembered, was the plan to reduce the rate of interest to 4 per cent; and the chief, best-known advocate of the reduction was Josiah Child, who became so important a figure in the debate because of the strong impression that his *Brief Observations* made on contemporaries.

Matters of trade naturally fell under the ministerial scrutiny of Ashley, who was at this time well ensconced in his eleven-year term as Chancellor of the Exchequer. It is tempting to suppose that when Child's pamphlet—and the Bill tabled in Parliament at the same time—began to stir discussion, Ashley turned to his intelligent and learned secretary for a critique of the proposal. The memorandum that Locke wrote on this occasion soon reached Ashley, whether or not he commissioned it, and was handed on to other high officials; the copy that found its way to Henry Coventry is endorsed, 'By Mr Locke, directed by Ld Ashley.'[11]

11 Locke, 'some of the consequences that are like to follow . . .'; BM Add. MSS 32,094, f. 289.

This first effort—which went under the name, 'Some of the consequences that are like to follow upon lessening of interest to 4 per cent'—was the work of an amateur. Locke had no direct acquaintance with business except such as came from managing the minute and uncomplicated estate that his father had left him; aside from this he had been as insulated from business as any cloistered scholar is likely ever to have been. Nor had he, so far as appears, remedied this lack of direct personal experience by much reading. Later on, especially during the 1690s, he became an avid collector of economic tracts, but it does not appear that by 1668 he had read anything on the subject besides Child. That from such slender familiarity with the material Locke was able to produce a work as penetrating and original as he did is a tribute above all to the quality of his mind. But it may also be accounted for, though in lesser measure, by a mental habit that stemmed from his particular philosophical training—the disposition to consider moral and political problems from the standpoint of 'natural law'.

Locke himself took a modest view of this piece of work, for he wrote that its favourable reception showed what came of 'prefixing a great name to my trifles and sending them abroad in the world'.[12] And as to part of the piece, especially the opening pages, this was not excessive diffidence. He began by tracing the effects of an artificially reduced interest rate on various parties; the catalogue is blunt, bald, and unsophisticated—though it has the great merit, as compared to Child's partisan sophistication, that it does not fudge the issues.

For instance, Child had argued that a lower rate would benefit merchants and all other useful members of society, injuring only the usurers, against whom he trotted out the ancient objections—they are 'idle persons that live at as little expense as labour, neither scattering by their expenses so as the poor may glean anything after them, nor working with their hands or heads to bring either wax or honey to the common hive of the Kingdom. . . .' Since, Child continued, everybody knows 'how unprofitable it is for any

---

[12] Bod. Lib. Ms. Locke b. 3, f. 1.

nation to suffer Idleness to suck the breasts of Industry', he felt comfortable in his conclusion 'that the abatement of interest doth tend to the enriching of a nation'. Locke cut through all of this rhetoric of superstition, answering that the abatement

> will be gain to the merchant, for if he borrow at 4 per cent and his return be 12 per cent, he will have 8 per cent and the usurer 4; whereas they divide it now equally at 6 per cent. But this neither gets nor loses to the Kingdom in the trade, supposing the merchant and usurer to be both Englishmen.

Locke, in other words, was able in a simple and straightforward way to distinguish between the good of either a merchant or usurer and the general good—not, in principle, as difficult a distinction to perceive as the common practice of his contemporaries would suggest, yet for just that reason an unusually clear-minded one.[13]

And yet in other passages, Locke falls into gross errors of his own. Child had argued that if the rate of interest were reduced to 4 per cent, the value of lands would double; his reasoning apparently having been that as the value of land is the capitalized value of its income, to lower the lawful interest rate would be equivalent to raising the rate at which landed incomes were to be capitalized—although why he should have assumed that a decline of one-third in the rate would increase the capitalized value by 100 per cent rather than by 50 per cent is not easy to explain except as an arithmetical slip.[14] Locke's reply is a wonderful melange of sophisticated analysis and utter confusion, all the more remarkable for being condensed in so few words.

He considers first the effect of the proposed abatement on landed income:

> It will be a loss in the yearly income of lands, annuities, etc.; for £100 per annum will be [proportionately?] ⅓ less worth; unless the merchant, making more profit

[13] Child, B.O., 13. Locke, 'Some of the consequences . . . ,' f. 289; see pp. 98 ff. above.
[14] Child, B.O., 10.

by low interest, will sell his consumable commodities
at 2 per cent cheaper than he doth now; which is not
likely as long as the consumption of England is as
great and the buyers as many as are now; which must
be an effect of good husbandry and not low use.[15]

The passage opens with a conclusion—the abatement will
reduce 'the yearly income of lands'—that is much less obvious than it looks. Since rents in England were then as
now expressed in terms of so many shillings per acre per
year, no change in the interest rate could be expected to
effect, in the short run, the money rent; landlords would not
lower rents just because the rate of interest declined, nor
would tenants be less willing or able to pay the prevailing
rent. A decline in the interest rate would reduce landed
incomes only if the price of land were to rise proportionately
to the decline in the interest rate. This result would be
brought about if men who had previously lent out cash at
6 per cent, finding their returns cut to 4 per cent, now
started to buy land, because the rate of return from land
would still, for a while, continue high; in doing so, they
would bid up the price of land, until the yield from land
dropped to 4 per cent, at which point the bidding up would
cease. This mechanism would in time result in landowners
earning a *rate of return* one-third lower than before. But
Locke certainly did not explain the mechanism, and it is by
no means clear that he understood it; for if he had, he
should have agreed with Child that all those who owned
land at the moment the interest rate was abated would gain
by the rise in the value of their estates. Indeed, had Locke
understood the mechanism, he could hardly have mistaken,
as he did, a decline in the *rate of return* from landed property, a decline brought about by a rise in the value of the
estate, for a decline in *money income* from that property.

The next step in Locke's implicit reasoning is that real
incomes from land would decline as money incomes did—
'unless the merchant, making more profit by low interest,
will sell his consumable commodities at 2 per cent cheaper'.
To recognize that a decline in money incomes would be

15 'Some of the consequences . . . ,' f. 289.

immaterial if its cause simultaneously forced money prices down in the same proportion—to introduce, in short, the then still recondite notion of real income—is another instance of Locke's native talent for economics. But the rest of the remark is full of flaws. If the interest rate were reduced by one-third, the merchant's profits would rise by exactly the same proportion only on the perverse assumption that the merchant had no expenses except interest charges. Moreover, the emphasis that Locke places on *consumable* commodities is misleading, unless landowners spent their whole incomes on consumption. Locke's price theory becomes still more suspect when he adds that merchants will not reduce their prices 'as long as the consumption of England is as great and the buyers as many as are now'—thus introducing the assumption that the total demand for goods would be unaffected by the decline in landowners' money incomes— that is, that their income elasticity of demand was zero. And finally, the passage which argues that prices of goods will decline only because 'of good husbandry and not low use' seems to assert the curious view that technical savings can reduce costs whereas financial savings cannot.

This particular passage can, to be sure, be restated in such a way as to make it more palatable to the modern economist and more revealing to the historian. Let us suppose that what Locke really meant, as distinct from what he said, is this: The total demand for food will not decline perceptibly even if the incomes of landowners decline somewhat, since landowners will continue to buy as much food as they please. The supply of food would be increased if farmers were more efficient, and this would reduce prices. But the price of food is not perceptibly reduced when merchants' costs decline. Merchants do not compete with each other; nor would the law abating interest increase the supply of capital, thus enabling existing merchants to expand their trade; nor would increased profitability of merchandizing at all quickly induce other men to become merchants; in short, the merchants as a group are monopolists. Moreover, their monopoly power is strong because the price of their services makes up so small a part of the price the consumer pays for the product, because of which the price elasticity of demand for merchants' services is very much lower even than the already low price elasticity of demand for foodstuffs. Had Locke said this, it would probably have been a fair statement of the case at his time; and Locke may have *meant* something like this; but the distance between it and what he actually said measures the weakness of his analytic power when he was writing the paper.

It is hardly necessary, however, to attempt to salvage a coherent meaning from the passage, for Locke very quickly abandoned it. A short supplement that he added to the paper later in the same year begins, 'Upon a review of the foregoing particulars, I guess the third consequence should be stated thus brief: That lessening of use will very much alter the value of men's estates in land, annuities, and money in reference to one another . . . but will not at all alter the value of the yearly income of those lands and annuities in reference to commodities purchasable by it. . . .' In arriving at this correct statement of the case, Locke had excised the more subtle questions that had so badly confused his first attempt; later he returned to them with surer powers.[16]

Despite its flaws, the 1668 paper is distinguished by two innovations of the greatest importance. The first is the concept of a 'natural' rate of interest, introduced after a series of arguments by which Locke aims to show that a legal rate of 4 per cent would merely redistribute income as between lenders and borrowers, or worse, restrict the supply of funds offered for loan. It would be better, he therefore concludes, if the legal rate of income were near the natural rate. He then defines it. 'By natural use I mean that rate of money which the present scarcity makes it naturally at. . . .' Subsequent remarks—such as, 'That which most sensibly raises the rate of interest of money is when money is little in proportion to the trade of a country'—fill out the definition.

16 The paper of 1668 in Bod. Lib. MS. Locke e. 8, ff. 1–17, is followed by the supplement, ff. 18–27, at the *close* of which stands, in Locke's hand, 'Sic cogitavit 1668 JL'. There then follows another supplement, ff. 28–31. Although the whole is endorsed, in Locke's hand, 'Interest at 4 per cent, 74', ff. 28–31 is the only section that seems to have been written in 1674. The text is given in Appendix V on p. 295.

Locke obviously meant that the 'natural' interest rate was the rate determined by the supply of and demand for money at any given moment. Why Locke should have called the free market rate the 'natural' rate, and what the implications of that adjective were, will be considered later. It is enough for the moment to say that this expression, which was not a mere usage but of a piece with Locke's theory of natural law, had an enormous influence on economic thought.[17]

Secondly, the notion of a natural interest rate, and the general tendency of his argument, led him to assert that there was some proper amount of money that a country needed in view of the extent of its trade at any given time. After insisting on 'the necessity of some proportion of money to trade', he goes on to say, 'but what proportion that is is hard to determine'. His explanation of why it is hard to determine, and the way he tries to surmount the difficulty—these are, as pure economic theory, what is best in the paper.

> . . . but what proportion that is is hard to determine. Because it depends, not barely on the quantity of money, but the quickness of its circulation—which since it cannot easily be traced . . . to make some probable guess we are to consider how much money it is necessary to suppose must rest constantly in each man's hands as requisite to the carrying on of trade.

Part of the quantity theory of money is stated here more clearly than it had been before. For although the notion that the level of national economic activity is a function of the supply of money was not in the least unusual in Locke's time,[18] to bring the velocity of circulation into the discussion as explicitly as Locke did was, if not altogether unknown, nevertheless as good as the best thinking then going on about the subject. Moreover, the remainder of the paper, which Locke devotes to a most ingenious inquiry into how much money Englishmen usually keep on hand—into the size of what under the present dispensation would be

[17] 'Some of the consequences . . . ,' f. 290; see pp. 184 ff. below.
[18] Vickers, *Studies in the Theory of Money.*

called 'transactions balances'—is a very elegant piece of abstract reasoning.

Unfortunately, the better half of the paper has practically no bearing on the policy question from which he started; it tells the reader nothing about why interest should or should not be reduced by law. The paper as a whole, therefore, was not well designed for rhetorical effect; on the contrary, it shows at work a mind more prone to go off chasing theoretical hares than to keep steadily at the business of driving the political cows home. And so it always was with Locke, at least in his economic writings: objectivity and disinterest arose not from outward compulsion but from an ingrained habit of speculating.

III

During the years after Locke joined Shaftesbury's staff, he came increasingly into contact with the economic problems that pressed on his master's attention. Many of these were official, and Locke, raised from private physician to private secretary, worked with the petitions, complaints and reports that besieged a great minister, some as exotic as Collins' scheme for elaborate national economic accounts, others concerning the most practical details of commerce and the largest questions of foreign trade. He was introduced also to colonial problems, for Shaftesbury, part owner of the Carolinas, persuaded him in 1668 to become secretary to the Lords Proprietors. Aside from being elevated to the abortive peerage of the colony, Locke lent a hand in writing its constitution and managing its administration. And in 1673 his standing as an expert was sealed by his first official appointment, as Secretary to the Council for Trade and Plantations.[19]

This body was formed, apparently at the instance of Shaftesbury, to replace the Council of Trade on which Child had served and which had been dissolved after turn-

[19] Collins to Shaftesbury (Nov. 1667), in PRO 30/24/4/160; endorsed in Locke's hand, as are many papers in the Shaftesbury MSS. CAROLINA: Cranston, 119 ff.; C.S.P. Col., 1669–74, passim.

ing into a battleground of the East India and Levant companies. The Council for Plantations, commissioned on 30 July 1670, consisted of ten members, courtiers, members of Parliament, and experts on mercantile and marine affairs. Five of them had served on earlier councils; but one group that had been heavily represented, and indeed dominant, in the past was now conspicuously absent—the merchant magnates, excluded perhaps because their previous misbehaviour had demonstrated that 'working merchants' were after all too partial to attend to the public good, perhaps also because they were not distinctively qualified for the Council's chief function, to advise and aid in governing the colonies. The Council had for its President the diplomat and admiral, the Earl of Sandwich, and as Secretary, Henry Slingsby, Master of the Mint, who appointed as chief clerk his protege, John Collins. The staff was completed by an Assistant Secretary, that great link in commercial policy, Dr Benjamin Worsley—propagator of the Navigation Acts, Child's mentor, Petty's old antagonist, and more recently, consultant to Shaftesbury.[20]

Before Locke joined it, the Council had undergone a series of alterations. In March of 1671, it had been enlarged by the addition of dignitaries. The Duke of York, Prince Rupert, Buckingham, Ormond, Lauderdale and Culpeper were authorized at all times to 'enter and vote'; John Evelyn was added as a regular member. These new appointments were greeted plaintively by John Collins, who by way of apology for delay in answering a letter, wrote: 'it fell to my lot to transcribe copies of the commissions and instructions for their use'. Others may have found the recruits objectionable on other grounds, for although the new members could not help but augment the Council's prestige and were, several of them, qualified by previous interest in colonial

[20] DISSOLUTION OF 1668 COUNCIL: See chap. 1, p. 27 above. SHAFTESBURY'S INFLUENCE: Andrews, 96. MEMBERS OF THE COUNCIL OF PLANTATIONS: Sandwich, Lord Gorges, Lord Allington, Thomas Grey, Henry Brouncker, Sir Humphrey Winch, Sir John Finch, Silius Titus, Edmund Waller, Henry Slingsby. C.S.P.D. 1670, 538–39 (18 Nov. 1670). WORSLEY AS SHAFTESBURY'S ADVISOR: L. F. Brown, *The First Earl of Shaftesbury*, 141 et passim.

affairs, the fact that they were strong supports of the Court suggests that the Council was being packed to prevent it from following Shaftesbury's lead rather than the King's. The body was reconstructed in 1672, shortly after Sandwich was killed in the battle of Solebay. It became a Council for Trade and Plantations, with much the same membership as before but Shaftesbury as President. Its work was expected now to be heavier, and Slingsby—foreseeing this and also that the financial pressures of the Third Dutch War would make the payment of the Council's salaries less likely than ever—resigned. Collins, as usual unpaid, left with him. Worsley succeeded to a short term as Secretary, which closed the next summer when, being a dissenter, he refused to take the Tests. Locke became Secretary in his stead.[21]

Every sort of economic and administrative problem was grist to the Council's mill, issues being introduced by way of questions referred from the Privy Council and officers of government, memorials and petitions from merchants, companies or colonial planters, and inquiries initiated by the Council itself. The gravity of the subjects that might come before it is indicated by the great debates in earlier, similar bodies, on fixing the legal rate of interest or revising boundaries between the trading areas of great merchant companies. Smaller problems were regular fare. Merchants complained of rampant piracy and unjust exactions by supposedly friendly governments. One Doddington touched off a fight by urging that no more currants be imported from

---

[21] APPOINTMENTS OF 1671: *C.S.P.Col. 1669–74*, 178 (20 Mar. 1671). Collins to Gregory (25 Mar. 1671), in Rigaud, II, 217. James, aside from being proprietor of New York, invested in the Royal African, Hudson's Bay and East India companies; Rupert invested in the two former companies as well; and among other members of the Council, Sandwich, Grey, Shaftesbury and Locke invested in or were officers of the Royal African Company (Davies, *Royal African Company*; Rich, *Hudson's Bay Company*, Vol. I). COUNCIL OF 1672: Thomas Grey was omitted, Halifax and Culpeper were added to the earlier roster of regular members. *C.S.P.Col. 1669–74*, 407 (16 Sept. 1672). SLINGSBY'S RESIGNATION: Collins to Dr Beale (20 Aug. 1672), in Rigaud, I, 200 ff. LOCKE'S APPOINTMENT: *C.S.P.Col. 1669–74*, 527 (14 Oct. 1673); but see *Acts P.C. (Col.)*, I, 591 (20 June 1673), 'Dr Locke, secretary to the Council of Trade and Plantations.'

Zante, because the Venetians mistreated English sailors and England's balance of trade with Venice was unfavourable; both of which assertions several merchants denied, producing accounts to prove that the balance of trade with Venice was really favourable. Colonial questions constantly preoccupied the Council, the chief and perpetual problems, then and later, being to determine, in the first place, even the gross facts about what was happening in the colonies—how many inhabitants they had, where they lived, by what occupations, and under what local ordinances—and secondly, infinitely more difficult, to impose on colonial governments the declared will of the home government, or, to descend to what was more practicable though nevertheless seldom achieved, merely to discover whether the colonial governors were following the official policies established in London. Some of the Council's work was uncommonly practical: it planned the arming and equipping of military expeditions in the colonies, down to the number of bullets and rations to be provided; it phrased orders to colonial officials in the most scrupulous detail, reaching out from London to settle boundary disputes between two small landowners in Virginia. It also operated on a much broader scale of policy. When the merchants and seamen of the western coast, on whom a monopoly of Newfoundland fishing rights had been conferred, complained of interlopers, the Council offered its opinion that the King should open the trade to all his subjects, but that immigration to Newfoundland should be prohibited and the existing immigrants—who set off the complaint by underselling the official monopolists—be encouraged to move to Jamaica or other colonies.[22]

[22] DEBATES ON RATE OF INTEREST AND EAST INDIA QUESTIONS: see pp. 6 and 27 above. ZANTE: PRO, C.O. 388/1 contains these and various other petitions, etc., before the 1672 as well as other councils on trade. COLONIES, ETC.: The minutes of the 1670 and 1672 Council are in the Library of Congress (Washington); they are described in 40 *Eng. Hist. Rvw.* 93 (1925). Papers submitted to it are in PRO, C.O. 388/1 and elsewhere in the C.O. series and Shaftesbury papers, also in the Bodleian, MSS Locke, c. 9, 30, 36, d. 7, etc. Many of the problems before the Council for Trade can also be traced, insofar as they arose before the Privy Council, in the 'Privy Council Registers' (PRO), calendared in *Acts of the Privy*

Such were the Council's deliberations during the two years of Locke's service. When Shaftesbury was dismissed from all offices at the end of 1674, the Council was dissolved and its functions transferred to a committee of the Privy Council, where Danby could keep such matters under firm control. Shaftesbury retired to the country, and Locke returned to his private life after these seven years of interruption.[23]

The next sixteen years, his forty-second to fifty-eighth, Locke spent away from London and economic affairs. From 1675 to 1679, he travelled about France as bearleader to the son of Sir John Banks, a great London merchant. He spent some years enjoying his sinecure at Oxford, and when the Reaction of 1683 threatened all notorious Whigs, he retired to Holland, whence he returned only after the Revolution. During all that time he worked steadily on philosophy, so that within a year of homecoming he published all his chief works, the first two *Letters on Toleration*, the *Treatises of Civil Government*, and the *Essay concerning Human Understanding*. The latter, the only one to which he signed his name, immediately established him as England's great philosopher. His known affiliation with Shaftesbury, now reckoned an honourable martyr, his meritorious exile, some service he may have done William of Orange while in Holland, his splendid return in the company of Queen Mary—these, together with his sudden philosophic fame, made him a sort of minor prophet.

Soon after Locke's return the monetary problems that had been overlooked during the political crises of the past ten years began once again to claim attention. The deterioration of the coinage was already noticeable, and though it was not yet approaching a crisis, Locke was very afraid that it would become much worse. Another monetary question was more urgent. On 10 October 1690, the House of Commons gave

---

Council (Colonial). The system as a whole is analysed in C. M. Andrews, *The Colonial Period of American History*, Vol. IV (1938). NEWFOUNDLAND: *C.S.P.Col.* 1669–74, 143–44 (2 Mar. 1671).

[23] For dissolution of Council and formation of its successor, see PRO, C.O. 391/1.

leave to bring in a Bill for reducing the rate of interest from 6 per cent to 4 per cent, the Bill to be drafted by Sir Edward Hussey, Sir Mathew Andrews, and Thomas Papillon, veteran of the campaign of 1668. The auspices suggest that the renewed effort was led by the greater foreign traders; but they did not have everything their own way, for another Bill was coupled with theirs, to prevent the export of bullion, and encourage its importation and coinage. The movement for the Bill was moreover aided by Child, who chose this moment to publish an augmented version of his 1668 tract. Locke, reacting immediately to the reappearance of these old antagonists, acquiesced when an MP, perhaps Sir John Somers, asked him to expand his own paper of 1668 into a substantial attack, this time for publication. Long before his counterblast could be published, the Bill was narrowly defeated. But the proponents of the Bill reintroduced it during the next session, in time for Locke's book, *Some Considerations of the Consequences of the Lowering of Interest and Raising the Value of Money*, to have some influence on the outcome. His friend Edward Clarke, after distributing copies to MPs, wrote Locke at the end of 1691 that there 'is already a doubt whether the Bill . . . will ever be read a second time or not, and all that have read the *Considerations* are clearly of opinion the arguments therein are abundantly sufficient to destroy that Bill and all future attempts of the like kind'. The House of Commons proved that this was much too friendly a compliment, for in January 1692 it passed the Bill. Clarke now wrote Locke:

Several attempts were had . . . to have thrown it out, wherein all imaginable reasons were used to that end. In which debate I was not a little pleased to hear the arguments used that are contained in the *Considerations*. . . . But I am satisfied that if an angel from heaven had managed the debate, the votes would have been the same as now. For it is not reason, but a supposed benefit to the borrower that has passed the bill, and I believe it is that will carry it through the House of Lords. . . .

Clarke was wrong again. The House of Lords did not pass it.[24]

The *Considerations,* influential or not, was a vast improvement on Locke's paper of 1668. It shows a degree of sophistication about commercial affairs that can reasonably be attributed to his years of practice in the administration of the Carolinas and the Council for Trade and Plantations. The basic outline of his objections to a legal limitation of interest was still the same, but the arguments were now stated much more fully, correctly, and with the certainty not as before of a bright young man but rather of a confident expert.

The degree of improvement is clear, for instance, in how he now dealt with the price of land. This subject became the chief matter of a longish treatise, and, what is more important than the amount of space devoted to it, the con-

[24] BILL OF 1690: Leave to introduce, 10 Oct. 1690; first reading, 13 Oct. 1690; second reading, and rejected, 158 votes to 155, 26 Nov. 1690; 10 *C.J.* 433, 440, 484. CHILD'S DISCOURSE: Licensed 18 Nov. 1689, published 1690; cf. Appendix, p. 250 below, for relation of this work to Child's *Brief Observations.* It may be Child's *Discourse* that Locke bought from the bookseller Churchill on 5 Mar. 1691; Bod. MS. Locke b. 2, f. 118. SIR JOHN SOMERS: The *Considerations* opens with a letter addressed to 'A Member of Parliament,' in which Locke says that the MP 'put me upon looking out my old papers'. The conclusion that this MP was Somers is a mere surmise, founded on the close association of these two and on the well-documented fact that Locke wrote some of his later tracts on coinage at Somers' request; what makes it questionable is that Somers was not the only MP who asked Locke's opinion in such matters; see, for instance, the paper endorsed by Locke '*Mony* 95 Written at Sr Wm Trumbulls request and given him in Sept 95' Bod. Lib. MS. Locke b. 3, ff. 62. DATE OF CONSIDERATIONS: In the prefatory letter, dated 7 Nov. 1691, Locke speaks of having put the notions in writing 'above twelve months since'; October, 1690, seems the time indicated, although he may have started a bit earlier. He does not, however, appear to have finished it at once, for the letter refers to more recent additions; moreover, his correspondence with Benjamin Furly shows that he kept asking the knowing merchant about details of currency and foreign exchange between Nov. 1690 and Oct. 1691; Bod. MS. Locke c. 9, *passim,* and b. 3, f. 28. Clarke's letter, cited below, shows that the *Considerations* was published before 11 Dec. 1691. CLARKE TO LOCKE: (11 Dec. 1691) and (23 Jan. 1692), in Benjamin Rand, *Correspondence of John Locke and Edward Clarke* (1927), 323–24, 330–31.

clusions were founded on a long chain of theoretical reasoning. Instead of rushing precipitately at the assertion that a statutory reduction of the rate of interest would not raise the value of land, he passed stage by stage through an abstract analysis of how prices of land are arrived at.

The analysis proceeded according to the following scheme. The value of land depends on the income that can be derived from it, and bears the same relation to that income as the principal of a loan does to the interest it earns. Therefore, in principle, land should sell at twenty years purchase when interest is at 5 per cent, at ten years purchase when interest is at 10 per cent, and so on; the reason being that if £100 loaned out as cash would earn £5 per year, then a piece of land that yields a rent of £5 per year must also be worth £100; or in short the number of years purchase of a piece of land should, in principle, be the reciprocal of the rate of interest. Not, however, of the *legal* rate of interest, if that differs from the actual rate that lenders are getting. Nor, for that matter is the value of land fully determined by the *market* rate of interest; different plots of land vary in their capitalization rates, according to variations in the supply and demand from place to place. The supply is increased when, as a result of ill-husbandry, owners go into debt and are forced to sell out; the demand is decreased if merchants are spendthrift and so cannot afford to buy. Moreover, as the value of land depends also on the rent, anything that reduces the rent will reduce the value. Rents may decline because, among other things, demand for products of land falls—as it may, for instance, because of competition from foreign products—or because the supply of money falls.

From this analytic structure, Locke then drew his conclusion. Insofar as the value of land is determined by the rate of interest, an artificially low statutory rate does nothing to raise it; men will not pay £100 for a farm that yields £4 in rent when they can get £6 in interest by lending the same amount of money—even if the law prohibits taking more than 4 per cent in interest. Moreover, since an arbitrary lowering of interest rates will lead to hoarding and thus reduce the supply of money in circulation, it will reduce the prices of crops and thus the income of land; therefore, insofar as the value of land depends on rent, the abatement of interest will also tend to reduce the values.[25]

From the standpoint of technical analysis, the argument suffers from excessively broad assumptions and occasional logical leaps. Nevertheless, it has an analytic character extremely unusual among economic writings of its time, in that instead of consisting of a jumble of ill-assorted bits of reasoning, however brilliant some or many of the separate pieces might be, the *Considerations* is a sustained analysis, in which—aside from the meanderings to which Locke was always prone—each stage is firmly erected on the last, the whole rising by deduction from premises to conclusion. It was a method natural enough to a philosopher, at least to one trained in disputations, but that method had not previously been applied to the subject matter of price and capital theory.

In the second and shorter part of the *Considerations*, Locke turned to the coinage question, and particularly to the remedy being proposed as early as 1690, that the depreciation of the coinage be stopped by 'raising the coin', that is, by raising its denomination, lightening its weight, or debasing its alloy—in short, devaluing the currency. This proposal he regarded as not only mistaken but almost loathsome, because its supporters, as he thought, were putting their faith in a stupid and ineffectual form of magic. They supposed, he said, that by calling a coin by a larger name, the nation would have more money. They forgot, he said, that what determined the value of money was not the name of a coin, but the amount of silver in it; change the name however you liked, men would still take it in exchange at the value determined by its silver content. Supposing that coin were devalued by one-twentieth, 'when men go to market to buy any other commodities with their new, but lighter money, they will find 20s. of their new money will buy no more than 19 would before'. The principle, in short, on which Locke grounded his entire discussion of the question was that the buying power of money depends on the 'nat-

[25] Locke, *Considerations*, especially 32, 37–39, 53–54, 65, 69–74.

ural market value' of the silver or gold it contains. He insisted, therefore, that the only possible remedy for the deterioration of the coinage was to remint the bad coins at the old standard, while so controlling foreign trade that coin and bullion would not be carried abroad to cover an unfavourable balance of trade.[26]

Locke's argument on this score, although it has sometimes been admired, was mistaken. It is true enough that if men accepted a coin only according to the true value of its metallic content, then devaluation would have no effect whatsoever. But it certainly was not true that Englishmen at Locke's time treated money in that way; if they had done, no debasement, no deterioration could ever have injured anyone, nor could the rule of legal tender ever have worked. There is no shortage of evidence that Englishmen in Locke's time bought, sold, and settled debts according to the face value of coin. Devaluation would, therefore, have had real economic effects. Locke was simply wrong, not in advocating recoinage at the full standard, but in arguing that everything but restoration would be a futile gesture. Probably he was wrong in supposing recoinage at the old standard to be beneficial at all, although that is a matter of judgment as to which it is no easier to feel certain now than it was then. Locke's analysis of the question is interesting chiefly as it shows his dependence, in still another area of economic policy, on the notion of 'natural value' as a true and beneficent guide to action.[27]

The *Considerations* of 1690 was only the beginning of Locke's participation in the recoinage controversy. In the course of the controversy he became the Government's mouthpiece and perhaps the architect of its ultimate decision to recoin at the old standard. He entered into the later stages of the debate at the request of his admirer, Sir John Somers, who in 1694 was appointed Lord Keeper in a new Whig ministry. William Lowndes, who as Secretary of

[26] Locke, *Considerations*, 87. NATURAL MARKET VALUE: *ibid.*, e.g. 99. BALANCE OF TRADE: *ibid.*, e.g. 109, 71–73.

[27] On the relative merits of devaluation and restoration, see Horsefield, especially chap. 3.

the Treasury was the Government's internal expert on these matters, urged devaluation; Somers urged Locke to contest Lowndes' position, in the fall of 1695, before the regency Council. Later in the year, after Lowndes published his report, Locke published his answer, which was so well received that it went into a second edition almost immediately and a third edition in the next year. His objection here as before was that the value of coin could not be altered to any effect; 'one may as rationally hope to lengthen a foot by dividing it into fifteen parts instead of twelve, and calling them inches . . .'. The core of the objection was that coin had a natural value, unchangeable by statute, determined by the natural price of silver. 'Men in their bargains contract not for denominations or sounds but for intrinsic value, which is the quantity of silver, by public authority warranted to be in pieces of such denomination. . . .'[28]

'Intrinsic value' was the key to Locke's analysis of monetary problems, just as the fundamental idea from which it stemmed, the idea of 'natural value', was the key to much of his economic thought. This idea, in turn, can be understood only as a reflection of Locke's theory of Nature, or more precisely, the Law of Nature.

IV

The conviction Locke held, that if a thing is 'natural' it is right—a conviction unnatural, yet become so habitual that it has been codified in the usage of English and most other European languages—depends on the particular doctrine of Nature evolved in Western philosophy, especially in the theory of natural law. That theory stems, within the tradition of philosophy, from a text in Aristotle.

---

[28] [Lowndes], *A Report containing an Essay for the Amendment of the Silver Coins* (1695; Horsefield 226). [Locke], *Further Considerations concerning Raising the Value of Money* (1695; Horsefield 155); passages quoted are in Locke, *Works*, V, 144–45. On Locke's part in the controversy, see Horsefield, 58 ff.; and see pp. 77 ff. above.

Political justice is partly natural and partly legal. The part which is natural is that which has the same force everywhere and is independent of opinions. The part which is legal is that which, in the beginning, may indifferently take any form, though it matters once it has been laid down—as, for instance, that the ransom of a prisoner shall be a mina, or that a goat and not two sheep shall be offered in sacrifice. . . . It is easy to see what kind of thing is natural and what is not natural but legal and conventional. . . .

A natural law, in Aristotle's instance, is the law requiring all men whatsoever to offer sacrifices to the Gods; conventional or 'positive' law is that expression of the natural law that specifies in each community at any given time what animals shall be sacrificed, the manner of doing so, and other such details. The main components of this distinction—that natural law is inevitable and universal, though its expression in positive law is optional and changeable—have been preserved in all subsequent natural-law theories.[29]

Subsequent theories have varied greatly however on many other aspects of the problem. For instance, some later theorists—most prominent among them the Roman jurists who developed the notion of *jus gentium*—took the position that the mandates of natural law could be discovered by induction from the common consent of mankind. Natural law, for them, was the least common denominator of the positive laws of all, or at least all civilized communities.

Others produced anthropological evidence to show that the common consent of mankind was a very dubious guide, and that the natural law could only be known by deductive reasoning from the nature of God and man—this, in brief, was Locke's view. Such reasoning might identify natural law with practical necessity. Instead of maintaining that natural law can be known to prohibit murder because

[29] Aristotle, *Ethics*, 1134 b. 18–21. On the general history of natural law doctrine see A. d'Entreves, *Natural Law* (1951); Otto Gierke, *Natural Law and the Theory of Society*, 1500–1800, trans. E. Barker (Cambridge, 1934); J. Bryce, *Studies in History and Jurisprudence* (1901), vol. II, Essay XI; F. Pollock, *Essays in the Law* (1922); and the sources cited by Taylor, *op. cit.* n. 41, p. 194 below.

all or most communities do in fact have laws against murder, the advocates of this position urged that natural law must prohibit murder because no community could survive if the members were free to kill each other. Natural law, in this view, simply states the minimal facts about what a man and community must do in order to survive, or even more, to attain a high level of their proper development. This style of reasoning about natural law is perhaps best exemplified in the work of Hobbes, for whom the law of nature is nothing but a rational formula for creating peace and order.

Yet whatever disagreements developed in time—and they were many—as to how men could know the law of nature, or what its source is (God's reason or God's will, for instance), or any of its other qualities, one feature consistently attributed to it was universal inevitability. Yet inevitability, when ascribed to law, is a delicate notion. Even though a natural law might be inevitable in the sense that every community has some positive law on the subject (a strong position, denied by those who declined to accept the proof from common consent), it could not be inevitable in the sense that no man ever disobeyed it. If then one said that natural law was inevitable, one must hasten to clarify the term by adding that it was not immune to violation. The ambiguity might be dispelled by saying that insofar as it was law it was evitable, insofar as natural, inevitable. It does not control men, but commands them; in short, it is a moral injunction, pointing out the necessary path toward goodness.

This moral character of natural law is illustrated in a classic passage from Cicero:

> True law is right reason in agreement with nature. It is of universal application, unchanging and everlasting. . . . It summons to duty by its command, and averts from wrongdoing by its prohibitions. . . . We cannot be freed from its obligations by Senate or People, and we need not look outside ourselves for an expounder or interpreter of it.[30]

[30] Cicero, *De Republica,* iii. xxii. 33.

The natural law, in short, stands independently of anything men may do, its authority arising from its correspondence with the nature of things. It bids men act in accordance with the nature of things, but men, being what they are, may close their ears to its bidding.

The notion of natural law as having moral force was strengthened by the Scholastics, who, incorporating it in Christian theology, maintained that it was in some sense or other derived from or an expression of divine law. The effect of this development on subsequent philosophers of Christian persuasion was to enhance the degree to which the dictates of natural law corresponded to virtue, and all that was good. But there was another effect, which was to draw at least an analogy, and perhaps to indicate an absolutely parallel relation, between the law of nature in the realm of jurisprudence and the law of nature in the realm of natural science.

That relation cannot be an utterly comfortable one. One law of nature commands a man not to murder; another commands a star not to deviate from its course. Both laws are inevitable; but the man can violate the one, while it is questionable whether the star should be praised for not violating the other.

The distinction is emphasized by the pains to which Greek philosophers are said to have gone in maintaining it. When, as was rarely the case, they used the word 'nomos' to describe a law of the scientific sort, they apologized for speaking in dubious metaphors. They preferred to express the idea of scientific law with words signifying 'necessity', 'principle', or 'natural process'. Their successors, far from imitating these precautions, overlooked or rejected them. Whatever the process of intellectual development may have been, by the seventeenth century, 'law of nature' had come to include two disparate notions, moral laws and scientific laws. Bacon, Newton, and Locke—as well as many of their contemporaries—used the terms natural law in their scientific sense, regularly and with no apology for depending on an analogy, or worse, a strained analogy. Indeed, within the framework of the view that the universe and everything in it is dominated by one omnipotent God, no apology was needed.[31]

From the standpoint of social science, as it developed during the century after Locke, the most important result of this fusion of ideas, which bracketed scientific laws with moral precepts, was that the goodness originally attributed to the latter was now imputed to the former.

To suggest that this transfer of attributes came about always accidentally would be to deny that any economist or social theorist of the seventeenth and eighteenth centuries accepted the premises of Christian theology. Certainly some of them, who regarded the operations of Nature as being benevolent, did not deduce this benevolence from the principle that Nature was the creation of a benevolent God. But whatever the individual's warrant for his views on the rightness and propriety of nature, Locke and his successors did on the whole agree on this premise.

The fundamental moral kinship between scientific and juridical laws of nature, Locke asserted as a premise in the opening lines of his *Essays on the Law of Nature.*

> Since God shows Himself to us as present everywhere and, as it were, forces Himself upon the eyes of men as much in the fixed course of nature now as by the frequent evidence of miracles in time past, I assume there will be no one to deny the existence of God, provided he recognizes either the necessity for some rational account of our life, or that there is a thing that deserves to be called virtue or vice. This then being taken for granted, and it would be wrong to doubt it, namely, that some divine being presides over the world—for it is by His order that the heaven revolves in unbroken rotation, the earth stands fast and the stars shine, and it is He who has set bounds even to the wild sea and prescribed to every kind of plants the manner and periods of germination and growth; it is in obedience to His will

[31] W. A. Heidel, *The Heroic Age of Science* (1933), 22–24. Locke, in a manuscript, *De Arte Medica* (quoted by Cranston, 92–93), wrote that Man tries to discover 'the operations of nature, and thus vainly expect[s] that nature, or in truth God, should proceed according to those laws which his maxims had prescribed to him'.

that all living beings have their own laws of birth and life; and there is nothing so unstable, so uncertain in this whole constitution of things as not to admit of valid and fixed laws of operation appropriate to its nature—it seems just therefore to inquire whether man alone has come into the world altogether exempt from any law applicable to himself, without a plan, rule, or any pattern of his life.

In short the laws that govern the movement of the stars and the growth of plants are like the laws that define human virtue and vice: all of them alike are divine orders setting for each thing 'valid and fixed laws of operation appropriate to its nature'.[32]

This view Locke restated and reinforced in one of the proofs he offered for the existence of natural law:

The third argument is derived from the very constitution of this world, wherein all things observe a fixed law of their operations and a manner of existence appropriate to their nature. For that which prescribes to every thing the form and manner and measure of working, is just what law is. Aquinas says that all that happens in things created is the subject-matter of the eternal law, and, following Hippocrates, 'each thing both in small and in great fulfilleth the task which destiny hath set down', that is to say nothing, no matter how great, ever deviates from the law prescribed to it. This being so, it does not seem that man alone is independent of laws while everything else is bound.

The argument here again is that physical laws of nature and moral laws of nature alike derive from divine law and share the attributes of inexorability and permanence, reason and appropriateness, that mark their common source.[33]

This doctrine of natural law, with its fusion of scientific

[32] Locke, *Essays on the Law of Nature,* ed. W. von Leyden (1954), 109. That the natural law doctrine contained in these essays, which Locke wrote early and never published, persisted into his later work is shown by von Leyden (60–82), who concludes that 'it became an important premiss of several of his mature theories' (82).

[33] Locke, *Essays on the Law of Nature,* 117.

principle and moral standard, Locke carried over into economics. He asserted that economic affairs are governed by certain natural laws, which determine the natural prices of goods. He asserted further that economic affairs would be misgoverned by any positive laws that do not accord with natural law. This was the foundation of his arguments against a positive law to reduce the rate of interest below that formed by natural law, and against a positive law to change the face value of coin from the intrinsic value that the operation of natural law gave it. These natural laws, that furnished his criterion of goodness for social policy, he described as 'the laws of value'.[34]

Not stopping at the assertion that such laws must exist, Locke went on to state them:

> The 'intrinsic' value of a good does not affect its price.
> The 'marketable' value of a good depends on the proportion between the supply and demand for it.
> The price of a good is determined by the amount of money relative to the supply and demand for the good.[35]

To these laws of value and the natural prices established by them Locke attributed just that sort of inevitability that his philosophy attributed to all natural laws whatsoever. For example, in discussing the effects of a positive law that deviated from the natural law—in this instance a statute limiting interest to 4 per cent when the natural rate was in the neighbourhood of 6 per cent—he maintained that the positive law would be ineffectual.

> The first thing to be considered is, 'Whether the price of the hire of money can be regulated by law?' And to that I think, generally speaking, one may say, it is mani-

[34] Locke, *Considerations*, 36: 'Money therefore, in buying and selling, being perfectly in the same condition with other commodities, and subject to all the same laws of value. . . .'

[35] Locke, *Considerations*, 42–45 and ff. Although Locke did not use the terms 'supply' and 'demand', they are fair approximations, the one for 'quantity', the other for 'vent', that is, 'sale', especially in view of his qualification that 'vent' is to be understood not as any transaction in a good but as a purchase for consumption (43–44).

fest it cannot. For since it is impossible to make a law, that shall hinder a man from giving away his money or estate to whom he pleases, it will be impossible, by any contrivance of law, to hinder men, skilled in the power they have over their own goods, and the ways of conveying them to others, to purchase money to be lent them, at what rate soever their occasions shall make it necessary for them to have it; for it is to be remembered, that no man borrows money, or pays use, out of mere pleasure: it is the want of money drives men to that trouble and charge of borrowing; and proportionably to this want, so will every one have it, whatever price it cost him.

The only persons who would be compelled by this positive law, contrary as it is to the indications of natural law, are those who least ought to be subjected to it: 'those who most need assistance and help, I mean widows and orphans and others uninstructed in the arts and management of more skilful men, whose estates lying in money, they will be sure, especially orphans, to have no more profit of their money than what interest the law barely allows'. In short, this unnatural positive law would either be nugatory or injurious, and ought therefore to be rejected.[36]

For the development of a science of economics, the statement of a body of fundamental laws was roughly equivalent to the importance for chemistry of Boyle's law and for physics of Newton's laws of motion. That the work should have been done by Locke, who was not merely a contemporary but an intimate friend of Boyle and Newton, satisfies one's sense of historical fitness. Locke's laws, it must be granted, lacked the mathematical precision of Boyle's and Newton's. On the other hand, they were bolder; for while Boyle and Newton needed to assume only that inanimate nature acted according to the physical necessities, Locke was implying that human beings—to whom his philosophy required that he attribute free will—acted, at least in part of their behaviour, just as much under the determining influence of law. Locke implicitly assumed, in other words, that economic

[36] Locke, *Considerations*, 4–5.

relations are akin to the facts of nature. Some tincture of this assumption has lingered in the work of economic theorists ever since; but more important is the fact that Locke first invested economic theory with the substance, in the form of his laws, that marked it off as a self-sufficient science.

The theory of natural law in economics carried Locke to the conclusion that the State ought not to tamper with interest rates or vary the value of coins. Did it carry Locke to the conclusion that the State ought not, on the whole, to intervene in economic affairs at all? Or to put the question more abstractly, did the idea of natural law necessarily imply *laissez-faire?*

That there was some tendency among contemporary economic writers to use symbols associated with natural law in order to justify policies that might be associated with the general principle of *laissez-faire* is true enough. But using the catchwords of a theory is not the same as believing in its general principles, and the desire to stop Government from installing a particular regulation need have nothing to do with a principled objection to all regulations. Many writers on economic questions before and during Locke's time complained that certain particular economic regulations defied natural law. An early and very explicit instance is the comment in 1550 by one John Mason:

> I have seen so many experiences of such ordinances [fixing price ceilings], and ever the end is dearth and lack of the thing that we seek to make good cheap. Nature will have her course *etiam si furea expellatur;* and never shall you drive her to consent that a penny-worth . . . shall be sold for a farthing. . . . For who will keep a cow that may not sell the milk for so much as the merchant and he can agree upon?[37]

Statements of this character became more and more common during the next century. Roger Coke, for instance, was one of the many to invoke a slogan that followed the words of a Latin proverb, its ultimate intellectual justification resting in natural law doctrine and its current popularity de-

[37] *Tudor Econ. Docts.,* II, 188.

riving from Francis Bacon; no 'man or nation', Coke said, 'ever well attain their ends by forceable means against the nature and order of things'. In the same vein was a declaration by the Council of Trade of 1660 against bullionist regulations. 'The result at last would be no more but what experience has already taught, that money and bullion have always forced their way against the several laws, that the trade of the world will not be forced, but will find or make its own way free to all appearances of profit.'[38]

But those who use such language did not let it get out of hand. The Council that said trade could not be forced did not refrain from forcing England's trade on to English ships exclusively or forcing economic matters of all sorts into the desired mold. Similarly Josiah Child, in urging the legal abatement of interest, used the slogan, 'Nature must and will have its course', but used it to support his conclusion that 'the matter in England is prepared for an abatement of interest, and it cannot long be obstructed'. This was an entirely permissible use of the logic of natural law doctrine, for just as the law of nature commands men not to pass positive laws that contradict it, it commands them to pass positive laws to implement it. For this reason, Child's way of using natural law doctrine shows even more than the uses that were merely empty rhetoric why to believe in natural law was not necessarily equivalent to believing in *laissez-faire*.[39]

Natural law might father *laissez-faire* in a man who believed that nature, left to its own devices, tends to an ideal state; or in the much more sophisticated man who held that the effects produced by nature, however far from ideal, would yet be much better than those produced by the special interests and bungling of men who set about to improve on nature's work. Neither of these views necessarily follows from the principle that scientific laws of nature, being devised by God, who is good, must also be good. Perfect optimism, of the sort that lent itself to lampooning in the figure

[38] COKE: *England's Improvements . . . Treatise III* (1675, Kress 1380), 57. COUNCIL: *Advice of H.M. Council of Trade,* in McCulloch, *Select Collection of . . . Tracts on Money* (1856), 148–49.
[39] CHILD: *B.O.,* 17; and see p. 47 above.

of Pangloss, is possible only if one ignores or denies free will, that is man's power to behave contrary to moral laws of nature. Locke did not deny free will. He held that the state of nature was far from perfect, that government was necessary to impose the dictates of natural law on erring men; and in view of this reasoning on political theory was neither logically compelled nor inclined to go to the length of suggesting *laissez-faire* in the range of economic policy. Quite the contrary. The State papers he composed while a Commissioner for Trade—especially his famous proposal to suppress the woollen manufacture of Ireland and replace it with linen—as well as the repeated insistence in the *Considerations* that the Government must regulate trade in order to assure a proper balance of trade: these show that he was very much an advocate of government intervention in economic affairs.[40]

In the absence of inane optimism, the link necessary in order to believe in *laissez-faire* is something which can assure the believer that the natural condition of things would be, if not ideal, at least not chaotic, and very possibly better than what most men could produce or improve on by design. That link was ultimately supplied by the notion of a natural tendency toward equilibrium. As the mere assertion that nature acting freely tends toward equilibrium would not have satisfied scrupulous minds, the link could only be satisfactorily welded by an explanation of how equilibrium comes about and a demonstration that it naturally does come about. To furnish such explanations required a mechanistic theory, which neither Locke nor Petty ever supplied—even though both of them often asserted that economic variables such as prices and the stock of money were naturally controlled.[41]

To offer an explanation of economic affairs based on the

[40] STATE OF NATURE: Locke, *Of Civil Government*. IRISH WOOLLENS: Cranston, 407–8.

[41] For Petty's use of natural law doctrines, see A. F. Chalk, 'Natural Law and the Rise of Economic Individualism in England,' 59 *JPE* (1951), 332, 342–44. On the place of natural law doctrines in the development of economic theory generally, see O. H. Taylor, *Economics and Liberalism* (1955), chaps. 2 and 3.

operation of self-stabilizing mechanisms, however important this might be in establishing a firm intellectual foundation for *laissez-faire,* was equally important for the disinterested scientific understanding of economic affairs. Locke's laws of value were a vital contribution to economic science, but even assuming that they had been correct and exhaustive, they would have left one huge gap. They could at most describe the end conditions of a process; they did not explain how the process worked or why it led to the correctly described results; they did no more for economics than Boyle's finding that the pressure of a gas is proportional to its temperature did for chemistry. It was much, but more was needed, and it remained to be done by Dudley North.

Chapter 7

SIR DUDLEY NORTH:
A DEDUCTIVE THEORY

I

IT HAS BEEN said, with greater authority than justice, that economic theory emerged from the thinking of two groups of men, philosophers and merchants. About the rôle of philosophers there cannot be any question: Locke, Berkeley, Hume, Smith, Mill form an unbroken succession whose contributions to economic theory are fundamental. But the place of merchants in the history of economics is much more dubious.

There is of course a superficial reason for expecting that a man engaged in the practice of trade would have special aptitude for analysing the theory of price or of aggregate output; but the reason is superficial indeed. To make very much of the merchant's 'familiarity' with the substance of economic theory is to suggest that a shotmaker, a fruit farmer, or some other craftsman used to seeing things fall ought to have been among those who first devised the theory of gravitation. To do so is to confuse practice with theory, the manipulation of real things with the effort to understand, the mentality of a craftsman with that of a scientist. Even supposing that merchants were in an especially favourable position to understand the subject matter of economics, what would make them put aside their work so that they might devote their energies to reflecting on it? If a merchant wandered into public office or put himself forward as a pamphleteer, then perhaps rhetorical needs would require him to invoke general principles; but still the challenge to move in the direction of science did not usually bring forth any special ability to move in that direction.

The evidence on this score has been misinterpreted. That great trio of early seventeenth century writers on economic matters, Malynes, Misselden, and Mun, were certainly merchants. As merchants they knew a great deal about the craft and institutions of trade, and, a rarity in their time, they understood the mechanics of foreign exchange. But their books were to economic theory as an engineer's manual is to theoretical mechanics. Child too was a merchant, able and knowledgeable, but his writings on economic questions were equally irrelevant to the development of economic theory.

One merchant only among the seventeenth century writers on economics freed himself from the habits of mind common to his profession: that was Dudley North. His career, his training, experience, and personality, illustrates how unlikely it was that a merchant should have been able to solve the concurrent problems of rhetoric and analysis that needed to be solved in order to arrive at an economic theory, however primitive, which can fairly be called scientific. Why he, in particular, should have been able to do so is as irreducible a mystery as why it was Malthus, for instance, rather than any other man, who did just what he did. Just as saying that Malthus was a clergyman in no way explains his accomplishments, so the fact that North was a merchant fails utterly to explain his ability to solve a problem that many other merchants confronted without success.

Stemming from a family distinguished by intellectual and artistic talent, Dudley North gives the impression of having had virtually none. His eldest brother, Francis North, Lord Guilford, aside from being an eminent judge, ultimately Lord Chancellor, was among the best amateur musicians of his time, and a patron of art and science. John North, his younger brother, was a scholar, Professor of Greek and Master of Trinity College, Cambridge, having moved to Trinity for the company of Isaac Barrow and Newton. Roger North, Dudley's youngest brother, was one of the most competent political writers of his time, an admirable biographer, and an eminent connoisseur. Yet their brother Dudley knew nothing of literature, art, scholarship or science. At Roger's urging he once did a little experiment with the barometer;

he set up a vinegar refinery in his study; he had a nodding acquaintance with Sir Christopher Wren—these were the sum of his interest in the arts and sciences, aside from economics.[1]

His formal education had been a failure. He had been sent by his father, the fourth Baron North, to the grammar school in Bury St Edmunds, but the master took a strong aversion to him, and whether this or his own tastes were the cause, his aptitude for schooling was slight. Roger, a fond biographer, recorded that, though not absolutely stupid, Dudley was 'a kind of dunce at school'. He was dismissed at about twelve, and that was the last of his classical education. As if his education were not already deficient, North was isolated from English life by a residence in Turkey which began in about 1660, his nineteenth year. When he returned to England at forty, he looked a barbarian, and was not much more cultured than one. Although he recovered enough Latin to read some of the classics, he never seems to have done or enjoyed much reading.[2]

What he knew was trade. When his parents withdrew him from grammar school, they decided that he 'had learning enough for a merchant, but not phlegm enough for any sedentary occupation'. He was sent to a writing-school in London to study penmanship and accounting, and at the age of sixteen, was apprenticed to a minor Levant merchant. He spent the ordinary three years learning the trade from the London side, after which, as the second phase of his apprenticeship, was sent out as supercargo on a ship bound for Smyrna via Archangel, Ireland, and Leghorn. After a trip of little less than a year, North arrived in Smyrna, where he took up his post as factor or agent for the London principal. The stay in Smyrna was unrewarding, and North returned to England, probably at the end of his apprenticeship, to drum up business on his own account. He was discouraged, and ready to settle for a cheap peaceful retirement in Italy, if only he could get an annual income of £200; but Cavalier families of the second rank generally

[1] For North's life, the chief source is Roger's biography, *Lives*, III, 204–5, 208, 214.
[2] *Lives*, II, 291–93; III, 213. Wood, 229 ff.

had just enough income to maintain themselves decently, and North's family was no exception. They could not give Dudley an income, they could not even give him enough money to set up in trade. All the capital he could gather was a loan of £200 from an elder brother and a gift of £60 which his mother had saved ever since his birth. With these funds and some agency agreements with London merchants, he returned very shortly to Smyrna, presumably by then a full-fledged member of the Levant Company.[3]

Luckily for North admission to the Company, and so the right to trade in Turkey, did not require any great initial charge. Unlike the East India Company, or the African Company—in which North later made substantial investments—the Levant Company had no common capital stock, but was one of the regulated companies, given a monopoly of the English trade to a certain area on the grounds that discipline was needed for the proper conduct of foreign trade. Only the company's members could trade in its area, but in principle any Englishman could become a member on agreeing to observe its regulations and paying an entrance fee, which in North's case was probably one pound. Each member traded with what capital he could command, so that he competed not only against French, Dutch, and Venetian counterparts, but also English colleagues. There was always some tendency however to resent newcomers to the trade, and the elder merchants in Turkey were inclined to join forces against the novices; North had been subjected to such designs as a young factor, and later, as a leader of the community, opposed them because, he said, there was enough trade for all if they minded their business.[4]

Soon after returning to Turkey, North accepted the offer of a partnership in a Constantinople trading house, of which, due to the incapacity and laziness of its senior members, he soon became active manager. The reputation for honesty and efficiency which he made in this position assured him a thriving trade when a few years later he opened

[3] *Lives*, II, 293, 299 ff., 361. Wood, 215.
[4] *Lives*, III, 48, 106. ENTRANCE FEE for one who had served three years of apprenticeship in the East was £1, for others it ranged up to £50; Wood, 40.

his own firm, and by the age of thirty he had become the most substantial of the English merchants in Constantinople, the centre of the Turkey trade, and was elected their treasurer. North's business, like that of his colleagues, consisted of selling English woollens and metals, and buying silk, cotton, wine, spices, and currants. Besides, he engaged in several 'extraordinary methods of trade, by which he obtained superabundant profit'. He lent money to Turkish officials, who, forced to pay for their positions but knowing that once armed with the authority of office they would quickly recover the outlay, were quite ready to pay interest of 20 to 30 per cent. He also traded in jewels, and struck up some connections which enabled him to palm off rotten cloth. Throughout his stay in Turkey his aim was to establish a going concern which could be left in charge of a younger brother while he withdrew with his profits to a life of comparative leisure in England. By 1680 he had accumulated enough, and returned to England, where he kept up a lively interest in trade for the rest of his life. Almost immediately after his return he was elected a director of the Levant Company, and soon became one of its more influential officers, as he was of the African Company also; so that although he no longer did much trading on his own account, he became involved in the statesmanship of trade.[5]

If one wants to estimate what mental abilities North's mercantile career would have required and fostered, perhaps the best indication is the instructions that Thomas Mun, one of the more successful merchants of his time, left for the training of his son. In the first chapter of *England's Treasure by Foreign Trade*, Mun catalogued the 'qualities which are required in a perfect Merchant'. The evidence strongly suggests that Dudley North had them. The merchant, Mun said, should be a good penman, arithmetician, and accountant. Presumably North's writing-school had taught him these skills, at least his biographer frequently remarked on

<hr/>

[5] *Lives*, II, 366 ff., 398 ff., 408. Levant Company Court Book, 1676–1695 (PRO, SP 105/154), f. 238 *et seq*. AFRICAN COMPANY: North not only bought shares but served as a director and assistant governor between 1681 and 1686; K. G. Davies, *Royal African Company* (1957), 385.

his ability to make sense of a confused set of financial books. The merchant, Mun continued, should know measures, weights, and moneys of foreign countries—North, like most of his more aggressive colleagues, did a bit of speculating in the Turkish money market, and it may be presumed that he was no tyro in these matters. He should know the taxes and duties which fall on imports and exports; as the Levant Company's treasurer at Constantinople, North's function was to collect the consulage fees which the Company charged on all goods entering by English ships, and North took part in the frequent negotiations on such matters with Turkish officials. He ought to understand remittance by Bills of Exchange; part of North's duties as treasurer consisted of collecting the Company's moneys from all of Turkey and sending them home to London. If he had not acquired these and the analogous skills which Mun mentions while an apprentice, certainly North's election to the Treasurership showed that he had acquired them during his stay in Turkey. North had also followed Mun's injunction 'to attain to the speaking of divers languages'; he wrote fluently the bastard Italian which was the *lingua franca* of the Near East, and for years after returning to England broke into Turkish whenever provoked. His letters show him to have been, as Mun recommended, 'a diligent observer of the ordinary revenues and expences of foreign princes, . . . their laws, customs, policies, manners, religions, arts, and the like . . .' Mun's last recommendation was to learn Latin, although he allowed that 'there be no necessity that such a merchant should be a great scholar'. That North was indeed no great scholar is evident. He had, however, all the technical information and skills that a merchant of his time thought necessary, and he had them to a distinguished degree. He was keenly aware of what trade was about, and how men acted in commerce. In short, he was the perfect merchant: he knew everything he should have known, and nothing more. It was this that made him independent of traditional views about trade, yet provided him with the materials and ability to construct his own conception.[6]

[6] Mun, *England's Treasure by Forraign Trade* (1664: Kress, 1139), 1-4.

North's mercantile skills figured largely also in his brief political career. At the time he returned to England, Charles II was opening his great campaign to shake free of the Whig opposition. But when in 1681 the King attempted to have Shaftesbury indicted on a charge of treason, the London grand jury dismissed the charge; for the grand jurors were appointed by the sheriffs of London, who, reflecting the prevailing views of the tradesmen and merchants of the City, were also Whiggish. The King decided that in order to have justice as he understood it, he must have a loyal sheriff; and Dudley North was an obvious candidate, being a freeman of the City, wealthy, and closely linked by family to the Court party. His brother, Guilford, then Lord Keeper, persuaded Dudley to accept the candidacy which, if successful, was certain to make him unpopular; and in 1682, after a famous, tempestuous and irregular election, in which Papillon figured as one of the Whig candidates, North was installed in office. He served for a year, during which—if Macaulay can be believed—North's juries and hangmen inflicted heavy casualties on the Whigs. At the end of the year, he was knighted for 'remarkable courage and tact' and certified for higher office.

The next step up was an appointment in 1683 as a Commissioner of the Customs. This position, which combined the control of trade with protection of the King's revenues, was equally suitable to North's talents and politics. He worked by the maxim that the King's customs revenues were driblets, and unless every drop was guarded the whole would run away. He had the patience and neatness to watch each item, and it may have been partly due to his skill that the yields began to rise. North's mercantile training was indispensable for the post; he was the only commissioner with enough knowledge of accounting to understand the customs books, and the only one sufficiently conversant with commerce to interpret to the Treasury changes that affected income from particular duties. He was so efficient that in 1685 he was promoted Commissioner of the Treasury; but the Commission was dissolved a few months later when Rochester was appointed Lord Treasurer. North returned to the Commission of Customs, where he remained the leader un-

til the Revolution. In the meantime he was elected to the
Parliament of 1685, and although his support of James' government was not unqualified he was assigned the important
'place of manager for the Crown in all matters of revenue
stirring in the House of Commons . . .'[7]

It was during this term of service in government, and
through his family connections with high political life, that
he began to see trade not only as a private vocation, but also
as a public concern. He was first struck by the coinage question, and wrote an address to Parliament, which, never delivered, lay idle in manuscript for over five years. Then, like
Locke, he was excited by the renewed agitation in 1690 for
a law to reduce the rate of interest. He wrote a discourse
against usury legislation, which together with his paper on
coinage, was published anonymously as *Discourses upon
Trade*, most probably in 1692. His conclusions were in many
respects quite similar to Locke's. His mode of argument, on
the other hand, was remarkably original.[8]

II

The *Discourses* of North is a pamphlet of forty pages, com-
prising four parts: Preface, a discourse on interest, a discourse on coin, and Postscript. The preface, which fairly
describes Dudley's method but goes distinctly beyond the
text in its purported summary of Dudley's conclusions, was
written, after the rest, by Roger North. No better description can be given of Dudley's method than the one that
Roger offered.

He seems [Roger wrote of Dudley] to be of a temper
different from most who have meddled with this subject
in public; for it is manifest his knowledge and experience of trade is considerable, which could not be at-

---

[7] *Lives*, III, 132 ff., 147, 153–54, 160, 180–82. The revenues of
the customs, which fell from £558,346 in 1682 to £544,665 in 1683,
rose in the next year to £591,653; C. *Treas. Bks.*, Vol. VII, Pt. I,
xv–xvii.

[8] On the bibliographical history of the *Discourses*, see Appendix
IV, p. 271.

tained unless he were a trader himself; and yet it is not to be collected, from anything he says, of what nature his dealing has been; for he speaks impartially of trade in general, without warping to the favour of any particular interest. It has been observed formerly, when merchants have been consulted and the questions concerned only trade in general they agreed in opinion, but when opposite interests were concerned they differed *toto coelo*. As for his opinion touching interest of money, wherein he is clear that it should be left freely to the market and not be restrained by law, he is liable to the same suspicion which attends those of a different judgment, that is, partiality to his own interest; the difference is only in the supposed cause, which in the one is wealth and in the other want. *He has given his judgment with his reasons, which everyone is free to canvas; and there is no other means whereby a wise and honest person can justify his opinions in public concerns.*

In the next place, I find trade here treated at another rate than usually has been; I mean philosophically: for the ordinary and vulgar conceits, being mere husk and rubbish, are waived; and he begins at the quick, *from principles indisputably true*; and so proceeding with like care comes to a judgment of the nicest disputes and questions concerning trade. And this with clearness enough, for he reduces things to their extremes, wherein all discriminations are most gross and sensible, and then shows them; and not in the state of ordinary concerns, whereof the terms are scarce distinguishable.

This method of reasoning has been introduced with the new philosophy. The old dealt in abstracts more than truths, and was employed about forming hypotheses to fit abundance of precarious and insensible principles, such as the direct or oblique course of the atoms *in vacuo*, matter and form, privation, solid orbs, *fuga vacui*, and many others of like nature, whereby they made sure of nothing. But upon the appearance of Descartes' excellent dissertation *de Methodo*, so much approved and accepted in our ages, all those chimeras soon dissolved and vanished.

And hence it is that knowledge in great measure is become mechanical, which word I need not interpret farther than by noting it here means, built upon clear and evident truths. But yet this great improvement of *reason*, which the world has lately obtained, is not diffused enough, and resides chiefly with the studious and learned, the common people having but a small share; for they cannot *abstract*, so as to have a true and just thought of the most ordinary things, but are possessed and full of the vulgar errors of *sense*, except in some few things that fall within the compass of their day-labour and so gives them an experience, as when a common seaman, with all his ignorance, proves a better mechanic, for actual service, than the professor himself, with all his learning.

The case of trade is the same. For although to buy and sell be the employment of every man more or less, and the common people, for the most part, depend upon it for their daily subsistence, yet there are very few who consider trade in general upon true principles, but are satisfied to understand their own particular trades and which way to let themselves into immediate gain. And out of this active sphere nothing is so fallacious and full of error as men's notions of trade. And there is another reason why this matter seems less understood than in truth it is. For whenever men consult for the public good, as for the advancement of trade, wherein all are concerned, they usually esteem the immediate interest of their own to be the common measure of good and evil. And there are many who, to gain a little in their own trades, care not how much others suffer; and each man strives that all others may be forced, in their dealings, to act subserviently for his profit, but under the covert of the public.[9]

In all of this, Roger fastened on two main problems of method, which would succumb, he held, which had suc-

[9] *Discourses*, 'Preface' [pp. iv ff.]. (Italics added.)

cumbed already in Dudley's discourses, to a common solution. Men confuse their private interests with public good:
the only evidence a man can offer that he is not doing so
is to show how his conclusions follow from his premises, ex-
posing to public view the foundations and course of his
argument. Men are prone to be led from the truth by common prejudices, unreasoned beliefs, and the findings of
practical experience rather than theoretical truth: the only
way to avoid this is by close reasoning founded on simple,
indisputable abstraction, 'clear and evident truths'. Arguments from self-interest and from ignorance or error are alike
dispelled by reasoning from principles so fundamental as
to be virtually axiomatic: so Roger North said and so, he
said, Dudley North had done.

Dudley North's adherence to the method described by Roger
is evident from the beginning of the first discourse, which he
opened, after a few preliminaries, with this fundamental
abstract principle: 'Trade is nothing else but a commutation
of superfluities.' If the statement varied at all from Roger's
methodological apologia, it was in this only, that the principle was not, at the time, considered 'indisputably true'.
Not that it was a revolutionary novelty; as much as a century earlier another Englishman had asserted that 'to vent
the superfluities of our country and bring in the commodities of others' was the purpose of trade. Indeed North's statement comes close to being a definition of trade, and as such
indisputable, for 'commutation' is indisputably a necessary
ingredient of the notion of trade. What made the proposition debatable was the word 'superfluities'. Anyone who
attached special significance to gold and silver was bound
to deny North's statement; he would have argued that although in trade one country might be disposing of superfluities, the other might be giving up gold and silver, which
he would have asserted, could never be superfluous; no
country can have too much of them. Assuming that the
world's stock of gold and silver is more or less fixed, or increases very slowly, the proponents of this view—mercantilists, roughly speaking—insisted that trade was a sombre
game in which one nation gained only by another's loss.

This was presumably what Child meant when he said, 'All trade [is] a kind of warfare'; it was what Locke meant in urging the Government to regulate the balance of trade; it was what most men at the time believed. Dudley North's assertion of the contrary, therefore, though abstract and simple, was not self-evident. It becomes so if one interprets it, as modern economists have been taught to do, to mean that the thing a man gives up in a voluntary exchange must strike him as being worth less than the thing he receives, otherwise there would have been no sense in exchanging it. But that was not the interpretation that most of North's contemporaries would automatically have placed on it.[10]

Having denied the common view of his time, that men acquire riches by outwitting those with whom they deal— or to put it in the crudest way, that they acquire gold and silver by taking advantage of the stupidity or sloth of others —North required some other criterion of wealth and explanation of enrichment. He arrived again at a principle that is simple and, to the modern eye, obvious:

> He who is most diligent, and raises most fruits or makes most of manufactory, will abound most in what others make or raise, and consequently be free from want and enjoy most conveniences, which is truly to be rich, although there were no such thing as gold, silver, or the like amongst them.

The proposition would have seemed highly disputable to North's contemporaries. It was extreme enough to dissociate riches from gold and silver; it was much more so to attribute riches chiefly to production and especially to manufacturing. But North said it quite calmly and blandly, as though everyone already believed as he did, or would believe on first hearing. His casualness might suggest that he was unaware of the accepted conventions of economic thought, but it seems more likely that he was thoroughly indifferent to received opinion. When he was conducting James II's tax Bill through Parliament, a group of grocers came to him to protest that if sugar were taxed they would stop buying it.

[10] *Discourses*, 2. ANOTHER ENGLISHMAN: TED, III, 280–81. CHILD: see p. 47 above.

North asked their chief: 'Sir, if one comes to your shop to buy sugar, will you sell any?' Startled, he answered he would, whereupon North replied that if they sold sugar he was sure they would buy it. He wrote on economics in much the same spirit.[11]

Having set down his premises on trade and riches, North went on to analyse the real nature and function of money. Every metal has some value because it is useful in some way; gold and silver, having higher qualities, enjoy a special value and use. As North put it, they are 'by nature very fine, and more scarce than others', and 'imperishable, as well as convenient for easy storage and removal'. For these four qualities, 'and not from any laws, they are made a standard, or common measure to deal with'. In short, North's theory of money starts from the position that men naturally choose gold and silver for standards of value and not because those metals are unique, but because they possess in particularly high degree qualities that all metals share.[12]

To these premises North added one further, that the prices of all goods whatsoever, of silver and gold as well as corn or wool, are determined by demand and supply. At times he permitted himself to use the imprecise but current language of his time—'plenty of anything makes it cheap', or, when goods 'come to market in greater quantities than there are buyers to deal for, the price will fall'—but elsewhere he showed that he considered supply and demand perfectly co-ordinate in determining price.[13]

Armed with these general 'notions', North proceeded to analyse the usury question. His theory of wealth explained that in consequence of their industry and judgment, certain men accumulate property, which they tend to keep in the form of either land or money. In the course of this accumulation, some gather more land than they can cultivate while others end with no land at all. In a mutually convenient exchange, the former cede the use of their land to the latter in return for a payment. Others, again, accumulate their property in the form of money, and just as there are those

11 *Discourses*, 2. *Lives*, III, 162–63.
12 *Discourses*, 2–3.
13 *Discourses*, 4, 12, 'Postscript' [1].

who own more land than they can work, so some get more
money than they have the desire or skill to use in trade. As
some landowners let their lands, so some of these will let
their money. The return which the landowner takes for his
loan is called rent, and that which the 'stock-lord' receives is
called interest. But interest, North says, 'is only rent for
stock, as the other is for land'. And both are fundamentally
names for the price of using another's property. At this
point, the general theory of price applies, with the ruling
that rent and interest, like all other prices, depend on the
quantities of land and capital offered compared with the
quantities demanded. 'As plenty makes cheapness in other
things, . . . so if there be more lenders than borrowers, interest will also fall.' For North, the price analysis gives the
basic answer to the advocates of usury laws. Interest is a
price; like all prices it is determined by the supply and demand. To try to determine it otherwise is a ridiculous attempt to change effects without working through their
causes. 'It is not low interest makes trade, but trade increasing, the stock of the nation makes interest low.' Nothing can lower interest rates except an increased supply of
capital; and as no law can by fiat increase the community's
supply of capital, the proposed law is futile and injurious.[14]

This objection in principle North supplemented with a
series of unorganized and unrelated minor objections to
usury laws. They will reduce the supply of capital and
thereby raise the market rate of interest, they will help wast-
rels and injure merchants; they will diminish trade; and they
will lower the price of land. Like Locke, North also objected
to usury laws as unjust. Rents and interest are prices of the
same order; why then should one be reduced by law and
the other not? North implied that justice requires the law to
treat all prices alike, without singling out some for special
attention. But all these considerations are afterthoughts used

[14] *Discourses*, 4, 6–8. 'STOCK' is the seventeenth century term for
capital *funds*; it was not used in the sense of real capital goods. North
sometimes used it in the phrase 'stock of goods', where we would
write 'inventory'; and the term often implied also what is now called
circulating capital; but it was always fairly closely linked to money.

to bolster a case he had already made, and incidental to the main development of the *Discourses*.

In the 'Discourse upon Coined Money', North once again subordinated practical conclusions to a treatment of their theoretical substructure. The main body of this discourse and of the Postscript as well concern the general question of how much money a country needs and has, rather than their purported subjects of clipping and recoinage. At the outset, North recorded and quickly dismissed the common complaint that England lacks money. Beggars complain, of course, but it is food that they need and not money. On the other hand, if the complainants are farmers, shopkeepers, and merchants, what they mean is that they are not getting satisfactory prices for their merchandise. Because money is the medium of exchange, any deficiency of price seems to them a deficiency of money.[15] And to drive home his proof that such common complaints are founded on nothing firmer than popular misunderstanding and the personal troubles of the aggrieved, he proceeded to the question that haunted economic thinking in his era, the question that was assumed away by unmitigated merchantilists, that perplexed councils of trade, and evoked the best efforts of Locke and others who began to question received monetary doctrine: how much money *should* the nation have?

All the habits of mind and all the hopes cultivated by the Royal Society would have set Collins and Petty to counting up or estimating how much money England had in fact, and perhaps to the next step of determining, by an exercise in induction, how the supply of money related to other economic variables. Even Locke, who was otherwise less sanguine about the eventual success of the Baconian method —although his laborious collecting of weather reports for Boyle's natural history of the air might indicate some faith after all in the inductive method—even Locke set out to calculate as near as might be how much money England needed; and, as is so often the case, his important theoretical work, on velocity of circulation, was the by-product of an effort to bridge gaps in the data. But North, alien to the doctrine and hopes of the Royal Society, never considered a

15 *Discourses*, 11.

mathematical treatment of the question. He rested his analysis, as usual, on simple abstraction.

His analysis is summed up in the purely formal assertion: 'There is required for carrying on the trade of the nation a determinate sum of specific money, which varies . . . as the circumstances we are in. . . .' The broadness of the statement might make it seem an assertion of faith; in fact it is the theoretical end-product of North's analysis, which exposes a mechanism controlling the nation's supply of coin. North's explanation of the mechanism takes up first the factors determining a nation's need for money. One of these is the amount of trade the nation carries on: very little trade needs very little money, active trade needs more. For every increase in trade, a nation requires additional money. But this is not all. The amount of coin a nation needs may vary, even while the quantity of its trade is constant. In case of war, for example, men will desire to keep on hand a stock of money to cover contingencies. While they ordinarily depend on current income to provide them with sufficient stocks of cash, in war-time current payments are less dependable and current expenses less predictable; consequently men hold greater amounts of cash than usual, and the nation as a whole needs more. North's language in this passage suggests that he meant war to exemplify any circumstance which might interrupt the normal course of cash payments or increase the normal expectation of emergencies. Thus two general factors determine the nation's demand for money; they are what now go under the names of transactions demand and precautionary demand, and the fact that North's categories can be translated so readily into the terms of modern theory is a measure of the advances he made in the substance of economic doctrine.[16]

North now turned to analyse the supply of money. He began by reiterating his 'true notion' of trade, that it is 'commutation of superfluities'; in international trade, each country merely exchanges its surplus goods for those of other countries. The next step in the argument is supplied by the second axiom, the 'chief proposition' that silver and gold are

16 Discourses, 16–17, 'Postscript' [3].

used as money simply for their convenience as measures and instruments of exchange. But otherwise 'gold and silver are in no sort different from other commodities'. They, like any other goods, are commuted as superfluities; they 'are taken from those who have plenty, and carried to those who want, or desire them'. Consequently the nation's supply of gold and silver is largely determined by its ability to produce goods which it can exchange for the precious metals produced by countries having mines or colonies with mines.[17]

But gold and silver, North continued, are not necessarily held in the form of money. They may exist in 'logs or blocks' of bullion, or as 'plate', that is, as metal wrought for household use. The supply of *money* therefore depends not only on how much silver and gold enters the country, but also on what part of it is taken to the mint to be coined.

Logs and blocks of bullion are obviously not practical instruments of exchange, since their value can only be known by weighing and assaying. Because coin is 'more useful for commerce' it normally has a slightly higher price than the equivalent amount of bullion. This normal difference in value between coin and bullion is a special case of price relationship. The general law, North's 'universal maxim' that supply and demand determine price, applies as much to bullion and coin as to any other commodities. If there is plenty of coin, its price, in terms of bullion, will go down, and if there is not enough, its price will rise. As with every other commodity, both supply and demand have their effects. Accordingly, when trade or hoarding increases, the demand for coin rises, and its price in terms of bullion rises. Bullion is therefore brought to the mint for coining. This increases the supply of coin relative to bullion, and the price of coin drops. If individuals temporarily lose their urge to hoard, or too much bullion has been brought to the mint, or more coin is available than is required for the nation's trade, the price of coin will drop below the price of bullion. At that point, the coin is melted down for bullion, and the balance is redressed. To describe these fluctuations in quantity of coin as tending toward balance is not to take excessive

17 *Discourses*, 13, 16.

liberties with North. His summary of the mechanism is expressed in a similar, if more concrete simile: 'Thus the buckets work alternately; when money is scarce, bullion is coined; when bullion is scarce money is melted.'[18]

From his 'bucket' analysis, North could pass directly to his recommendations on monetary policy. It was evident in general, he argued, that any attempt to increase arbitrarily the country's stock of money was bound to fail because any excess coin would only be melted down. In this category he put the law of 1666 that eliminated seignorage, aiming to encourage increased coinage but producing in fact especially rapid fluctuations in the quantity of coin. The general policy that North advocated in coinage matters was that 'this ebbing and flowing of money supplies and accommodates itself without any aid of politicians'.

The buckets which work toward a balance, are, in short, a mechanism tending towards equilibrium. North's is the first full equilibrium analysis in the history of economic theory; or, more exactly, North was the first economic writer to construct a cogent analysis, founded on a few, broad, general principles of axiomatic simplicity, which enable him to provide a mechanistic explanation of an economic process, and to reach policy conclusions that are deducible strictly from the premises. Meager and excessively terse as the *Discourses* seem, they contain a theoretical structure of power unequalled in their time, the peak of economic thought during the seventeenth century.

III

The idea of a mechanism that works always towards equilibrium is a powerful asset for a doctrine of *laissez-faire*: if the economic machine looks after itself, the Government need not look after it; and if the machine keeps itself in good order, then officiously to tinker with it is worse than futile. But useful as this doctrine is for anyone who favours economic freedom, it is not essential. Most so-called free-traders

18 *Discourses*, 10–11, 17–18, 'Postscript' [3].

of the seventeenth century and earlier sustained their recommendations without its aid, indeed, most were quite prepared to urge the abandonment of some restrictive regulation or other without offering any particularly taut argument at all. Josiah Child's 'free-trade' proposals are a classic example of this type; not unreasoned, they were nevertheless advocated on the score of particular advantages they would procure to merchants and the nation rather than being deduced from any general and systematic doctrine. And it was in keeping with this mode of reasoning that the earlier free-traders confined their attacks to a narrow front, so that they are to be seen urging at the same time that some regulations be lifted and that others be extended or more strictly enforced.

Just as the policy of free-trade might be maintained without invoking the theory of a self-regulating mechanism, so the theory does not necessarily drive those who credit it to advocate *laissez-faire*. This is not only because no idea has ever been powerful enough to force a man's mind in directions he does not want it to follow, but even more so because equilibrium is an amoral notion. A guillotine blade is in equilibrium once it has come to rest at the bottom of the guides; whether that equilibrium is desirable or not depends on whose head has rolled. Machines that tend toward equilibrium will be given free scope only by those men who believe that the position at equilibrium is in some degree desirable. Locke's general theory of nature and natural law provided a ground for morally approving the results of economic freedom, in a few restricted areas at least; Dudley North's theoretical structure, on the other hand, included no such principle. If, nevertheless, Dudley North came closer than any other seventeenth-century economic writer to being an advocate of *laissez-faire*, thorough-going *laissez-faire* rather than the partial free-trade doctrines common at his time, he did so despite a gap in his theory of policy, or, at least, a gap in his statement of it.

North's chief policy conclusions in the *Discourses* as well as the policies suggested in his asides show both in substance and flavour the strength of his inclination toward *laissez-faire*. He argued that Government neither could nor should control interest contracts: 'It will be found best for the nation to leave the borrower and the lender to make their own bargains.' He opposed sumptuary laws of every description. He rejected all laws aimed at keeping forever inside the country any gold and silver that once entered it, because such laws inevitably fail. The only way, he held, for a nation to become rich was through the energy and prudence of its citizens, and this, he said repeatedly, was something laws might inhibit but could never promote. Men's activity and ingenuity have natural causes which laws could only diminish. To argue in this vein, as North consistently did, seems to go a long way towards *laissez-faire*.[19]

Roger North reported 'a detestation [Dudley] had of all projects, liberty and justice being his favourite patrons of trade'. Certainly the policies announced by the *Discourses* bear witness to some feeling for liberty, and in both the usury and coinage discussions he considered as an important argument against a proposal that it would create some injustice. But there are more striking passages in the *Discourses* that at first sight seem to prove that Dudley North took an extreme *laissez-faire* position:

> There can be no trade unprofitable to the public, for if it prove so, men leave off; and wherever the traders thrive, the public, of which they are part, thrives also.
>
> No law can set prices in trade, the rates of which must and will make themselves. But when such laws do happen to lay any hold, it is so much impediment to trade. . . .
>
> All favour to one trade or interest against another is an abuse. . . .

With these maxims opposing government interference are coupled others which outline the only proper functions of government in respect to trade:

> Laws to hamper trade, whether foreign or domestic, relating to money or other merchandises, are not the ingredients to make a people rich. . . . But if peace be

19 *Discourses*, 7, 13–15, 'Postscript' [2].

procured, easy justice maintained, the navigation not
clogged, the industrious encouraged by indulging them
in the participation of honours and employments in
the government, according to their wealth and characters, the stock of the nation will increase. . . .

It is peace, industry and freedom that brings trade
and wealth, and nothing else.

There can be no doubt that these statements are an im-
pressive outline and presage of the *laissez-faire* theory, such
as it was to become a hundred years or more later. They
insist that the community can achieve its best economic condition only when the Government restricts itself to assuring
peace, justice, and freedom. No eighteenth century liberal
could have put the case more pungently.[20]

As it happens, however, those strong words were almost
certainly written by Roger North rather than Dudley.[21]
In any case, they are almost completely unrelated to the
text of the *Discourses*. Dudley did object to certain specific
government interferences, but there is nothing in the text of
Dudley's two discourses to match Roger North's pleas in the
'Preface' for peace and freedom as requisites of trade; Roger's
remarks objecting to positive government intervention are
much more general and forcible than Dudley's, though there
is no reason to doubt Roger's assertion that he took his own
views on economic questions from Dudley. It must be said,
however, that general and sweeping as Dudley's faith in
laissez-faire may have been, remarkable as it is in being perhaps the very earliest pronouncement of its sort, it was not
integrated with his economic theory. The tight intellectual
link between classical economic theory and classical liberalism had yet to be forged.

IV

As to the method of Dudley North's work in pure economic
theory, Roger described it accurately in laying stress on the
generality and simplicity of Dudley's premises. No doubt

[20] *Lives*, III, 203. *Discourses*, 'Preface' [iv–v, viii–ix].
[21] See Appendix IV, p. 271.

Roger exaggerated when he described the premises as self-evident—or as one should say, in deference to his hostility toward the Old Philosophy, 'indisputably true'. No doubt the implication in Roger's remarks, that Dudley deliberately followed the method prescribed by Descartes, is a bit of friendly puffing or *post hoc* rationalization; and yet the chief argument in Roger's appreciation of Dudley's method holds without question. Generality there is in Dudley's premises, more than appears on the face of them. The statement that all prices are determined by supply and demand is general; it becomes more general if the minor premise is added that the rate of interest is a price; and still more so if another minor premise asserts that rent is a price. And Dudley's mind was such as to lead him constantly toward such generalizations whenever the material allowed. He believed the prices of rent and interest were determined in the same way. He believed that the loan of money and the loan of land were the same in origin and in nature. He was among the first to argue that home trade and foreign trade are inseparably connected and to state they were subject to the same economic laws. He extended the traditional analogy between the State and the individual so far that it became the maxim: 'A nation in the world, as to trade, is in all respects like a city in a kingdom, or family in a city.' He dealt throughout with a few clear and simple principles. All these evidences demonstrate the success of North's effort to write a general explanation of trade, general in the sense that its laws would subsume a wide variety of phenomena.[22]

But the generalizing mind has its own hazards, which North avoided because of his evident sensitivity to how men act in commercial matters, a sensitivity which prevented him from throwing together things that were too different. This happy balance stands out by comparison with Petty, who did not much notice other human beings, a failing that made trouble for him in business and politics and that accounts for the peculiarities, not to say weaknesses, of his economic thinking. Where Petty, for instance, frequently treated men as machines, which because they produce so much goods are worth so many pounds each, North drew some of his most

[22] *Discourses*, 14, 16.

important explanations from differences between men. His very conception of trade was one which implied that different men react differently to the same goods: one man's superfluity is another man's desire. His whole conception of enrichment was based on the assumption that different men have different capacities for work; some 'are more provident, others more profuse; some by their industry and judgment raise more fruits from the earth than they consume in supplying their own occasions'; and the industrious and ingenious become rich, even on the hypothesis that originally men shared all things equally. This distinction in economic ability and desires between men North repeated at various points, and he drew other distinctions in economic behaviour of different men. In explaining the effect of artificially lowered rates of interest on lenders, North distinguished between those who, being pressed for money, would take half a loaf rather than none, and others who, being less pressed, might choose to hoard their money rather than risk it at a low rate of interest. Differences in the economic position of men, he held, stimulate emulation and thereby production. Farmers, landlords, merchants, gentlemen, goldsmiths, all differ in their desire to keep stocks of cash on hand. In short, individual differences that affected man's economic behaviour were something North always took into account, no matter how much he may have misunderstood them.[23]

North's attention to the differences between men as economic actors is strikingly exhibited in his examination of coinage supplies. In the end he arrived at the conclusion that the nation always has just enough coin, a conclusion that Locke might have considered a natural law implanted in society by God. North never used the phrase 'natural law', and no explanation of natural economic order as a heavenly ordinance would have satisfied him. His explanation was in terms of a mechanism that tends towards equilibrium, but a mechanism that resulted from nothing other than reasonable human actions. When coin has a higher price than bullion, men take bullion to the mint for the very ordinary reason that they can make a profit by doing

[23] *Discourses*, 3, 6, 13, 15, 21–22.

so; when bullion is higher-priced than coin, men melt their coin because they can profit by selling it as bullion. It is men who, by carrying bullion to and from the Mint, operate the mechanism. A nation always has just enough coin, ultimately, because—and only if—men are willing to earn money by buying cheaply and selling dear. Ultimately the mechanism is nothing but human reactions to circumstances.

Dudley's method accomplished for him also what Roger put forward as the second of its great merits: by reasoning from a few clear principles to his conclusions on policy, Dudley came as close as anyone can to solving the rhetorical problem that faces any advocate, especially anyone whose expertise is made suspect by his personal interest in the matter—the expertise and self-interest alike stemming from his professional status, suspicion arising from the fact that his audience has no sound personal knowledge of him nor much faith that men prefer truth to riches. No method of reasoning can guarantee to such a writer the willing belief of his audience. But among methods of *rational* persuasion there is none more effective than demonstration by use of a continuous chain of syllogisms, founded on premises that are clear, simple, and few, as few as will serve.

Rational persuasion is best accomplished by deductive demonstration. It happens that scientific explanation also requires deductive reasoning from a set of a few clear and simple principles. The difference between the immediate purposes of the advocate and the scientist explains why men say that they *assent* to the argument of the one and *understand* the argument of the other; and this difference may obscure the fundamental similarity or identity, as it may sometimes be, in the logical structures of the two arguments. Yet the advocate of a policy can be likened to an engineer, and as the engineer's logic and the scientist's are the same, even though their purposes differ, so the advocate of economic policy may use exactly the same method of reasoning as the economic theorist. More, he may devise for the purposes of ultimate action the same scientific theory at which a pure theorist would have arrived under the impulse of pure speculation. That was exactly what Dudley North did.

His *Discourses* should have marked the birth date of economic theory; in one sense it did. But in the sense that a science is a live tradition rather than printed words in a lost book, it did not; the pamphlet fell out of sight soon after it was published, to be rediscovered only after others had learned all that North could have taught them and more.

PART III

The Legacy

Chapter 8

ECONOMIC THEORIES DURING THE EIGHTEENTH CENTURY

I

THE ECONOMIC WRITERS of the seventeenth century did not set out deliberately to create a science. Even Petty, the only exception, was not very exceptional. Announce though he would that he intended to establish a science of economics, that he had established it, the announcements told less about accomplished facts than about a methodological dogma consisting equally of piety and pride. As much of his work as faithfully followed Bacon's programme enriched economics little if any; his real contributions, which were many and important, he produced when Bacon's instructions had momentarily slipped his mind, or when the irritating absence of some necessary statistic forced him to bridge a gap with a brilliant, theoretical improvisation. Yet even in this quixotic effort, Petty was alone. His contemporaries were not intending to build a science; the possibility had never entered their heads. Quite the contrary. They knew that they were doing important work, solving urgent, timely, practical problems. They wrote pamphlets, little books designed as ephemeral, to be forgotten when the crisis was past. They could not have imagined that their occasional pieces would find a reader centuries later.

Within thirty or forty years the scene shifted entirely. By the time Joseph Massie wrote, a live tradition of economic theory, a self-consciously and deliberately scientific undertaking, had come into being. Men spoke of a science of economics, even if they did not yet use precisely that form of words; they recognized that such as it was it was embodied in a literature that anybody who presumed to be literate in the science would make himself familiar with; and, most important, they began to devote as much attention to speculative problems, that arose from within the scientific tradition and its literature, as to practical problems, that intruded into the study from the market place or the chambers of Parliament.

It is easy enough in the province of economics to recognize the difference between the problems thrown up by the state of the science itself and those proposed to it by the outer world, between what one may describe as the problems of the scientists' scientist and those of the man of the world's scientist. One clear example is the paradox that value in use and value in exchange seemed sometimes, markedly in the examples of water or air, to differ from each other. The paradox must, of course, have been familiar, since time immemorial, to the many men who had lived through famines. Yet it probably entered the stream of economic theory through Locke's *Considerations,* Locke having himself introduced the distinction in the course of dealing with the uncommonly practical problem of how to refurbish the coinage. Smith and the masters of the classical school preserved it as a useful and interesting observation; but from then on it must have been a pebble in a shoe, an intellectual irritant sure to discompose any cogent mind. How Jevons resolved the paradox by inventing marginal analysis is well-known, and well-known it is that Jevons was not seeking by that stroke to enlarge the wealth of nations but rather to put in better order an intellectual apparatus that interested him or might have done almost without reference to its relations with the rest of the world. To regularize the internal order of a system of thought is surely not the only impulse to scientific creation, and great scientific innovations never, perhaps, fail to change men's lives as greatly as they change men's thought, and yet the tempting analogy of Newton and Einstein suggests that the most notable jumps in science result from speculative rather than practical impulses. And speculative impulses flourish, it appears, not so much when a man begins to speculate *de novo* about the ways of the world but when he responds to an accumulated body of the

explanations men have offered of the world. It is too much
to expect a man to create an intellectual system out of
his own mind; it is a work of utmost genius if he can bring
into systematic form the scattered, contradictory, partial and
personal ideas of many men who have previously dealt with
his field of inquiry. A tradition of inquiry is not only useful
to a great scientist; a science sufficiently developed to be
worth the name is unthinkable without such a tradition.

The tradition, in the case of economics, was embodied in
stale pamphlets; and by the latter half of the seventeenth
century such pamphlets were already being recognized as
bearers of a tradition. To speak of such recognition as
though it could possibly mark a turning-point might easily
impress historians and lawyers, scholars and the bookish, as
treating something utterly natural and inevitable as though
it were a discovery or a contrivance. But the scholar's attitude to old books is not that of the scientist. An eminent
modern scientist need not know the classics of his discipline; there must be many Nobel Prize winners who have
not studied Newton, Faraday or Clerk Maxwell; many prime
economists have never read through Smith, Ricardo, Mill
or Marshall. They would consider the meticulous mastery of
those classics the proper work of an historian rather than of
a scientist, and properly regard the spirit of scholarship as
being antithetical to the spirit of science. Scholarship per-
tains, *par excellence,* to ancient, and even more so, to sacred
texts; the scholar's real business is with books that cannot be
improved on. A classical scholar does not aim to write a truer
history than Thucydides' or a better play than Sophocles'; a
Bible scholar does not aim to correct the witness of the
apostles or to bring the Ten Commandments up to date.
Scholarship is, to be sure, progressive, in that scholars hope
they will in time, as a group, understand their subjects more
fully and more correctly, but it is not progressive as a science
is, in that the effort of a scientist is to supersede his authorities. Even those scientists who recognize that at bottom every
scientist must begin from a faith in the authority of certain
books, would insist that all else being equal the most recent
authority is to be preferred and the oldest authority least
trusted—a canon exactly opposite to that of the scholar prop-

erly so called. Even those scientists who recognize that a science is a tradition of thought prefer the latest codification of that tradition, whereas for the scholar the final truth is in the original text he is dedicated to understanding, and everything since is merely gloss. It is not therefore impertinent for an economist, should he believe that modern treatises exhaustively sum up what economists have ever understood about economic life, to treat the knowledge of older treatises as an unessential luxury.

But at an earlier stage in the development of a scientific tradition, a proper reverence for its literature was, if not essential, extremely useful. In 1700 the tradition of scientific economics was still diffuse and totally disorganized: fragments of light were scattered helter-skelter through books not even as yet identified as parts of the same universe of discourse. What rational scheme, a merchant or civil servant of the seventeenth century might have asked, would dictate that a pamphlet on building be set on the shelf between a pamphlet on coins and a pamphlet on salt? And yet the development of economic theory required, or, at least, greatly benefited from just this unnatural juxtaposition.

That a nascent Literature of Economics was already identified as such during the seventeenth century is obvious from the work of many economic writers at the time. The sense that they were writing within a community of writers arose first of all, of course, from the fact that their subjects and intentions were nothing if not controversial. The tilt on the coinage question, in which Locke and Lowndes were the prime champions, and Barbon, North, and hundreds of others appeared as auxiliaries, was recognized everywhere as a great communal undertaking. But a sense of community based on such relations is not necessarily the best foundation for a scientific tradition.

The spirit of combat could, however, generate a somewhat more productive appeal to tradition, when a writer tried to arm himself with the authority of the past, a technique of which Child was especially fond. Although he drew his explanation of Holland's commercial excellence from the works of Henry Robinson, Benjamin Worsley and Samuel Lambe, and did so without acknowledging his dependence, he sought to support his chief proposal, to lower interest rates by law, with heavy authority. He invoked Petty's name, incorporated with his treatise the full text of Sir Thomas Culpepper's *Tract Against Usurie*, and quoted at some length from Samuel Fortrey's *Englands Interest and Improvement*. The spirit in which he levied on their work is displayed in his comment on the passage from Fortrey:

> Which I have here inserted for such like reasons:
> 1. That the world may see I am not singular in this opinion, although I thought I had been so when first I wrote the aforesaid *Observations*.
> 2. For confirmation of the truth, by the authority of a person of such known abilities.
> 3. To give the author his due honour of being the first observer. Etc.[1]

To believe, as Child evidently did, that the question 'How do you know?' may be answered 'So I've been told', is natural enough. Indeed, it is in some sense the only correct answer, since no matter how much of what he knows a man may have reasoned out and tested for himself, a vastly larger part of his knowledge he must have taken on faith. Yet the aim of a science is to build up a structure, every piece of which has been tested and found reliable, no piece being accepted on an ancient maker's warranty; this was the point of Bacon's insistence on dealing with Nature directly, without the mediation of inherited ideas, the thrust of Petty's dogma that one should consider only the evidence of the senses, as registered in 'number, weight and measure', rejecting all mental constructs. Anyone who did not share this hope, vastly exaggerated though it was, missed the point of the scientific movement of the seventeenth century as Child did. The quaintest position of all in this regard was that of John Collins, who, devoted Fellow of the Royal Society though he was, nevertheless hoped that the truth in eco-

---

[1] CHILD: see Appendix II, p. 259. For Child's use of Petty, see B.O., 17; of Culpepper, B.O., 21–30; of Fortrey, B.O., 37–38. Fortrey's tract (Kress 1337) was first published in 1663.

nomic matters could be arrived at by weighing pros and cons to find where the preponderance of authority lay.[2]

And yet Collins, whose bibliographic work in mathematics was extraordinarily fruitful in locating and bringing together from all corners of Europe the whole corpus of modern mathematics, and who hoped to turn his bibliographic talent to the service of economics, showed which way the wind was blowing. In Locke's working habits one can see the beginnings of scientific scholarship in economics, easier to recognize in his case perhaps because so much more evidence remains about how he worked, and easier to explain in a man trained as he was in the scholarship of classical learning. Given his training, but lacking as yet any direct experience of commerce, Locke had hardly begun to think about economic questions before he set himself to reading what others had said about the matter. At some time before 1674 apparently, he had read the tract by Thomas Manley, *Usury at six per cent examined, and found unjustly charged by Sir Tho. Culpepper and J. C.[hild]* . . . , which first appeared in 1669. The notes Locke took on reading Manley, which are preserved, make it appear possible—more than that is not justified by such evidence—that Locke learned some of his views from Manley. The notes begin with Manley's doctrine in general, 'How use [i.e. interest rates] the effect not cause of riches. Instance Holland where use fell without a law . . .'; they go on to register striking facts recorded by Manley, one of which, showing the relation between the interest rate and the rate of capitalization, Locke eventually used in the *Considerations*. He read with the same care Carew Reynell's treatise of 1674, *The True English Interest*. And the catalogue of his library shows that eventually he had acquired the works of Petty and Graunt, Child's *New Discourse*, the Discourses on Trade of William Petyt, Simon Clement, and John Pollexfen, and a number of other works on trade. The collecting impulse, the passion for bringing together as many examples as possible of plants, or metals, or records, or manuscripts; the impulse that motivated so much of the Royal Society's early work, that

2 COLLINS: See above, pp. 121–22.

created the great manuscript collections of the seventeenth century, that made every amateur *cognoscente* treasure his cabinet of curiosities; this impulse, so common in the early history of many sciences, can be seen at work also in Collins' bibliographic programme, in Locke's library, and for all we know in the still richer libraries of contemporaries.[3]

The visible peak of such collecting is the library formed within a generation or two of Locke's death by Joseph Massie, who collected some 2,500 tracts and manuscripts on trade. Massie, who was himself an unusually prolific writer of economic pamphlets, advocated in 1754—in a manner reminiscent of Collins—that the City of London should establish a public library on commerce to house his own collection, 'such a set of old, scarce, curious and valuable tracts and treatises on the history of commerce (the product of many years collections) as he humbly conceives are not to be found in many private hands'. The Government remained indifferent to this offer, even after many years of Massie's pressing it on them, and ultimately he recorded his sense of grievance in a broadsheet addressed to 'Messieurs Fog and Mist'. Yet despite his disappointment, Massie had drawn other great benefits from the collection. For instance, a booklet that he published in 1757, *Ways and Means,* carried with it 'An account of the ancient and present states of the most considerable branches of manufactury and trade belonging to these kingdoms, extracted from the commercial writings of various authors'—in short, he was mining his collection for the ends of economic history. Another of his pamphlets describes its relation to the literature in its title: *Observations relating to the coin of Great Britain; consisting partly of extracts from Mr Locke's treatise concerning money, but chiefly of such additions thereto as are thought to be very necessary at this juncture . . . whereunto is annexed Sir William Petty's Quantulumcunque concerning money. . . .*

³ MANLEY: Kress 1241. Locke's notes on Manley are in MS. Locke b. 3, f. 6; the excerpt from Manley is at Locke, *Works,* V, 81. REYNELL: Kress 1369. Locke's notes are in MS. Locke c. 30, ff. 18–19. LOCKE'S LIBRARY: the catalogue is at MS. Locke f. 16; see entries at folios 42 v., 60 v., 115, 176 v. and 226 v.; the three entries on the latter appear to be Kress 1521, 1873, and 2040 or 2041. See also the booksellers' bills at MS. Locke b. 2, ff. 115, 118.

And still another, the most interesting from the standpoint of pure economic analysis, was his *Essay on the governing causes of the natural rate of interest, wherein the sentiments of Sir William Petty and Mr Locke, on that head, are considered*. In that essay the collecting impulse had produced its most beneficial outcome: by collating and disengaging, and then critically comparing the interest theories of two earlier masters, Massie was able to display the theory as it then stood, in its strength and weakness. As systematic order and relation of principles is the essence of a science, so the assembling and systematizing of principles, however well they may have been understood singly, is the essence of scientific work; and it was such work, albeit in a very narrow field, that Massie did, and was, in a limited sense, enabled to do by his penchant for book collecting.[4]

To speak of the literature of a discipline presupposes that the scope of the discipline has been defined, otherwise it would be impossible to determine rationally which books are and are not pertinent. But this priority of the definition is logical rather than temporal: the domain of economics was not once and forever marked out by a great law-giver, nor did writers set out with no other design than to fill gaps in a preordained setting. What happened instead was that over the course of three centuries economics has been repeatedly defined, at first loosely and implicitly, later more rigorously, always variably. The definition has fluctuated, in the breadth of phenomena that it authorized the subject to examine, according as men thought that the central matter of the subject was wealth, prices, income, exchange, scarce resources, or anything else. The particular definition, obviously, depended on its author's substantive theories about the phenomena themselves. Moreover the collector of literature played his part as well, for while, on the one hand, the

4 [Massie], *An essay on the many advantages . . . of great and capital cities* (1754; Kress 5373), 19–21. Massie, *To Messieurs Fog and Mist* [1766; Kress 6360]. Massie, *Ways and Means . . .* (1757; Kress 5629). Massie, *Observations . . .* (1760; Kress 5873). Massie, *An essay on the governing causes . . .* (1750; Kress 5055). See also W. A. Shaw, *Bibliography of . . . Joseph Massie* (1937).

books he selected as fit for his purpose depended on what he thought the subject included, the definitions that other men drew up had to be broad enough to include all of those books, at least, that were thought to deserve a place in any library on the subject. In short, the limits of the discipline were established, are continually being re-established, by an interplay between extensive and intensive definition of the relevant subject-matter. Any definition of economics represents an interpretation of the whole tradition of economic theory.

The rubric under which economic writers, as we now call them, of the seventeenth century most commonly placed their works was 'trade'. The word had in their time two chief meanings: the buying or selling of goods; and occupations, especially workmanlike occupations such as shoemaking or carpentry rather than professions or farming. It was chiefly though by no means exclusively the former sense that economic writers had in mind when they used the term, as it appeared in the titles of many of the leading tracts: Thomas Mun's *A discourse of trade from England unto the East Indies* (1621) and *England's treasure by forraign trade* (1664); Child's *New discourse of trade* (1693); and Barbon's *Discourse of trade* (1690). But the use that they made of the simple rubric shows how elaborate and expansive their theory, at the very least their implicit theory, had already become. Barbon, for instance, opened his *Discourse* with this preliminary definition of his subject:

Trade is the making [of goods] and selling of one sort of goods for another. The making is called handicraft trade, and the maker an artificer. The selling is called merchandizing, and the seller a merchant.

This definition, extensive enough to include the categories we know as commerce and production (though, curiously enough, it omitted agriculture, the then preponderant branch of production), was not yet broad enough to cover all the phenomena Barbon felt impelled to treat, and felt warranted in treating as parts of the same whole. He therefore proceeded to a more expansive statement of the question:

The chief end or business of trade is to make a profitable bargain. In making of a bargain there are these
things to be considered: the wares to be sold, the quantity and quality of those wares, the value or price of
them, the money or credit by which the wares are
bought, the interest that relates to the time of per-
forming the bargain.

And even this catalogue, which linked with production and
commerce the additional subjects of price, money, and interest, did not exhaust the range of topics that the *Discourse*
in fact touched on, topics such as savings, expenditure pat-
terns, population, tariff policy, and the price of land.[5]
All of these subjects, which now seem naturally and inevitably to fall within the proper domain of economics, had
at some time forcibly to be brought together, for in the nature of things they are distinct. The fact that interest and
goods, for instance, bear different names is evidence, if one
needed it, that men were at some time or other more impressed by their dissimilarity than by any organic relation.
It needed a theoretical invention to link them together, a
theoretical invention which asserted, for instance, that interest is the price one pays for the use of goods, or, as it
might be, that interest is a rate enabling one to compare the
present value of a good with its value at some time past or to
come. In short, Barbon's view of the extent of his subject
represents the conclusions of a body of theory—not all of
which he himself devised, not all of which he did or could
explicitly state, not systematically co-ordinated—and yet a
body of theory—that is, a distinctly artificial contrivance.
A few other titles will indicate how much, during the
eighteenth century, economic writers broadened their conception of the subject. In 1700, one James Donaldson published a treatise on economy policy called *The undoubted
art of thriving*, which suggests that he took as the focus of
his study a notion resembling wealth or prosperity; a similar
view was presented in William De Britaine's *Human Prudence, or, The art by which a man may raise himself and
his fortune to grandeur*, also published in 1700. But despite

[5] Barbon, *Discourse*, 1-2.

the tendency to bring within the orbit of the subject more and more aspects of economic life, the most common heading for books about it continued, during most of the eighteenth century, to be *Trade*. Pollexfen's treatise of 1700 dealt with trade: trade in general and in particular, domestic and foreign, of specific trading companies, also of coin, bullion, wool textiles, and finally 'Of Ways and means to increase our riches'. John Law arranged his views under the heading of Money and Trade; David Black, under Industry and Trade; and William Wood, under Trade and Colonies. And finally, for what stands out as by far the most powerful work in economic theory up to its time, Richard Cantillon adopted the title which, so far as its original English wording can be reconstructed, must have read *Essay on the Nature of Trade in General,* under which heading he comfortably fitted most of the major subjects that economists have concerned themselves with since.[6]

It is worth a moment's pause to ask how 'the study of trade', which was the going name of the science, and an ample name, came to be replaced by Political Economy, the title under which the classical school worked, and which only less than a century ago gave way to Economics. 'Political Economy' was familiar to all close students of Aristotle and of classical Greek, and there are English writings throughout the seventeenth and eighteenth centuries showing that 'Economics' was used and understood in the Aristotelian and Greek sense: the art of managing a household. The art of managing a state was called, by direct analogy, Political Economics. But the habit of using the term to indicate the economic policy of the State was much stronger in France than in England: Antoine de Montchrétien, whose *Traicté de L'Économie Politique* (1615) is more famous for its title than its contents, was anticipated in this use by Mayerne-Turquet, as well, undoubtedly, as by others, and suc-

[6] Donaldson, Kress 2218; De Britaine, 2217; Pollexfen, 2249; Law, 2463; Black, 2492; Wood, 3082. CANTILLON: I follow Higgs' translation of the title (see his edition of Cantillon, 1931) though I am not aware that 'Commerce' in the French title would be less well served by 'Commerce' than by 'Trade' in English.

ceeded, though perhaps not followed, by many others. But curiously enough the term that came into use in France toward the middle of the eighteenth century to replace the settled French rubric, *commerce*, was *oeconomie*, spelled usually in the fashion that insisted on its Greek origins. The most important user, in terms of theoretical merit and influence, was Quesnay, whose *Tableau Oeconomique* was published in 1759, and whose school thereafter identified themselves as the *économistes*. In the English literature, the first writer of note to use the term was Sir James Steuart, who called his great treatise of 1767, *An Inquiry into the Principles of Political Oeconomy: being an essay on the science of domestic policy in free nations.* Steuart used the term, as the Greeks had, especially for policy; so too did Adam Smith, who defined it as 'a branch of the science of a statesman or legislator', the branch that 'proposes to enrich both the people and the sovereign'. Not until much later, such are the temptations of applied science, did economists feel quite comfortable about ignoring utterly all policy questions, and studying solely the abstract and purely speculative problems set by the internal structure of their theory; only then did economics come to have its present technical character and apolitical name.[7]

Nevertheless the idea that a science of trade was being created had already begun to spread early in the eighteenth century. Men had long been used to speaking of the 'mystery and art' of trade, a medieval formula often intoned over crafts and trades, whether tailoring, chandling, or silver-

[7] 'POLITICAL ECONOMY' IN ARISTOTLE: See above, pp. 91–92. MONTCHRÉTIEN: See J. E. King, 'Origin of the term "Political Economy",' 20 *Jour. Mod. Hist.* 230 (1948). OECONOMIQUE: Noël Chomel's *Dictionnaire Oeconomique* (1709, 1718; Kress 3050) still used the term, as did Dudley North's father (see above, p. 91), to mean 'household hints'. The newer sense of the term, however, made its appearance in Germany at about the same time as in France. Cf. Justus Ch. Dithmar, *Einleitung in die öconomischen-policey-, und cameral wissenschaften* (5th ed., 1755; Kress 5431). Justi, . . . *staatswirtschaft; oder, systematische abhandlung aller oeconomischen und cameral-wissenschaften* . . . (1755; Kress 5448). D. G. Schreber, . . . *Sammlung verschiedener schriften, welche in die öconomischen, policey-und cameral auch andere wissenschaften einschlagen* . . . (1755; Kress 5471). SMITH: *Wealth of Nations*, IV, Introduction; Cannan I, 395.

smithing, as a reminder that the qualified craftsman had his own peculiar skills and accomplishments. When, towards the opening of the eighteenth century, however, men began to speak of a 'science of trade', they referred no longer to the esoteric skill of the practitioner, passed from hand to hand by hard apprenticeship, but to the knowledge of trade 'in general' that an educated man could now acquire from books. In short, when they used the name 'science' so as to oppose it to 'art', they meant by art not a branch of humanities, but the skill of applying that knowledge which a science cultivates for the sake of understanding.[8]

Although Petty had declared before the close of the seventeenth century that economics could and should be made into a science, it is not surprising that some time elapsed before others became habituated to saying that such a science already existed. The lag can almost be measured. In 1695 the Bristol merchant John Cary opened his essay on trade by referring to 'the general notions' of trade, by which he meant known theoretical principles of trade. But when in 1717 he issued under the usual title of *A Discourse on Trade* a revised and enlarged version of the essay, he opened with a more robust assertion about the status of economic knowledge: 'Trade has its principles, as other sciences have.' The feeling that a science of economics existed apparently began to come upon Englishmen during the first decade or two of the eighteenth century. In 1740, Joseph Massie, who, as a great bibliographer, was in a better position to judge, wrote: 'Some writers have considered Commerce as a science and endeavoured to deduce the knowledge of it from axioms, maxims, etc., while many others have treated it as a branch of history, and given narratives of transactions, occurrences, etc.; but the former have made only light essays on the elementary part of commercial knowledge, and the latter have given only scraps of a commercial history. . . .'

[8] The flavour of the early modern use of 'art', which runs through the documents of the guilds, can be gathered from a booklet, *The art and mystery of vintners and wine-coopers: containing one hundred and fifty-eight approved receipts for the conserving and curing all sorts of wines, whether Spanish, Greek, Italian, or French* . . . (1682; 1750 ed., Kress 5005).

Most writers, so Massie continued, fell into a third class, who 'have not considered commerce as a science or as a branch of history, but have mixed personal with national affairs and blended principles, history and practice together'. To correct this deplorable situation, Massie proposed to improve and regularize the commercial history of Britain, and also to write a 'treatise, wherein I shall endeavour to establish upon fixed principles that branch of commercial knowledge which may properly be called elementary because it is deducible from self-evident truths, and not at all connected with either the historical or the practical branches'. Within his lifetime the idea that such a science existed had spread through Europe. Dithmar, Justi, Schreber and others were comfortably writing of *oeconomis-chen-wissenschaft*; an anonymous French writer wrote an account of how modern Frenchmen had gone about 'forming the science of political economy'; and Beccaria wrote a mathematical essay on smuggling and tariffs as an example of 'how economic science can be analytically considered'. Nor did British writers by this time hesitate to assume the mantle: Steuart called his work an essay on 'the science of domestic policy', and Smith referred repeatedly to a science of political economy, which he subsumed in his *Lectures* under Jurisprudence, 'that science which inquires into the general principles which ought to be the foundation of the laws of all nations'.[9]

Despite, however, the strong tendency of later eighteenth-century writers to use the word 'science' preferably for the practical use to which theoretical knowledge could be put, and the tendency of their writings to be directed ultimately toward practical use, they nevertheless devoted much more

[9] CARY: *An essay on the state of England, in relation to its trade, its poor, and its taxes* . . . (1695; Kress 1870). *A discourse on trade* . . . (1st ed. 1717; 1745 ed., Kress 4742). MASSIE: *A Representation concerning the knowledge of commerce* (1740), [ii]. DITHMAR *et al.*: See n. 7, p. 234 above. FRANCE: 'Notice abrégée des differens écrits modernes qui ont concouru en France à former la science de l'économie politique,' *Ephémérides du Citoyen* (Paris, 1769), Part I. BECCARIA: 'Tentativo analitico sui controbbandi' (1764), quoted in R. D. Theocharis, *Early Developments in Mathematical Economics* (1961), 22. SMITH: *Lectures on Justice* . . . ([1763], 1896), 1.

effort and attention than had their seventeenth century for-
bears to the purely theoretical side of the discipline. Indeed,
their way of dealing with policy had become a much more
theoretical one; for instead of addressing themselves to concrete and timely problems, such as a particular Bill before
Parliament or a momentary crisis in commerce or the money
market, they laid down rules for dealing with general and
durable problems, how populous a nation should be, how it
should control its balance of trade, or, how much credit its
banks should be permitted to create.

This spirit suffused Cantillon's *Essay on the Nature of
Trade in General*. It has a strong and complex framework
of pure theory, the parts of the book being neatly divided
into the theory of value, of price and money, international
trade, and banking. The architecture reveals itself most
clearly, as it will, at points of articulation, for instance:

> In Part I an attempt was made to prove that the real
> value of everything used by man is proportionable to
> the quantity of Land used for its production and for the
> upkeep of those who have fashioned it. In this second
> Part . . . it will be shown by comparing exchanges
> which may be made, wine for cloth, corn for shoes,
> hats, etc., and by the difficulty which the transport of
> these different products or merchandises would involve,
> that it was impossible to fix their respective intrinsic
> value, and there was an absolute necessity for Man to
> find a substance easily transportable, not perishable,
> and having by weight a proportion or value equal to
> the different products and merchandises, necessary or
> convenient. Thence arose the choice of Gold and Silver
> for large business and of Copper for small traffick.

The general problem before Cantillon, in short, was not
suggested to him by reasons of state, much less by current
reasons of state, but in large part rather, as he repeatedly
indicated, by his dissatisfaction with the analysis offered by
earlier economists, chiefly Locke and Petty. He was quite
ready to pronounce on policy questions, he often did, but
always in general terms; after showing why a nation ought
to avoid exchanging raw materials for foreign manufactures,

he added, 'But I have no intention of entering into detail as to the branches of trade which should be encouraged for the good of the State.' The *Essay*, in its applied as in its pure theory, shows no sign of being a piece written for a special occasion. Even his analysis of economic policy tokened that Cantillon had retreated from the market into the study: the door was not shut, but the shop was left to the management of others. And as Cantillon, so his successors, Tucker, Steuart and Smith became, what no one had been before, economists.[10]

II

All the efforts of seventeenth and eighteenth century economic writers culminated in the *Wealth of Nations*. Everything useful that they did, Adam Smith incorporated; everything worth doing that they left undone, he accomplished. His was the achievement, and yet it was his partly because luck placed him at that moment in the development of a tradition when all the materials lay ready to his hand.

Fortune saw to it, for one thing, that Smith faced no special problem in establishing his credentials. Granted that his use of deductive demonstration would have guarded him, as it did North, against the charge that he wrote to feather his own nest; still he needed no protection. He certainly took none. Not one word in his book follows the apologetic formula that seventeenth century writers used, as he must certainly have known from reading them, to say that their thoughts aimed purely at the public good. He was a scholar, had long been a professor and more recently a recluse. A never dissipated awe of learning, enhanced by the special respect which learning enjoyed during the Scottish enlightenment, and a trust founded on the evident unworld-

[10] Cantillon, *Essay* (Higgs ed.), 115, 235. Among Cantillon's motives for writing the *Essay*, it should be mentioned, may have been resentment toward or at least distrust of John Law, by whom he had been injured (see pp. 368 ff. of Higgs' ed.); the latter chapters of Part III of the *Essay* and especially the sharpness of the *Essay's* closing paragraph may have been directed at Law.

liness of professors, especially at a time and place when university teachers were still commonly divines—these must have come to Smith's aid, warding off any embarrassing questions about the purity of his motives or the objectivity of his observations. He was the first economist to benefit from the credit the world so kindly extends to academics, assuming on faith that they love truth and put the public good before any desires of their own. Smith did not need this aid, but it did not injure him.

Fortune had a more useful gift as well. By the time Smith came to his work, the main substantive principles needed for an economic theory had been laid down, not once but many times, in the literature; a man who knew how to see could not overlook them. Vast efforts, induced by natural piety, have been invested by generations of scholars in tracing back all of Smith's ideas to some intellectual ancestor or other; it need hardly be said that for each of his main ideas and for many details scholars have been able to locate substantial pedigrees. Consider, for instance, the division of labour, the pivotal idea in Smith's theory of economic growth and the subject of his opening chapter. Cannan, an admiring and self-effacing editor, commented on 'division of labour' that it was not a familiar phrase, but added that the name, as well as the idea that the thing is of great importance, both probably came from Mandeville's *Fable of the Bees,* and that the idea though not the name was used in 1757 by Joseph Harris. In his notes to the first chapter, Cannan also pointed out that Smith's famous example of pin-making was undoubtedly drawn from the *Encyclopédie,* that the three types of efficiency which Smith attributed to the division of labour had previously been recognized in the *Encyclopédie,* that Smith's story of the boy who improved the operation of a steam engine originated in the misreading of a passage that involved a 'boy' and a 'buoy' (i.e. a float valve), and finally that the resounding end of the chapter, in which Smith pointed out how division of labour enables European peasants to live more comfortably than African kings, is founded on Mun, Locke, Mandeville and perhaps also Joseph Harris. An editor more ambitious and less prudent than Cannan would be able to trace out much more, and to trace it much further back, to show, for instance, that the idea of division of labour is at least as old as Plato, who insisted on it in his state of pigs, and to show every link in the seventeenth-century chain of hands that passed down to Smith the explanation of why gold and silver are preferred for money. But it hardly needs an editor to point out to us how much Smith owed to other authors: he himself quoted authorities, quoted them by the dozens. These acknowledgments, coupled with the reconstructed catalogue of his library, show how widely he had read in the economic literature, how firmly he stood on the shoulders of his predecessors.[11]

He added to what he had inherited, but much of what he added was by way of tying together loose ends, bringing into sensible relation principles and intuitions that had been left standing isolated. One of his great feats in this way was to combine the idea of natural economic laws, as given by Locke, with mechanistic explanations of the sort given by North and later by many others, notably Cantillon, to combine them with other elements into a tenable case for *laissez-faire*. The way he went about this work can best be seen by examining the celebrated passage on the invisible hand.

In considering monopolies of home manufactures, Smith asserted that though they might encourage the favoured industry they could not encourage home manufactures in total; he went further and asserted that no regulation of any sort could encourage home manufactures, and indeed that the result of any regulation must be to reduce the output of industry. He proceeded to justify the assertion. Every individual, he said, seeks to get the highest possible return to his capital. This moves him to keep his capital as close as possible to home, where it is least subject to loss; so that if the rate of return for funds invested in domestic trade is equal to the rate of return on investments in the carrying trade or trade of foreign consumption, then he will prefer the former. Earlier in the *Wealth of Nations* Smith had established the principle that a given fund of capital contrib-

[11] *W. of N.*, I, i; Cannan, I, 5–14. James Bonar, *A Catalogue of the Library of Adam Smith* (2 ed.; 1952).

utes most to national income if it is invested in the home trade, contributes less if invested in the 'foreign trade of consumption', and least if invested in the carrying trade. He now combined the two principles to arrive at the conclusion that 'Upon equal, or only nearly equal profits, therefore, every individual naturally inclines to employ his capital in the manner in which it is likely to afford the greatest support to domestic industry, and to give revenue and employment to the greatest number of people of his own country'. Every individual does so 'naturally', in that when he follows his natural desire to maximize his own satisfactions, the economic mechanism translates his actions into unintended benefits for others.

Moreover, Smith continued, every individual who invests in domestic production is naturally inclined to invest in the most profitable way, in the way, in other words, that maximizes his profit by maximizing the total value of his output.

At this point, Smith summarized his argument in the famous paragraph:

> But the annual revenue of every society is always precisely equal to the exchangeable value of the whole annual produce of its industry, or rather is precisely the same thing with that exchangeable value. As every individual, therefore, endeavours as much as he can both to employ his capital in the support of domestic industry, and so to direct that industry that its produce may be of the greatest value; every individual necessarily labours to render the annual revenue of the society as great as he can. He generally, indeed, neither intends to promote the public interest, nor knows how much he is promoting it. By preferring the support of domestic to that of foreign industry, he intends only his own security; and by directing that industry in such a manner as its produce may be of the greatest value, he intends only his own gain, and he is in this, as in many other cases, led by an invisible hand to promote an end which was no part of his intention.[12]

[12] W. of N., IV, ii; Cannan, I, 418–21.

To say that this is a tenable argument for *laissez-faire* is not to deny that Smith's argument rests on gaps and errors. One gap is his failure to deal with the case, less happy than the one he supposes, where the rate of return on capital invested in the carrying trade is much higher than on capital in domestic trade; were that the case, the private incentives of merchants would lead them to invest in such a way as to reduce the national income. But this issue, which Smith neatly bypassed, was a mirage in any case, arising as it did from the deeper mistake of believing that investing in the home trade is necessarily more productive than investing abroad. Another gap, which weakens his second argument, was his conclusion that an entrepreneur necessarily maximizes his profit when he maximizes the value of his output. If the entrepreneur is in a position to force down the cost of capital, labour or materials, or to force up the price of the product, then he can raise his profits without simultaneously and in the same degree raising his firm's contribution to national income. Smith's argument on this score, in other words, depends on the assumption of a perfectly competitive economy in stable long-run equilibrium, the condition that sees to it that the pie is cut, in Smith's terms, correctly.

Yet these difficulties do not in the larger sense mean that his argument for *laissez-faire* lacked firm intellectual foundations. What he was asserting was that men's natural tendency to follow their self-interest, together with the fact that capital, labour and land all contribute jointly to national income, mean that every man in looking after his own good inevitably benefits others. The invisible hand is introduced as a literary embellishment, an elegant way of summarizing an argument already stated, and not, as it has often been misrepresented, a dogmatic assertion of 'natural harmony' in economic life. To say that Smith required or even believed in natural harmony is to neglect *The Theory of Moral Sentiments* as a whole, as well as passages in *The Wealth of Nations*, and they are many, such as that in which he showed that although the interests of landowners and labourers are 'strictly and inseparably connected with the general interest of the society', the interest of merchants is 'always in some respects different from, and even opposite to, that of the public'.[13]

The importance of Smith's doctrine of *laissez-faire* for the development of economic theory as such, however, is much less than the influence of his assumptions and the style of his analysis. It was Smith who taught Bastiat to speak of the 'social mechanism', Cairnes to analyse Ricardo's work as an exercise in mechanistic explanation, and Jevons to describe the science of economics as the 'mechanics of self-interest'. But, of course, Smith in turn learned it from his own predecessors.[14]

It has often been said that Smith was a systematizer. The structure of *The Wealth of Nations* shows how consummate was his skill. The books are divided with the most perfect clarity into the pure theory of production and distribution, the theory of capital, the history of economic development, and the theory of economic policy, the latter being divided between two books, the fourth refuting false policies, the fifth presenting the correct policy. The internal structure of each book and of each chapter shows, on examination, the same clarity of organization.

Nevertheless there is no doubt that this precision of structure does not present itself forcibly and immediately to the reader; it is somewhat veiled. The veil is there partly because Smith put it there, partly because he could not avoid it. Insofar as he deliberately veiled the structure, he did so to suit the audience that he most wanted to convince: not scholars, technicians, or scientists, who might be depended on to wade through any material, no matter how cold or dry, if only they caught a glimpse of light at the far end; not students, who as Smith made poignantly clear, must learn whatever is lectured at them; but gentlemen and squires, members of Parliament, busy, not excessively intelligent or

---

[13] *W. of N.*, I, xi, Conclusion; Cannan, I, 248–50.
[14] F. Bastiat, *Harmonies of Political Economy* [1850] (trans. Stirling, 1860), I, 18. J. E. Cairnes, *Character and Logical Method of Political Economy* (2nd ed., 1875), 81 ff. Jevons, quoted by W. Stark, *The History of Economics* . . . (1945), 53.

devoted, who would take instruction at length only if it were presented in a pleasurable form, perhaps under the guise of sheer pleasure. It was they who might eventually revoke the whole system of government intervention and protection, and it was to reach them that Smith spent years reworking his Edinburgh lectures, tricking out the bare propositions in stately prose and enlivening them with colourful illustrations. In doing this, Smith sacrificed no clarity, but he exchanged some economy for palatability.

But even were one to strip *The Wealth of Nations* of all its non-scientific rhetoric, the organization would not stand out as clearly as the mere outline of its topics would suggest. That is because the topical organization has been interwoven with an organization reflecting Smith's doctrine on economic development. Viewed from the latter standpoint, the books are dedicated to demonstrating these propositions: national income increases accordingly as the division of labour increases; the division of labour can increase only in proportion to the accumulation of capital; capital is not necessarily acquired more rapidly or more securely in commerce and manufactures than in agriculture; mistaken economic policy alone explains why too much capital is forced into trade and into particular branches of trade; correct economic policy would have government do nothing except provide services that the beneficiaries could not buy separately, and finance those services by methods that least distort the natural increase and flow of capital. This second scheme of organization accounts for the titles that Smith gave to some of the several books, the first scheme for the others; still other leading doctrines, such as the dominant rôle of self-interest, further complicate the titles and even more particularly the transitional passages that connect successive chapters and books. An apparent lack of clarity on the surface, in other words, was the cost of extraordinary richness and intricacy in Smith's analytic system.

But if Smith was so emphatically a systematizer, a man who merely collated and ordered ideas inherited from others, then why should he deserve high regard as a scientist? Was

he not, perhaps, as is a librarian to novelists or a journalist
to soldiers, one who reports and neatly files the work of
creative men? Such questions are suggested by the strictures
of Schumpeter, who wrote that no matter what Smith 'actually learned or failed to learn from predecessors, the fact
is that the *Wealth of Nations* does not contain a single *analytic* idea, principle, or method that was entirely new in
1776'. Schumpeter concluded that Smith, by nature a methodical professor, was fit to do well only a task that required
no great understanding. 'His mental stature was up to mastering the unwieldy material that flowed from many sources
and to subjecting it, with a strong hand, to the rule of a
small number of coherent principles.' Schumpeter did not
fail to praise Smith, but it is praise for the great perform-
ance of work that, whatever its merits, has made no contribution to pure economic theory.[15]

This criticism misses the relations between system and
science. Not every systematizing effort is a scientific one:
it may result in nothing more than a telephone directory or
a chronicle if the ordering principle is trivial and obvious.
But to master unwieldy material and subject it to the rule
of a small number of coherent principles, as Schumpeter
rightly said Smith did, is to put the material into a system,
and if that material is itself theoretical, then it is to create a
work superior in scientific merit to any of its component bits.

What Schumpeter confused, and it is a confusion as common in the history of science as it is dangerous in the practice of science, is the scientific character of a work with its
truth. Newton's *Principia* is not absolutely correct, but it is
perfectly scientific. *The Wealth of Nations* is far from perfectly correct, but it too is perfectly scientific. The relation
between the scientific character of a work and truth is that
a theory represented in scientific form exhibits its weak
spots, invites testing, and so aids the process of rejection and
amendment by which a science approaches the truth.

The Wealth of Nations contains perhaps nothing that

[15] Schumpeter, *History of Economic Analysis* (1954), 184–85
et seq.

will survive forever as the closest approach economists can make to understanding the world. It deserves its reputation, not as in any way an ultimate statement, but as a turning point, the beginning of all that came after as it was the end of all that came before.

Appendices

Appendix I

A BIBLIOGRAPHY OF SIR JOSIAH CHILD

THE ENTIRE BODY of Child's published writings is comprised in the *New Discourse of Trade*, which reprints the *Brief Observations* as well as the *Discourse of Trade*, and particular chapters of which were later published separately. The only remaining problem about this group of books, to ascertain their precise dating, can be disposed of with some precision. The more substantial task is to disentangle from Child's writings a number of books that have been attributed to him falsely or gratuitously.

A. *WORKS BY CHILD*

1. *Brief Observations concerning trade, and interest of money.* By J. C. London. Printed for Elizabeth Calvert . . . 1668.

The pamphlet consists of four parts:

(a) the main text, pp. 1–16;

(b) 'Suppliment', pp. 17–20;

(c) a reprint of an anonymous pamphlet [by Sir Thomas Culpepper, Sr.], preceded by its own title-page, reading 'A Tract against Usurie, presented to the high court of Parliament, London, printed in the year 1621, and now reprinted for Elizabeth Calvert . . . 1668'; pp. 21–37;

(d) 'Postscript', by Child, pp. 37–38.

According to the 'Suppliment' (1b), p. 17, the main text (1a) was written 'in the sickness-summer', that is, the plague summer of 1665. The publication of the whole *Brief Observations* probably took place early in 1668, since Sir Thomas Culpepper, Junior, refers to it in his pamphlet, *A Discourse showing the many advantages which will accrue to this Kingdom by the abatement of usury.* He writes that having come to London to forward the scheme so dear to his father he found himself 'happily prevented by one Mr Child, a merchant, of known abilities in trade, and choice conversation; who (rising as it were out of my father's dust) did, by his own sagacity, find out this hidden vein'.[1] Since Culpepper's pamphlet was licensed on March 9, 1668,[2] the *Brief Observations* were evidently ready for publication or already published by the end of March of that year.

2. *A short addition to the observation concerning trade and interest of money.* By the same hand. London, Mortlock, 1668.

Child considers several further objections to the reduction of interest. This material was not reprinted in any subsequent book.

3. (Anon.), *A Discourse about Trade, wherein the reduction of interest of money to 4£ per centum is recommended* . . . Never before printed. Printed by A. Sowle . . . 1690. 'Licensed, Nov. 18, 1689. . . .'

4. *A New Discourse of Trade* . . . By Sir Josiah Child. London . . . John Everingham . . . 1693. 'December 24, 1692. Imprimator, Edmund Bohun'.

These two works are identical, except for title page, numbering, the publisher's preface in the 1690 book, and pp. 159–60—in fact, with these exceptions, the 1693 book is a reissue of 1690 sheets. Their bibliography has been definitively established by Bowyer,[3] who describes also the subsequent printings and editions of the *New Discourse*, which appeared in 1694, 1698, 1718, (1718–1751), 1751, 1775, and 1804.

---

[1] Culpepper, *Discourse* (1668), Preface, ix.

[2] *Ibid.*, 34. The licence date is written 'March 9, 1667', which is 1668 according to the new calendar system of dating years from Jan. 1 instead of March 25.

[3] T. H. Bowyer, 'The published forms of Sir Josiah Child's *A New Discourse of Trade,' The Library*, XI (Fifth series), (1956), 95–102. See also S. Helander, 'Sir Josiah Child', *Weltwirtschaftliches Archiv*, vol. 19, pt. 1 (1923), 233.

Both books include the material of the *Brief Observations*, the text (1a) and 'suppliment' (1b) being printed before Chapter I, as 'A Discourse concerning trade, etc.', while Culpepper's tract (1c) and the postscript (1d) are printed at the very end of the book. The additional material consists of a long preface, and ten chapters which intervene between 'A Discourse . . .' and Culpepper's tract.

The preface opens, 'The following answer to that treatise entitled, *Interest of Money Mistaken*, I wrote long before the last session of parliament that began the 19th of October 1669 . . .' The 'answer to that treatise', which is Chapter I of the *New Discourse*, must have been composed after March 1668, when the *Interest of Money* appeared, for the *Interest of Money* itself was a reply to the *Brief Observations*.

The 'Preface' itself seems to date from 1670. It is an answer to Manley, and as such was composed in or after 1669. It criticizes ideas expressed in 'a treatise writ about thirty years since by Lewes Roberts',[4] a reference to Roberts' treatise of 1641,[5] which would place Child's Preface 'about' 1671. Finally, it refers to testimony before the Lords' Committee on the Decline of Trade,[6] which places it after the autumn of 1669. All in all, 1670 seems the most plausible date for the Preface.

Similar bits of internal evidence[7] make it quite clear that all the additional material in the 1690 and 1693 books was written between 1668 and 1670. It is apparent that when Child wrote the additional material, that is, the Preface and the ten chapters, he conceived of them as a book in themselves, which would defend and enlarge the notions expressed in the *Brief Observations*, which he refers to in several places as his 'former' discourse.[8] Written soon after

[4] *N.D.T.*, Pref., p. [xxix].

[5] Lewes Roberts, *The Treasure of Trafficke* (1641); the material to which Child referred is at pp. 32 ff.

[6] *N.D.T.*, Pref., pp. [xvii, xxxvii].

[7] E.g., the Act of Navigation is said to be 'now of seventeen or eighteen years standing'; *N.D.T.*, 119. As the Act was passed 1651, the passage dates from 1668 or 1669.

[8] *N.D.T.*, 147, 177.

the *Brief Observations* and perhaps intended to be published then, there would have been little need to reprint the earlier work. But when the second manuscript finally went to press over twenty years later, it was necessary to reprint the *Brief Observations* after all, and a paragraph explaining this change was thrown, hastily and with no care to find a proper place for it, into the middle of the Preface.[9]

5. *Sir Josiah Child's proposals for the relief and employment of the poor.* (n.d.)

The text is identical with Chapter II of (3) and (4) except for the omission of the chapter's last paragraph. Numerous subsequent editions are listed in Scroggs' bibliography,[10] which ascribes the date 1670 to this one. That it was not published as early as 1670 is certain from the fact that Josiah Child was not called 'Sir' until 1678. Bowyer points out further that the appearance of Child's name in the title is not consistent with Child's 'custom of semi-anonymity preserved up to 1693', and therefore supposes some date after 1693.[11] But the reasons that made Child preserve *complete* anonymity in the 1690 *Discourse* would not have pertained to his reflections on the poor law, so that Bowyer's conclusion may be mistaken. A date after 1678, and possibly after 1690, is the best estimate that can be made.

B. *WORKS INCORRECTLY ATTRIBUTED TO CHILD*

6. *The East-India-Trade a most profitable trade to the Kingdom* . . . London, 1677.

This pamphlet was written by Robert Ferguson.[12] Subsequent editions appeared in 1680 and 1696 under slightly altered titles, the 1696 title including the words, 'Wrote at the instance of Thomas Papillon, Esq.'

[9] N.D.T., Pref., p. [xxxii].
[10] E. E. Scroggs, 'Bibliography of Sir Josiah Child,' *Bulletin Brit. Lib. of Pol. Sci.*, No. 14 (May, 1921), 15–17.
[11] *Op. cit.* n. 3, p. 250 above, p. 96.
[12] Cf. p. 36 above.

7. Philopatris, *A Treatise wherein is demonstrated, I. That the East-India trade is the most national of all foreign trades; II. that the clamors . . . against the present East-India Company are sinister, selfish, or groundless. . . .* London, T. J., for Robert Boulter . . . 1681.

7a. (The same.) London. Printed by J. R. for the Honourable the East-India Company, 1681.

8. *A supplement, 1689, to a former treatise concerning the East-India Trade, printed 1681.*

The Philopatris book, and by implication all its appendages, including (9) p. 237, is the only false attribution worth seriously considering. The evidence for Child's authorship consists of two sorts, attribution by contemporaries and similarities of style. Of the first sort there are two bits. A reply to (7) published in 1681, is prefaced by a mocking letter, addressed to 'Sr. J. C.', who is styled 'Commander of the East-India privateer', and accused of not loving his country as much as 'Philopatris' should.[13] In addition, Charles King later referred to the *Treatise* as 'a pamphlet wrote by Sir Josiah Child, or at least by his direction'.[14] Neither allegation can be taken as very competent evidence, since both merely credit Child, who was well known to be governor of the company, with a pamphlet written in the company's defence. Nor is the deduction from similarity with Child's other work much more satisfactory. Anderson says merely that the author was 'probably Sir Josiah Child, as appears from the style, scope, etc.'; and McCulloch, who repeats King's remark, adds, 'whoever compares it with his "Discourse of Trade" will be satisfied that Sir Josiah was its author'.[15] That there are certain similarities between the views of Child and Philopatris is undeniable, but not surprising. Both were defending the East-India Company and both adhered to the popular principles, or rather *clichés*, of mercantilist doctrine.

[13] *An arrest on the East-India privatier* . . . (16 Sept. 1681).
[14] Charles King, *The British Merchant* (1721), I, 182.
[15] Adam Anderson, *Historical and Chronological Deduction of the Origin of Commerce* (1787), II, 551; J. R. McCulloch, *Literature of Political Economy* (1845), 99.

But between Child and Philopatris there are also such wide divergences of doctrine that it is difficult to believe that the two were one. For instance Child had commended, in the *Brief Observations,* the Dutch practice of appointing to their councils of state 'trading merchants', merchants actively engaged in business.[16] Philopatris, on the other hand, flatly contradicts this view; he asserts that 'trading merchants' are not the best judges of the Kingdom's interests, and that the Dutch do not employ them: 'their councils are made up of few or no trading merchants, but of civilians or sons of merchants, that have long since left off their active trades'.[17] Again, Child asserts that the value of land always rises or falls as trade increases or declines, a proposition essential to his argument.[18] But Philopatris seems to question this view implicitly when he urges that 'all domestic or foreign trade . . . that doth not . . . increase the value of our English lands . . . ought not only to be discouraged, but totally rejected'.[19] These and other disagreements in doctrine make it hardly likely that the same author wrote both.

Beyond this, Philopatris' specific comments on East-India affairs are altogether at odds with what are known to have been Child's views at the time. The pamphlet appeared in August or September of 1681,[20] just before the great conflict between Child and Papillon concerning the offer to wind up the Company's old stock. Child opposed the measure and led the Company into a closer alignment with the court; Papillon favoured the measure, and became more and more a spokesman for the parliamentary opposition, until two years later the court party forced him into exile.[21] Now Philopatris expresses on these points just the views that Child most vigorously opposed and that a minority led by

16 *B.O.,* 3.

17 Pp. 1, 3.

18 *Discourse* (1690), Preface, at sig. B2.

19 P. 2.

20 It was published between 17 Aug. 1681, when the Turkey Co. presented their *Allegations* (cf. p. 33 f. above) and 16 Sep. 1681, the date of the *Arrest* (*op. cit.* n. 13, p. 253 above). It mentions the former and is mentioned by the latter.

21 See above, p. 37 f.

Papillon favoured. 'I shall not stick to declare,' says Philopatris, '(though it be against the sense of most of the now adventurers) that in my judgment I am for a new stock . . .' and he invites Parliament—not the King, from whom the Company's charter issued—to alter the Company's constitution as it sees fit.[22] Elsewhere he says that 'a company in joint-stock are a corporation by charter (and if it were by act of parliament, it would be much better for the Kingdom in general, as hath been said)'.[23] These sentiments are echoed moreover in the very pseudonym, 'Philopatris', which had distinctly republican connotations.[24] Neither the doctrines nor policies of Philopatris are compatible with Child's position, and if one were forced to ascribe the pamphlet to someone, Papillon or some 'Whiggish' member of his contingent would be a more plausible guess. But there is no direct evidence for any particular author.

9. *A Discourse concerning trade, and that in particular of the East-Indies* . . . London . . . Andrew Sowle . . . 1689.

This is an abstract of (7) and (8), by another hand, according to the author. Since it abstracts (8)—which was not published until 1689—the date placed at its conclusion, 'June 25, 1686' is evidently a misprint for 'June 25, 1689', and this is all the more certain since the year 1689 is mentioned in the text.[25]

10. *An essay on wool and woolen manufacture for the improvement of trade* . . . London, H. Bonwicke, 1693.

Attributed to Child by the *London Bibliography* (III, 1215) and Kress catalogue (Kress, 1810).

The author insists that the Government should forcibly maintain high standards in wool manufacture, a view directly contrary to that which Child advocates in the *New Discourse*, Chapter VIII. He also argues, contrary to Child,

[22] P. 10.
[23] P. 31.
[24] Dryden, for instance, wrote: 'Gull'd with a Patriots name, whose Modern sense Is one that wou'd by Law Supplant his Prince.'
[25] The correct date is entered as an emendation by the *London Bibliography of the Social Sciences*, III, 904.

that independent merchants are ruining the trade, which should therefore be confined to a company.

11. *A Discourse of the nature, use and advantages of trade* . . . London . . . 1694.

The chief ground for attributing this to Child seems to be that it proposes policies like those of Child: a registry of lands, reduction of interest rates, and naturalization of foreigners. If this were, however, a sufficient guide, then a large part of the economic literature of the period and much of the attempted legislation would have to be attributed to Child. Moreover, the author's fourth chief contention is that the export of coin should be prohibited, which runs directly contrary to Child's express statement in the *New Discourse* (p. 73). It is ludicrous to suppose that Child would have published a second, anonymous pamphlet in 1694 to reproduce some of the ideas and contradict others that were currently appearing under his name in the 1693 and 1694 editions of the *New Discourse*.

In addition, this *Discourse* differs widely from Child's both in style and general doctrine. Its opening words read: 'When fallen man was driven out of Paradise, the heavy charge imposed on him was, that in the sweat of his face he should eat his bread: and he who first was made of clay, must receive his nourishment and sustenance from the earth.' In this stately and mellifluous style, utterly contrasting with Child's vehement and disorderly prose, the author continues to develop a theory, perfectly foreign to Child, that the land and its produce are the fundamental source of all wealth.

Foxwell, incidentally, appended a note to his copy to the effect that it was 'wrongly attributed to Sir J. Child'.[26]

C. WORKS OF DOUBTFUL AUTHORSHIP

12. 'Answer of the said East-India Company' printed as part of *Allegations of the Turkey Company* . . . *against the East-India Company* . . . *presented to the* . . . *Privy Council, the 17th of August,* 1681. (1681; Kress, 1526.)

[26] Kress, 1842.

This book was said by Khan to be Child's composition, on account of general considerations of style and context.[27]

The only external evidence on its composition is an entry in the East-India Company's Court Book,[28] according to which the Turkey Company's 'Allegations' were read to the directors, 'as also a paper drawn up in answer . . . which was referred to the Governor, Deputy, and Committees, to make such amendments therein as they shall think fit . . .' This does not identify the author of the first draft, and only says that Child, the governor, Papillon, the deputy, and the directors (or committees, as they were known)—all or any of them—may have altered or completely rewritten the draft.

There is nothing in the 'Answer' that either confirms or disproves Child's authorship, although there is every reason to think that he was in perfect accord with the views it expresses.

13. 'The humble answer of the Governor, Deputy-Governor, and Court of Committees of the East-India Company . . .' May 20, 1692; in *Somers' Tracts*, 3rd Series, III (1751), 181.

Attributed to Child by Scroggs and others, possibly under the misapprehension that Child was still governor at this time. In fact this work alludes to Child as having been the singlehanded ruler of the Company, a practice which is defended, though the unflattering consolation is offered that he will soon die, and any fear that the Company will fall under a hereditary succession is allayed by the reminder that sons of opulent India merchants become landed gentlemen.[29]

The paper is undersigned for the Company by Robert Blackborne. It is a strong polemic, containing little of interest to historians of economic thought and no evidence of its author's identity.

[27] Khan, 195.
[28] Ct. Bk. 32, f. 140a (19 Aug. 1681).
[29] P. 189.

14. J. C., *The Great honour and advantage of the East-India trade to the Kingdom asserted.* London, T. Speed, 1697.

Attributed to Child by *London Bibliography* (III, 908). The inference seems to be based on the author's monogram, the thesis, and date. There is nothing more to identify the pamphlet with Child, nor anything to refute the inference.

Foxwell's surmise that J. C. may have been John Cary must be dismissed, for Cary opposed the East-India trade on the grounds that it was inimical to the wool trade.[30]

[30] See Foxwell's notation on Kress, 2018. Cf. John Cary, *Discourse concerning the East-India trade* (1696; Kress, 1945).

Appendix II

INDEX OF SOURCES FOR CHILD'S
LIST OF DUTCH PRACTICES

Child's List	Robinson[1]	Worsley[2]	Lambe[3]	Dutch[4]
1. Merchants council	p. 4, #16 Cf. p. 46	p. 9, #4	p. 7, #1	
2. Gavelkind		p. 10, #3A	p. 8, #2	
3. Exact making	p. 4, #6	p. 7, #3	p. 8, #3	
4. Inventors	p. 4, #7 Cf. p. 18	p. 10, #6	p. 9, #5	
5. Shipping		p. 3, #1		p. 52, #1
6. Parsimony				p. 53, #5 Cf. pp. 56–7
7. Education of children				p. 55
8. Taxes[5]	p. 4, #3 Cf. p. 9	p. 9, #5	p. 8, #4	
9. Poor	p. 4, #4			pp. 55–6
10. Banks	p. 4, #11	p. 10, #2A	p. 9, #6	
11. Toleration				pp. 48–9
12. Law merchant	p. 4, #10		p. 13; PS, p. 3	
13. Bills of debt	p. 4, #12		pp. 12–13?	
14. Register of titles	p. 4, #13			
15. Low interest	p. 4, #2 Cf. p. 6	p. 10, #1A		
Objection 1	pp. 7 ff.			
Objection 2	pp. 7 ff.			
Objection 3	pp. 7 ff.			

[1] Henry Robinson, *England's Safety, in Trades Encrease* (1641; Kress, 597).

[2] [Benjamin Worsley], 'Philopatris', *The Advocate* (1651; Kress, 837).

[3] Samuel Lambe, *Seasonable Observations* . . . (1657; Kress, S. 429).

[4] *The Dutch Drawn to Life* (1664; Kress, 1133).

[5] In addition to other sources, see [William Petty], *Treatise on Taxes and Contributions* (1662; Kress, 1098; 1667 ed.), 35, 72, and *passim*.

Appendix III

THE GREAT RECOINAGE:
AN ALTERNATIVE ESTIMATE

THE ACCOUNT I have given (see pp. 69–77) of money and prices during the Great Recoinage is based in large measure on data gathered by Mr J. Keith Horsefield in his excellent book, *British Monetary Experiments, 1650–1710* (1960). As, however, his estimates of changes in the money supply during the period of the Recoinage seem to me erroneous in certain respects, I take this opportunity of correcting a few errors and, more important, of suggesting an alternative line of inference from the data.

SILVER COIN

Horsefield does not distinguish altogether clearly between coin in circulation and coin in hoard. Although he writes that *his* figures (p. 14) 'exclude hoards', the base that he adopts does not seem to exclude hoards. That base is an estimate by Sir Isaac Newton, who placed at £13.7 million 'the total amount of silver money in existence' at the end of 1689. 'In existence' are Horsefield's words (p. 258); and Craig's report (Craig, *Mint*, p. 193) appears to confirm that Newton's estimate included all the silver coin in all possible forms, without distinction between money in hoard and money in circulation. Yet after reducing this estimate by £200,000 to adjust for wear and tear 1690–93, Horsefield describes the resulting £13.5 million as the amount 'remaining in circulation' at the end of 1693.

Hoards must in any event have sequestered a much larger fraction of the supply of coin during the seventeenth century than now. In the absence of banks, life insurance companies, and a stable and easy market for securities, the desires to

have at least some of one's savings near to hand and to hold
a fund of cash against emergencies of all sorts must have
been as great in England as they still are in parts of Asia.
I have, accordingly, in the accounts below, made a very
generous allowance for hoards. The precise size of the
hoards is purely conjectural and illustrative but the principle that they must have been relatively large is not. It is
borne out by the testimony of, among others, Lowndes, who
reported that of the heavy money left in the Kingdom 'a
great part . . . is supposed to lie in Hoards . . .' (*Report*,
106.)

Another difficulty has to do with the rate at which coin
was being privately melted down or exported. It is introduced when Horsefield divides Newton's total into classes
of coin, arriving at the estimate that £2.5 million of it was
'old full-weight', and £11 million 'old clipped' (p. 14), of
which, more precisely, £10 million was clipped and £1 million was 'condoned and acceptable counterfeits'. (Cf. Craig,
258.) But £2.5 million seems a very low figure for 'old full-
weight' coin. This category must include full-weight hammered coin, and all of the milled coin issued between 1663–
93; we cannot tell how much of the former remained in
existence, nor for that matter how much of the latter. But
it is known that about £4.0 million of milled silver coin was
issued between 1663 and 1693, and it is a bit hard to believe that this had dwindled to less than £2.5 million in so
short a time.

Yet Newton himself appears to have made a still stronger
assumption about the disappearance of milled silver coins.
If one takes his estimate for the end of 1689 and adjusts it
for the changes wrought by the Mint between then and the
end of 1701, the result is:

	£ million
End 1689, Newton's estimate	13.7
Add coin issued 1690–1701	7.0
Less coin melted down 1696–1701 (Craig, 193)	10.2
End 1701, stock	£10.5

Granted that this figure is an upper limit, since it makes no allowance for coin lost or melted by private persons (other than the goldsmiths referred to by Craig), yet it comes as a surprise that Newton estimated the stock of silver coin in 1701 at only £6.75 million. If his estimates were meant to be consistent, then he was willing to assume that £3.75 million of silver coin was privately destroyed or exported between 1690 and 1701.

But Horsefield, though he accepts Newton's estimate for 1689, implicitly rejects the estimate for 1701. He gives as the figure for silver *in circulation* (hoards presumably excluded) at the end of 1698 the sum of £9.0 million, a figure which, if it were to tally with Newton's 1701 estimate, would mean that as much as £2.25 million of coin was privately destroyed in only the three years 1699–1701. One piece of information may appear to make this estimate of loss plausible: namely, that in 1700 and 1701, bullion to the value of £834,000 and £751,000 was exported from England and Wales (E. B. Schumpeter, *English Overseas Trade Statistics 1697–1808* [1960], 14). But two considerations suggest that even if £2.25 million of bullion was exported during those three years, as may well have been the case, this export would not have required that an equivalent amount of English silver coin be melted down. For one thing, the figures are for *gross* exports; since bullion and coin could be imported freely, no record was kept of imports, but bullion and coin must have continued to flow in at least from areas, such as Spain, with persistently adverse balances in commodity trade; (cf. Ashton's comment, *ibid.*, 7). Secondly, the total of bullion export appears to have included at least some gold (see p. 264).

The Newton estimates for 1689 and 1701 are, it seems to me, sufficiently difficult to reconcile so that it is worth constructing an estimate on another set of data. It appears from the Newton Mint Manuscripts (Craig, 193) that during the Recoinage the Mint recovered £9.6 in face value of clipped hammered coin and condoned counterfeits. In addition, hammered coin to a value of £500,000 or £600,000 'reached London goldsmiths as bullion in the years 1699 to 1701' (Craig, 193) and a further £1,000,000 was thought to remain outstanding. Now if this sum of £1,600,000 (un-recovered prior to 1699) had been clipped coin, there would have been every reason for the holders to get rid of it at once; why then did they hold it until at least 1699, or longer? The only good reason for keeping it would have been that the holder could lose nothing by doing so, and this would have been the case with *full-weight* coin: its full value could always be captured by melting it down, even after it was demonetized in 1698. The total inventory of silver coin, in and out of circulation, at the end of 1695 may therefore be estimated as follows:

	£ million
Hammered clipped, and counterfeit	9.6
Hammered, full-weight	1.6
Milled	3.7
	£14.9

The figure given above for milled coin is the total pro-duction from 1663 to 1695 inclusive, adjusted to allow for a standard rate of wear of 0.3 per cent per year (Horsefield, 258, fn. 3); this figure is an upper limit, since it makes no allowance for export or melting down.

The figure for clipped and counterfeit coins, £9.6 million, following the Newton Mint papers cited above, also seems to be too high. Lowndes reported that when some 500 bags of silver coin were weighed at the Exchequer, they were found to be almost 50 per cent underweight. (Lowndes, *Report*, 159.) But the £9.6 million that was returned to the Mint contained enough silver, or almost enough, to al-low for recoining into £6.8 million of full-weight coin; in other words, if one accepts the figure of £9.6 million face value, then the coin was only about 30 per cent under-weight in 1696. What seems more likely is that £9.6 million is too high, a possibility confirmed by the estimating pro-cedure used in arriving at it. Of the £9.6 million, £4.7 million was received at face value, but the remaining £4.9 million was accepted at the Mint only by weight, and it is hard to believe that the officers of the Mint, already driven to despair by the rush of recoining, would have set themselves the perverse and futile labour of counting up the face values of some 50,000,000 or more coins which had already been weighed in. Very likely, therefore, the figure they assigned was an estimate, and, it appears, an overestimate.

If, however, for want of better evidence one accepts the figure of £9.6 million for coin retrieved by the Mint, then the inventory of silver coin immediately after the Recoinage, say on 31 December 1698, must have fallen to the following total:

	£ million
Hammered, full weight	1.6
Milled, made before 1696	3.7
Milled, made during 1696–98 inclusive	6.8
Total	£12.1

This again is an upper limit insofar as it makes no allowance for export of milled coins.

GOLD COIN

In order to estimate its value, Horsefield: (1) takes Newton's estimate for 1688 as his base, (2) adds to it the output of guineas for 1689 to 1698, (3) first, however, reducing the annual output by one-quarter—because Newton estimated that each year one-eighth of the guineas produced, 'being above the average weight, were culled out and melted down, and one-eighth exported'—and (4) values the stock of guineas according to the price of guineas as quoted by Houghton. (Pp. 259–60, 14.)

Now the calculations themselves appear to contain two errors. According to the Mint records as published by Craig (which, except for 1694, Horsefield seems to accept), guineas to the value of £417,562 were minted in 1689–1693 inclusive; and as the Mint valued them at 21s., this is equivalent to about 398,000 guineas; whereas Horsefield (259) gives 382,000. Furthermore in his calculation for 1694, 57,000 guineas have mistakenly been treated as 570,000, and consequently all the subsequent figures for the number of guineas (Table G, 260) are erroneous.

Unfortunately, however, Newton's estimates, considered as a group, do not themselves inspire perfect confidence. He estimated that the stock of gold coin in 1688 was worth £6 million, and in 1701, £9,250,000. (Craig, 193.) Now if one supposes that his estimates were for 1 January 1688, and 31 December 1701 (were one to assume that the 1701 estimate is as of January or June, the estimates could not possibly be consistent with each other and with the data on Mint issues), then guineas worth £3.45 million were coined in the interval. If Newton had started with his estimate for 1688 and assumed that one-quarter of each year's issue was lost, then his 1701 estimate would have been £8.59 million; or, if the loss rate were one-eighth, £9.02 million. As it is, he gave £9.25 million; which implies that the loss was about one-fiftieth of each year's issue. It follows, therefore, that Newton's estimates have either been incorrectly reported, or one or both of them are mistaken, or that the *average* loss by export was not one-eighth of the year's production over the whole period 1688 to 1701.

The fourth element in Horsefield's calculation, the series of prices for guineas as given by Houghton, is also very dubious, in view of evidence which Horsefield gives elsewhere. By a set of Acts passed during the first half of 1696, the official value of the guinea was reduced to 28s., then 26s., and finally 22s. But there is reason to believe that this official rate was honoured about as strictly as other such rates have been; indeed Horsefield says that 'the law was widely evaded' (pp. 81–82). Houghton's figures for 1696–98, which give a constant price of 22s., probably estimate Parliament's wish better than the public's behaviour.

An alternative series for the value of gold coin is given below. It corrects Horsefield's errors; assumes, for want of reliable estimates, that on the average no native gold coin was lost by export or gained by re-import, and uses, also for want of better, Houghton's series on prices of guineas.

MONEY STOCK, 1694–1698

The arguments above establish the total dimensions of the stock of silver and gold coins; in the table on p. 267 these

STOCK OF GOLD COIN

	No. of coins (millions)	Value of Guineas (in shillings)	Total Value (£ millions)
Dec. 31, 1688			
(Newton's estimate)	5.58		
Coined 1689–93	.40		
Dec. 31, 1693	5.98	22	6.58
June 1694	6.01	22	6.61
Dec. 1694	6.04	22.6d.	6.80
June 1695	6.40	29.6d.	9.44
Dec. 1695	6.75	29.6d.	9.96
June 1696	6.82	22	7.50
Dec. 1696	6.89	22	7.58
June 1697	6.95	22	7.65
Dec. 1697	7.01	22	7.71
June 1698	7.25	22	7.98
Dec. 1698	7.48	22	8.23

stocks are divided among hoard and circulation, the division being conjectural, as are shifts in and out of hoard. The other data given, on foreign gold coin, bank notes, and bankers' vault cash are adapted from Horsefield (pp. 14, 258 ff.). The only one that requires comment is foreign gold coin, where I have supposed, contrary to Horsefield, that the entire amount of £1.5 million stayed in circulation throughout these years. Given the shortage of currency, there is no overwhelming reason why it should have been exported before 1699; foreign coins were not unknown, and as they were gold they may very likely have been preferred to bank notes and possibly even to native silver.

Assuming that hoards were large and that full-weight coins were preferred for hoarding, I have allocated to hoards as of 31 December 1694, the sums of £3 million for full-weight or approximately full-weight hammered silver coin, £3.7 million for milled silver coin (which was presumably not clipped), and £0.8 million for gold coin, that being the amount of old hammered gold coin supposed still to be in existence (Craig, 193). The old gold coins would have been

MONEY STOCK, 1694–1698
(£ million, Dec. 31)

	1694	1695	1696	1697	1698
Silver Coin					
In hoards					
Hammered, full weight	3.0	1.6	1.6	1.6	1.6
Milled, struck before 1696	3.7	3.7		1.0	1.0
Milled, struck after 1696				1.0	1.0
Total, in hoards	6.7	5.3	1.6	3.6	3.6
In circulation					
Hammered, light weight	7.2	7.2			
Hammered, full weight		1.4			
Milled, struck before 1696			3.7	2.7	2.7
Milled, struck after 1696			3.1	4.9	5.8
Counterfeit	1.0	1.0			
Total, in circulation	8.2	9.6	6.8	7.6	8.5
Total stock of silver coin	14.9	14.9	8.4	11.2	12.1
Gold coin, English					
In hoard	.8	4.0	2.0	3.0	3.5
In circulation	6.0	6.0	5.6	4.7	4.7
Total	6.8	10.0	7.6	7.7	8.2
Gold coin, foreign, in circulation		1.5	1.5	1.5	1.5
Bank notes, in circulation	3.6	4.0	3.6	4.1	4.3
Summary					
Total stock of money	25.3	30.4	21.1	24.5	26.1
In hoard	7.5	9.3	3.6	6.6	7.1
In circulation	17.8	21.1	17.5	17.9	19.0
Less bankers' vault cash	.9	.8	.4	1.0	1.1
Net in circulation	16.9	20.3	17.1	16.9	18.0

peculiarly apt to be hoarded, since by this time they were almost all a century old or older (from 1600 to 1663, when guineas superseded them, less than £50,000 worth were produced; Craig, 415), were of different weights and fineness from the prevailing guineas and could have circulated only with the greatest inconvenience.

During 1695, because of the flight from hammered silver, all but the best of that which was hoarded must have come into circulation; since £1.6 million appears to have stayed in hoard (see above), £1.4 million must have emerged. The holders of hoards would, of course, be inclined to conserve the value of their holdings, if they could, though the sharp inflation of 1695 might have moved them to replace some of the money hoards with hoards of imperishable goods. However, because at the same time guineas also rose sharply in price, anyone who held guineas might consider the accretion of value as a windfall gain, and I have therefore assumed that guineas equivalent in value, at the new price, to the profit on guineas were transferred to hoard. The result, in other words, of the greatly increased stock of money during 1695—its total value rose during the year from £25.3 to £30.4 million, or by over 20 per cent—was to increase both the amounts in hoard and in circulation.

Once the recoinage began in 1696, the stock of money fell sharply, and the need for circulating media would have forced money out of hoards. Evidence as to how much came out is suggested by Houghton's price series, which show that while prices fell during 1696, they did not fall below the 1694 level, remaining if anything a bit higher. I conclude therefore that all of the milled silver and £2.0 million of guineas were dehoarded, thus providing a total of money in circulation slightly higher than in 1694. Some confirmation that the old milled silver had been in hoard and now entered into circulation is afforded by a comment of the contemporary, William Stout, who wrote that these emerged from hoards in 1696, 'and for some years after this there was as much of that money in all payments, as of the old money new coined'. (Quoted by Prof Ashton, in his review of Horsefield, *Econ. Hist. Rev.*, XIII, 119 ff.)

During 1697 and 1698, as the Mint continued to issue guineas and new milled silver coin, the hoarders acted so as to re-establish their hoards. I have assumed—it is a perfectly bald assumption—that increments to hoards were equally divided during 1697 between old milled silver, new milled silver, and guineas; but that during 1698 only £500,000 was added to hoards, because by this time they had been rebuilt almost to the level of 1694.

PRICES, 1694–1698

These changes in the supply of money in circulation correspond reasonably well to the price series constructed by Horsefield from Houghton's data (7, 252). They account for the sharp increase in prices from June 1695 to April 1696, an increase of about 18 per cent; money in circulation increased, according to the table on p. 267, by about 20 per cent from December 1694 to December 1695. They account for the milder decline in prices from the peak in April 1696 to the low in February 1697, a decline of 13 per cent; money in circulation fell during 1696 by about 16 per cent. They account also for the slight decline in prices from 1696 to 1697 and for the sharper increase during the succeeding year, years for which the Phelps Brown-Hopkins index numbers are 1696, 697; 1697, 693; 1698, 767. Phelps Brown and Hopkins, 'Seven Centuries of the Prices of Consumables', XXIII (N.S.) Economica, 313 (1956).

The estimates I have given for money in circulation correspond rather better to the price series used by Horsefield than do his own estimates of the money supply (p. 18, Table 3), although he adjusts his by estimates of changes in the velocity of circulation and in the volume of substitutes for money.

It seems to me entirely plausible to argue, as Horsefield does, that both velocity and the volume of substitutes rose during 1696, when the total stock of money was suddenly cut by about one-third. It does not seem so plausible that velocity fell between June 1694 and June 1695 because 'of the reluctance with which clipped coins were accepted' (p. 14). This reluctance, to the extent it existed, need not have affected velocity of circulation; if it meant that some of the clipped coin was acceptable only by weight, then the effect should rather be construed as a fall in the quantity of money, the size of the fall being equivalent to the difference between the face value and the bullion content of these coins that had ceased to be treated as money.

On the whole, therefore, velocity should be expected to have been at an unusually high level from June 1695, when the flight from hammered silver began, until after the Recoinage was well under way, say December 1696. The volume of money substitutes, largely in the form of extended credit terms for commercial accounts and private debts, must have been—as Horsefield argues—at a high level during 1696, when the stock of money was at its lowest. But Horsefield's estimates of changes in the quantities of money, even when they are taken with these changes in velocity and in quantities of substitutes, still do not account for the observed price changes during the first half of 1695 or at any time during 1696 to 1698 inclusive.

Appendix IV

THE AUTHORSHIP OF SIR DUDLEY
NORTH'S *DISCOURSES UPON TRADE*

SIR DUDLEY NORTH's *Discourses upon Trade*, published in 1691, have been lauded as the first great exposition of free-trade doctrines. Economists have extolled Sir Dudley for his profound understanding and precise logic, and have acclaimed him a great, if not the greatest, predecessor of Adam Smith. The tradition which assigns him such a high place, like many other traditions of interpretation, combines with its accumulated insight into the subject a highly developed body of myth.

The earliest printed study of Sir Dudley North is Roger North's biography. This work appeared in London as part of a group published in two quarto volumes: the first, *The Life of the Rt Hon Francis North, Baron Guilford*, in 1742, and the second, *Lives of the Hon Sir Dudley North . . . and the Hon and Rev Dr John North*, in 1744. Its author as well as its subjects were sons of Dudley, fourth Baron North, a Cavalier country gentleman, whose small claims to historical prominence rest on a few devotional and technical pamphlets, and on the eminence of his family.[1]

---

[1] The founder of that family was a Tudor courtier, created first Baron North by Queen Mary. His elder son followed the father's profession in the court of Elizabeth; the younger son, Sir Thomas, translated Plutarch, thus founding the family's literary pretensions. The second Baron was succeeded by a grandson, whose brother, Captain Roger North (1580–1652), was a colleague of Sir Walter Raleigh, and described by Aubrey (*Brief Lives*) as a great explorer and a 'most accomplished Gentleman'. Dudley, third Baron North, was a courtier to James I, who at the accession of Charles I retreated to the country to nurse his fortunes and practise a life of culture and refinement. He lived to crotchety old age, and surrendered the peerage only when his son was already sixty-six. This elderly son, the fourth

Of this distinguished family, the sons of the fourth Baron were undoubtedly the most eminent generation. The eldest son, Charles (1630–1690), is an historical nonentity. He lived a retired life, and because of the distance he maintained between himself and his biographer brother, Roger, little at all is known of him. The next brother in age was Francis (1637–1685), who was trained for the bar in the Middle Temple. Making himself useful to Attorney General Palmer and the King, he rapidly rose in his profession. He became Solicitor General in 1671, Attorney General soon afterwards, by 1675 was Lord Chief Justice of the Common Pleas, and in 1682, at the age of forty-five, was appointed Lord Keeper of the Great Seal, the highest law office in the realm. Although completely devoted to the Court, and consequently castigated by Macaulay as a prime mover in the Tory reaction, he was a brilliant and honest judge.

The next brother was Sir Dudley (1641–1691), the economist.

John North, his immediate junior (1645–1683), was the scholar of the family, collector of an especially fine Greek library, and brilliant critic and linguist. He entered Jesus College, Cambridge, in 1661, and became a fellow in 1666; by 1677 he was Professor of Greek and Master of Trinity.

The author of the *Lives*, Roger North (1653–1734), was not the least remarkable of these brothers. A lawyer, he was always overshadowed by Francis, but he was considered sufficiently capable to be King's Counsel and Queen's Attorney General. His greatest merits, however, appeared in his private life. Here he was the model of a devoted brother. Before a late marriage, he had shared quarters with each of his brothers in turn, and had benefited from each in some considerable way. He repaid those favours when, having long outlived all of them and left to manage the affairs of all the widows and orphans of the family, he bore, as he said, 'burdens to oppress porters'. He was as much concerned with his

---

Baron, was the father of the subjects of the *Lives*. The family distinction which those brothers magnified, was further enlarged by their descendants, William, Lord North and Gray, one of Marlborough's generals, and by Frederick North, second Earl of Guilford (1732–1792), George III's Prime Minister.

brothers' reputations as with their responsibilities. He answered the political attacks made on them by composing the *Examen*, a laborious justification of their political careers. Feeling that this was not enough, he also wrote the *Lives*, with the express purpose of rescuing 'the memories of these distinguished persons . . . and for that end, bring their names and characters above-board, that all people may judge of them as they shall appear to deserve.'[2] Roger North was in the best sense of that age a cultivated gentleman: sincerely pious, conservative, honest, kind, and active. He wrote voluminously, but published during his lifetime only one small treatise on fishing. There have since been edited from his manuscripts valuable books on music, accounting, the study of law, and the English Constitution. There remains in unpublished manuscript form a long series of essays on philosophical and scientific subjects.[3] It seems probable that but for this reticence a man of his character and accomplishments would not have remained so obscure and unrecognized.

The *Lives* are first-rate literary biographies. The author coupled with pride in his brothers an informed sympathy for their careers, based on his own experience. In addition, he was an accomplished stylist. As a result of his aims and abilities, the *Lives* are not mere compilations of appearance, act, and event; Roger North was anxious to show the probity, independence, and individual intellectual outlook of each brother. He consequently gives a full exposition of the subjects' ideas. In the course of discussing Dudley's political career, Roger mentions his views on trade and the pressing problem of the faulty coinage then current in England. He writes that Dudley published these views in 1691 in a pamphlet, titled 'Discourses upon Trade; Principally directed to the Cases of the Interest, Coynage, Clipping, Increase of Money'. He recalls that this pamphlet appeared some years before the coinage was finally reformed in 1696, and points out that the reform carried through was inferior to that which Dudley North suggested. He then adds:

2 *Lives*, I, xiv.
3 Cf. n. 30, p. 285.

And whether any use of his pamphlet was made or not,
. . . it is certain the pamphlet is, and hath been ever
since, utterly sunk, and a copy not to be had for money.
And if it was designedly done, it was very prudent; for
the proceeding is so much reflected on there for the
worse, and a better showed, though not so favourable
to abuses, as doth not consist with that honour and
eclat, as hath been held forth upon the occasion.[4]

Even if the pamphlet had been sunk, Dudley North's
views on trade and coinage were available in Roger North's
précis as early as 1744. No eighteenth century economist,
however, noticed them. Only in the early years of the nineteenth century, when economics had begun to be a recognizable discipline with its own pretensions and gospel, did
economists display any interest in the history of economic
theory. Only then was Dudley recognized.

His importance was first impressed on economists by
James Mill. In an article on 'Economists',[5] which first appeared in 1818, Mill diverted his attention from the Physio-
crats to mention 'some few minds in England, which, at a
comparatively early period, had attained to wonderfully correct notions on the principles of commerce'. Among them,
the most remarkable was Dudley North. Mill proceeds to
quote in full two long extracts from Roger North's *Lives*
which summarize Dudley's economic views. He also quotes
Roger's suspicions concerning the disappearance of the pamphlet and adds: 'The complete extinction of this pamphlet
is but too probable; for though the writer of this article has
made search for it in every possible way, for several years,
he has never seen it, nor met with an individual who had.'
Interest in Dudley as an economist was at this time still
slight, for although Mill himself had searched for the *Discourses,* he evidently felt that few others would even have
read North's *Lives,* or have noticed the passages which he
quoted.

Once refurbished, Dudley's reputation among economists

---

[4] *Lives*, III, 173.
[5] *Supplement to the Fourth, Fifth, and Sixth Editions of the
Encyclopædia Britannica* (1824), III, 709–10.

grew. In 1824 McCulloch published a work which treated earlier economic doctrines not merely as errors to be condemned or as truths to be affirmed, but as successive stages in the development of economic knowledge. This book, which was thus the first intentional history of economic thought, is the *Discourse on the Rise, Progress, Peculiar Objects, and Importance of Political Economy*. McCulloch re-used much of the material of this essay, only slightly revised, first in the *Principles of Political Economy* (1825), then in the 'Introductory Discourse' to his edition of Adam Smith's *Wealth of Nations* (1828), and again in the *Literature of Political Economy* (1845). In each work he reiterates his judgment that North's *Discourses* contain 'a far more able statement of the true principles of commerce than any that had then appeared. He is throughout the intelligent and consistent advocate of commercial freedom. . . . His system is consentaneous in its parts, and complete.'[6]

McCulloch's persistent efforts to establish Dudley's significance were very much aided by the discovery of the pamphlet, which McCulloch describes in these words:

Unluckily this admirable tract did not obtain any considerable circulation. Indeed it would appear from the statements in the very interesting *Life* of the author . . . that it had been designedly suppressed; and it was for a lengthened period supposed to be entirely lost. Fortunately, however, this supposition has turned out to be incorrect. A copy of the tract, which had found its way into the library of the late Rev Rogers Ruding . . . was purchased at the sale of his books by a gentleman of Edinburgh, who printed a few copies for distribution among his friends. We have since stumbled upon two copies of the original edition.[7]

The reprint to which McCulloch refers is that of 1822, of which it is said that eighty copies were issued.[8] Another reprint was published in 1846; McCulloch himself reprinted

[6] *Principles of Political Economy* (1830, 2nd ed.), 42.
[7] *The Literature of Political Economy* (1845), 43.
[8] Dr Lippert, 'North, Dudley (Sir)' in Conrad, *et al., Handwörterbuch der Staatswissenschaften* (1893), V, 37–39.

the *Discourses* in 1856; and J. H. Hollander edited the latest reprint in 1907.[9]

North's reputation was established by McCulloch. About North's stature as an early economist there has since been little debate; about the meaning of his *Discourses* there has been only a reasonable amount of disagreement; but about the historical facts concerning North and the *Discourses* there is a remarkable accumulation of misinterpretation and error.

There were in Dudley's life very few dates that are likely to interest economists: perhaps those of his birth, death, return to England, and certainly that of the publication of the *Discourses*. About the first three of these there can be little doubt. Roger North gives the birthday as 16 May 1641;[10] and the date of death as 31 December 1691.[11] There is clear evidence that Dudley returned to England in June or July 1680.[12] The date of publication of the *Discourses* is a more complex question, which will be considered later; it is sufficient to note here that the original edition bears the imprint '1691', and this date is confirmed by Roger North.[13] Even about these dates, however, the historical literature shows great confusion.[14]

[9] McCulloch's reprint is in *Select Collection of Early English Tracts on Commerce;* Hollander's in his *Tracts,* Baltimore.

[10] *Lives,* II, 289.

[11] *Ibid.,* III, 231; this is confirmed by a letter written that day. Add. MSS., 32,500 f. 139, and by that day's entry in Luttrell's *Diary.*

[12] Add. MSS. 32,500, f. 37 is a letter from his mother, dated 25 July 1680, speaking of his arrival at Tostock, as does f. 38. *Lives,* III, 97 indicates that he spent some time in London before going to Tostock. He probably landed in England in early July.

[13] *Lives,* III, 169.

[14] Dr Lippert (*op. cit.*) gives incorrect dates about both birth and death; with more precision than accuracy he states the former as 16 March 1644, and the latter as March 1691. A. Jessop in the *Dictionary of National Biography* ('Sir Dudley North'), has these dates right but makes Sir Dudley return to England in Autumn, rather than Summer, 1680. Raffel, in his study on *Englische Frei-händler vor Adam Smith* (*Zeitsch. Gesamte Staatsw.,* Tubingen, 1905), 46, repeats this error. Beer, *Early British Economics* (1938), 209, is in error about the date of the *Discourses;* he writes they were published in '1690, about a year before his death', and for no apparent reason attributes the 1822 reprint to McCulloch. According to the

These errors, though trivial, are indicative of more serious mistakes concerning the *Discourses* themselves. One of the most serious concerns the suppression of the pamphlet. The tradition about the disappearance of the *Discourses* starts with the statement, given above, by Roger North. The statement is ambiguous; Roger merely says that *if* the *Discourses* were suppressed, it was for a good reason. This view of the matter, Mill did nothing to change; he merely quoted North on suppression and remarked that he had not been able to find a copy of the pamphlet. McCulloch, on the other hand, added an ominous note: he found 'good reason . . . for supposing, that it was designedly suppressed'.[15] But it was left to Roscher, in 1851, to give the tradition an entirely new life. Sir Dudley, he wrote,

> may have believed that a Revolution, which used 'Freedom and Property' as its shibboleth, would have given the doctrine of free trade a very favourable reception. He was, however, badly mistaken. In England this very revolution contributed to the highest development of the system of protection and prohibition, which was applied equally to foreign nations and the British colonies. What a shock for North! A man of his character must have regretted bitterly having taken so much trouble to publicise such unpalatable truths. This situation suggests a fairly simple explanation of the enigmatic disappearance of his work for over a hundred years.[16]

According to Roscher, North must have suppressed his own pamphlet. But Roscher did not explicitly insist on suppression—he only insinuated an 'enigmatic disappearance'. Roscher's innuendo was made explicit by Lippert:

> Supposing that the economic consequences of the Revolution would be a victory of the principle of free trade,

---

D.N.B., the *Discourses* were published 'only a few months before his death', a statement for which no evidence is stated or obvious. Also the D.N.B. speaks of Sir Dudley's two sons, whereas the letter referred to in n. 12 above makes it clear that he had three sons.

[15] *Principles*, 44–45.

[16] *Zur Geschichte der Englischen Volkswirtschaftslehre* (1851), 86–87.

he published his treatise in 1691; but he was obliged only too soon to yield to the conviction that the result of the Revolution would rather be the extremest intensification of protectionist measures. This turn of affairs induced him, out of regard to his social well-being . . . to get rid of this pointed evidence of his free-trade opinions by buying up and destroying the whole edition.[17]

At this stage, Sir W. J. Ashley made an attempt to deflate the myth. Criticizing Lippert's version, he insisted that Roger North simply meant that the Government had suppressed the *Discourses*. But Ashley's effort[18] was evidently not sufficient to curb the force of the myth, to judge by Heckscher's assertion, as recently as 1935, that the *Discourses* 'remained entirely unknown, and it is not even certain that it was ever published'.[19]

This whole critical tradition sprang from one fact and one statement. The fact was that until 1822 no copy of the *Discourses* was known to exist. But this should not have been thought strange. Many seventeenth century publications, never believed to have been suppressed, are today still 'utterly sunk'. In any case, there must by now be at least a dozen copies of the original edition of the *Discourses* in various libraries and private collections. In fact, the *Discourses* do not appear to be any more rare than many contemporary publications. The only other evidence is Roger North's statement. It is fortunate that the origin of that statement is almost as easy to trace as the genesis of the tradition to which it gives rise.

Roger North first wrote a life of Dudley in 1709. These 'Memorialls of the Liffe and actions of Sir Dudley North Kt.' were never published, but exist in manuscript in the

[17] Lippert, *op. cit.*, quoted by Ashley: 'The Tory Origin of Free Trade Policy', reprinted in his *Surveys Historic and Economic* (1900), 294. Ashley believed that Lippert took this suggestion from McCulloch, but the closeness with which Lippert follows even the organization of Roscher's account seems to demonstrate conclusively where he took his lead.

[18] *Surveys*, 296.

[19] *Mercantilism*, II, 322.

British Museum. The manuscript shows signs of at least two revisions. Roger North, who was a careful and patient worker, at some later date prepared a completely new manuscript, also available in the British Museum, from which the printed version was apparently taken. This second draft likewise shows signs of considerable revision, and a clean copy was probably made for the printer by Roger's son and literary executor.[20] The various stages in Roger North's composition of the suppression story can be traced through the two manuscripts, but the last version in the first draft is the most revealing. Roger criticises the proponents of the recoinage of 1696, and continues:

> And one circumstance almost persuaded me that the early promoters of that great work were at first enlightened and instructed by that pamphlet, which is that the impression hath been sunk. For at the time of the law passing I made inquiries after it and could not then or ever since hear of one. . . . I cannot say they were all bought up, with design to appropriate the notions, . . . as plagiarizers use to do, who arrogate to themselves the inventions of others without any recognition at all. Nor [can I say] that the thoughts were so inspired and not really and originally their own. But I may venture to say that either the one or the other might have been the case, and that it is most proper to conclude it was so, because the pamphlet appeared in public some time before the money-menders had anything to do with the public, and then disappeared.[21]

Whether this is a true or plausible picture, it is clearly not the same one implied by the version in the printed *Lives*. North dressed and re-dressed the incident, and finally settled on an account that made no mention of plagiarism, and only hinted at suppression. His evidence on this point seems far from trustworthy, and the constructions that have since been built on his insinuation accordingly lack adequate foundation.

[20] The 1709 draft is Add. MSS. 32,512; the later one, which is complete, is 32,513.

[21] Add. MSS. 32,512, f. 124.

With appropriate caution about the credibility of Roger North and the credulity of later historians, the evidence and the critical tradition bearing on the authorship of the *Discourses* may now be examined. The *Discourses* were published, their title page tells us, for 'Tho. Basset, at the George in Fleet-Street. London. 1691.' No author's name is shown on the title page or elsewhere. Since the original edition of the *Discourses* was published anonymously, the only explicit evidence bearing on their authorship is Roger North's statement in the *Lives* that Dudley 'put his sense in the form of a pamphlet, and, sitting the convention (or some time after it was turned into a parliament) in 1691, published it, printed for T. Basset, and entitled "Discourses upon Trade" . . .'[22] There is no reason to doubt Roger's assertion. There are, however, grounds for doubting that Dudley wrote the Preface to the *Discourses*.

This doubt arises, in the first place, from the opening lines of the Preface:

> These Papers came directed to me, in order, as I suppose, to be made Publick: And having transmitted them to the Press . . . I am absolved of that Trust.
>
> The Author is pleas'd to conceal himself; which after perusal of his papers, I do not ascribe to any Diffidence of his Reasons, the Disgusts of Great Men, nor overmuch Modesty, which are the ordinary Inducements for lying hid; but rather to avoid the Fatigue of digesting, and polishing his Sentiments into such accurate Method, and clean style, as the World commonly expects from Authors. . . .

The author of the Preface maintains throughout the distinction between himself and the author of the *Discourses*, his 'unknown confidant'. But that distinction has been either overlooked or denied by historians. McCulloch did not mention the question of authorship, although he quoted the economic maxims stated in the Preface as if Sir Dudley had written them. Although Roscher saw the problem, he gave a strange explanation. North, he said, hoped to in-

22 III, 169.

gratiate himself with the Whig Government by writing a
free-trade polemic. But frightened by the novelty of his own
views, North 'took the precaution to pretend that his book
had been written by a friend, and that he had only published it'.[23]

Roscher's theory leaves several questions unanswered:
How could North have pretended to publish the book, when
his name was nowhere present? If North was trying to in-
gratiate himself, why hide his name? Or, if he was hiding
his name, why pretend to have written the Preface? Roscher's thesis creates more difficulties than it explains.

Other historians of economic theory have followed Mc-
Culloch in treating the content of the Preface as though
Dudley were its author. Only Schumpeter explicitly con-
sidered the authorship of the Preface:

> The remarkable preface, though presented as the work
> of someone other than North, is of a style unmistakably
> similar to that of the text. It includes a familiar opposi-
> tion, in terms of the new scientific method, between
> realistic, scientific economic theory, and the 'ordinary
> and vulgar conceits being meer husk and rubbish'. And
> the whole train of ideas of both Discourses . . . hon-
> ours this methodological principle.[24]

Schumpeter rejects the explicit ascription of the Preface to
some unknown preface writer. He infers from the similarity
of style between them, and the adherence of the text to the
methodological prescriptions of the Preface, that the Preface
is a joke by Dudley, in which the already anonymous author masquerades as another anonymous character, the preface writer. The Discourses are then a monument to a passion for anonymity.

Those historians who have given the fourteen economic
maxims of the Preface as a summary of North's argument,
must either have accepted an argument like Schumpeter's,
or believed that even if the Preface writer was not Dudley,
the fourteen points are a fair summary of the conclusions

[23] Roscher, op. cit., 86.
[24] Schumpeter, 'Epochen der Dogmen- und Methodengeschichte',
Grundriss der Sozialökonomik (1924); I, 31. (My translation.)

of the text. In fact they are not; Preface and text disagree on important points.[25] If the ideas of the Preface are not Dudley's, then the history of economic theory must record two economists, the author of the Preface, and the author of the text. It is therefore pertinent to examine the two bases on which Schumpeter resolved the question for himself. The first of these is what Schumpeter described as an unmistakable similarity in style between preface and text.

The author of the Preface explains in a polished, sonorous paragraph, quoted above, that the author of the text did not desire to digest and polish 'his Sentiments into such accurate Method, and clean style, as the World commonly expects from Authors'. He continues that the author's anonymity saves him from being taken for 'either a careless or illiterate Person'. In fact, he spends the first third of the Preface defending the style of the *Discourses*. We are left to conclude that he had no high opinion of it.

An independent judgment of Dudley's style may be based on a sample such as the first lines of the first discourse:

Arguments for Abatement of Interest are many, viz.
  I. When Interest is less, Trade is incourag'd, and the Merchant can be a Gainer; whereas, when it is great, the Usurer, or Money-owner takes all.
  II. The Dutch, with whom Interest is low, Trade cheaper, and under-sell us.
  III. Land falls in value, as Interest riseth.
With divers others, whereof the Facts may be true, but proceed from another Cause, and conduce nothing to the purpose for which they are alledg'd.

This and similar passages bear out the Preface writer's contention that the text lacks precision and polish. The writing does have a certain force and breathlessness, but its pace is irregular. The *Lives* show other examples of Dudley's writing, all with similar characteristics: dryness of style, lack of grace, and complete absence of literary allusion. Thus a letter opens:

[25] See the table, p. 293.

We departed from the town by the ship's boats, which
had then lain a full week at the castles, where all the
day was spent in feasting and taking leave of our
friends. Towards night we all set sail; but, the wind being fresh out of the sea, by our short tacks to get out,
we made but little or no advantage. So we came to an
anchor again at night, and lay all next day, which was
Sunday. Our Smyrna friends had left us the day before;
so we went and dined aboard the Massingbird, and,
after dinner, walked on shore to the hot waters, some
two miles, or better, from the castle. It was a pleasant
walk, being all even, or else an undiscernible ascent.[26]

In fact all the writings of Dudley bear an unmistakable resemblance to each other, but none of them resembles the
rich, flowing, allusive style of the Preface. A further example will illuminate the contrast. Still defending the style of
the *Discourses,* the Preface writer remarks:

I grant also, that delicacy of Words, now most used in
Poetry, is useful for disposing way-ward People to
learn, or make them endure to read. But the World is
not at such low ebb of Curiosity in this age. Men are
forward enough to run their Noses into Books, especially such as deal in Faction and Controversie: And
it were well if they were either Wrote or Read with as
much Integrity as Industry; we have no need of Sugar-
plum devices to wheedle Men into Reading . . .[27]

On the grounds of style alone, the theory that the Preface
was written by Dudley seems to fail. The theory that Dudley was masquerading cannot explain away the difference
in style; no joke would make him suddenly capable of writing as he had never written before. For that matter, if he
could have written the Preface, why did he not write the
discourses in the style of the Preface, and so save himself
the long apology? Is it likely that Dudley, who was not over-

[26] *Lives,* III, 78.
[27] *Discourses Upon Trade; Principally Directed to the Cases of the
Interest, Coynage, Clipping, Increase of Money,* London: Tho. Basset, at the George in Fleet Street, 1691. Preface [iii]. (All citations
to the *Discourses* are according to the pagination of the original edition, which is preserved in the reprints of 1822 and 1846.)

educated and had never previously shown signs of wide reading, could suddenly quote Horace, Tully, and the other authors mentioned in the Preface? One can only conclude that Dudley could not and did not write the Preface.

Schumpeter's second ground for maintaining that Dudley wrote the Preface is that the text follows the methodological prescriptions of the Preface. Although this is true, it does not imply what Schumpeter suggests. The simple interpretation of the Preface is that it was written after the discourses themselves: 'These papers came directed to me. . . .' If we accept that Dudley did not write the Preface, then it must have been written after the discourses. This being so, the 'methodological prescriptions' of the Preface are not prescriptions. They are merely a description of the methodology used in the discourses, a description written by a man who was looking at the completed text and interpreting its logical pattern. The agreement between Preface and text about methodology, therefore, does not prove the single authorship, but only shows that the Preface writer correctly understood and described the methodology used by Dudley.

If then Dudley did not write the Preface, what theory about the *Discourses* is correct? To find the true author of the Preface we must return to the *Lives*. The history of Dudley's production of the discourses is there recounted as follows. Dudley was greatly offended, writes Roger, by 'the currency of clipped money'. He 'was resolved, that, if ever he sat in another session of parliament, he would bid battle' to the idea that the value of coin is determined by its face rather than by its metallic content. 'And, being full of the subject,'

> he eased his mind by laying down his reasons upon paper; and the fancy took him to do it in the form of a speech in the House of Commons. . . . But the parliament, in which he served, was dissolved; and he came no more within that pale. But afterwards, finding that the grievance of clipped money became insupportable, and with design that, since he could not, some other persons might push for a regulation . . . and to incite them to it, he put his sense in the form of a pamphlet,

and sitting the convention (or some time after it was turned into a parliament) in 1691, published it . . .[28]

Roger North's account is supported by evidence contained in the manuscripts which family pride, legal training, and interest in history prompted him to collect. He was so ardent a collector that he even violated his brother John's intention to destroy all his papers.[29] All Roger North's booty is collected in over fifty large volumes of manuscripts written by him and his brothers.[30] Among them is part of a draft of the 'speech' referred to, and in both drafts of his life of Dudley, Roger had originally included its full text. The separate draft is endorsed, 'A proposal intended to be made in parliament in order to regulate the coin, Jn, 1683'.[31] In the first draft of the life, Roger North refers to the speech as 'A representation intended to be laid before the parliament in the year 1683 concerning the bad condition of the money current in England, and the means to remedy it.'[32] Dudley may have written the speech in 1683, but he could not have presented it in Parliament that year, as none was in session between March 1681 and May 1685. Besides, Sir Dudley was first elected to Parliament in 1685.[33] But although the date is questionable, the manuscript version of the speech is certainly what North refers to in the printed Lives, and its content accords with his description. The speech is written in Dudley's style, and deals both with clipped money specifically and with the underlying theory of money. It differs from the text of the Discourses not in what it proposes, but in what it overlooks. It is nothing more than a well-argued proposal for reforming the coinage.

Continuing Roger's narrative, we find that Dudley, after failing to deliver his address, 'put his sense in the form of a pamphlet', which he published at a curious date: 'sitting the convention', that is, after January 1689; 'or some time after it was turned into a parliament', that is, between 1689 and

28 Lives, III, 168–69.
29 Lives, III, 343.
30 Add. MSS. 32,500 to 32,551.
31 Add. MSS. 32,522, f. 26.
32 Add. MSS. 32,512, f. 117b.
33 Lives, III, 159.

early 1690;[34] 'in 1691'. Before considering this question of dating it is interesting to examine the manuscript version of the *Discourses*, preserved with the North papers.[35] This is a final draft, which is, except for typesetters' errors, identical with the printed text. It is in Roger North's handwriting throughout, except for a dozen words in the second discourse which are in Dudley's handwriting.

The presence of Roger's handwriting on a final draft of the *Discourses* raises the question of his connection with the work. Was he simply employed as a secretary or copyist, is this manuscript only a copy he made for his own files, or did he have some more creative role in the writing of the *Discourses*?

The answer is suggested by some passages in the early drafts of the *Lives* which Roger suppressed in the printed text. First, in the early draft, after discussing the speech on coinage, Roger remarks:

> These were his first profers, but he went further, and composed a sort of tract upon the subject, which the writer of these papers digested, and a little touched the style (for he thought he had not one just enough for the public).[36]

This 'sort of tract', of which Roger 'a little touched the style' was the *Discourses*. Again, in the second draft of the *Lives*, Roger mentions the *Discourses*, then adds, 'The style was a little touched by me, but the whole sense, and chiefly the penning, were his own.'[37] These passages were excised and the *Lives* as printed do not mention Roger's connection with the *Discourses*.

In view of Roger's capability for harmless error and invention, it may be well to consider what other evidence there is of his participation in the *Discourses*. First, the state of the manuscript *Discourses* is revealing. In the Preface Roger made many bold changes. In the first discourse he

[34] The Convention Parliament was dissolved early in 1690.
[35] Add. MSS. 32,522, ff. 1–16.
[36] Add. MSS. 32,512, f. 123. 'To digest' was 'To put into good order'.
[37] Add. MSS. 32,513, f. 112.

added two paragraphs, but changed little else. The second discourse is most revised of all. Its margins are dotted with over a dozen 'q's' in Roger's hand, and only in this section does Dudley's distinctive handwriting appear. This suggests that unlike the other sections of the manuscript, here Roger had an opportunity to consult with Dudley about the text. He entered 'q' in the margin opposite any point about which he had a query, and Dudley made a few of the necessary amendments in his own hand.

Consideration of this manuscript suggests a hypothesis which explains why Dudley marked only part of the draft, why the *Discourses* happens to have a Preface at all, and who wrote it. The hypothesis is that Dudley dictated a draft of the two discourses and the postscript to Roger, that Roger then took it away for editing, returning with certain queries about the second discourse, which he discussed with Sir Dudley. At about this time the draft was shown to Basset, the printer, who announced it for publication in November 1691.[38] For some reason Roger and Sir Dudley were unable to meet again to discuss the rest of the draft before Sir Dudley's unexpected death on 31 December 1691. Roger then hastily revised the first discourse and the postscript, and wrote the Preface to defend the style of the text, to honour the trust which Dudley had left him, and to provide a badly needed introduction. The *Discourses* were then published before 25 March 1692.

Both internal and external evidence support this hypothesis. That Dudley dictated the draft to Roger is hinted at in the Preface, where in extenuating the style of the text, Roger wrote: 'Nor do I perceive that the Gentleman intended more than his Title holds forth; common Discourses, which possibly were taken by an *Amanuensis*, and dispatch't without much Correction.' Taken with the fact that the manuscript is written in Roger's hand, this appears at least quite likely. The idea is further supported by a suggestion elsewhere, that Dudley preferred to think on his feet.[39]

That Roger then took the draft away for polishing is a

[38] It is listed in the *Term Catalogue* for that date. See E. Arber, *The Term Catalogues*, 1668–1709 (1903–1906), II, 385.

[39] *Lives*, III, 168–69.

conjecture supported by his statement that he 'touched the style', and by the presence of the query marks in the margin. Why Roger and Dudley broke off their joint correction of the manuscript is not altogether clear. But Roger records that in 1691 he and Dudley parted late in September, that Dudley did not return to London until October or November, by which time his wife, already aware of his illness, reported that 'he had no heart or spirit to mind things . . .' On returning to town he caught cold, and remained constantly ill until his death.[40] It is certainly possible that Dudley was never well enough after autumn 1691 to undertake the revision.

Although the *Discourses* were advertised in the *Term Catalogue* for November 1691, and the *Discourses* bear the imprint '1691', they could have been printed as late as 25 March 1692. Stranger anachronisms have resulted from the confusion of Old and New calendars. In 1691, England was still going by the Julian calendar, according to which each new year was numbered from March 25th. 1 January 1691 was then the day *after* Dudley's death on 31 December 1691, and the year 1691 continued until March 25th. A book published after Dudley's death might just as well bear the imprint 1691 as, for instance, Roger's letter, dated 7 January 1691, which discusses Dudley's funeral.[41] Nor does the advertisement of the *Discourses* in November 1691 create any difficulty. More than one book was advertised in the *Term Catalogue* before its printer had so much as seen a final draft of it, and books advertised in November sometimes did not appear until the next year.[42]

The concluding proposition of the hypothesis about the authorship of the *Discourses* is that Roger wrote the Preface. Considerable support for this thesis is yielded by the Preface itself. First, it contains literary allusions, which the text does not. Whereas Dudley had little formal education, Roger had much. He entered Jesus College in October 1667,[43] in his

[40] *Lives,* III, 228–29.
[41] Add. MSS. 32,500, f. 141.
[42] Arber: *op. cit.,* I, xi, sect. 27.
[43] *The Autobiography of the Hon. Roger North* (ed. Jessopp, 1887), 14, fn.

fourteenth year, as was then common. He was under the tutorship and lived in the rooms of his brother, John, the Greek Professor, who kept him hard at work. At Cambridge, Roger became a devotee of the 'natural philosophy, which they call physics, and particularly Descartes'. Although Cartesian Philosophy was railed at and even forbidden, 'there was a general inclination, especially of the brisk part of the University, to use him, which made me conclude there was somewhat extraordinary in him, which I was resolved to find out, and at length did so . . .'[44] Roger maintained his admiration as late as 1706 when he wrote of Descartes' 'felicity in lucid expression, and his hints . . . clearer than the glosses of others'.[45]

In the Preface to the *Discourses*, we find the author expressing a similar interest in and admiration for Descartes. He commends 'Des Carte's excellent dissertation *de Methodo*'. He continues: 'Knowledge in great measure is become Mechanical; which word I need not interpret farther, than by noting, it here means, built upon clear and evident Truths.'[46] This is an interesting observation: its first clause seems to follow more than casually the words of the first English translation of Fontenelle, the popularizer of Descartes, 'Philosophy is now become very Mechanical';[47] the concluding phrase, 'clear and evident truths', was the Cartesian battle-cry. The Preface commends the author for his use of a method introduced by 'the new philosophy'; 'the Philosophy of Descartes, or the New Philosophy' is the way a contemporary puts it.[48] The explicit Cartesianism of the Preface conforms to Roger North's training and life-long interest in the new philosophy. [49]

Again, there is no Latin in the *Discourses*. The Preface, on the other hand, cites Horace and alludes to Cicero.[50]

[44] *Ibid.*, 15.
[45] *Ibid.*, 255.
[46] *Discourses*, Preface [vi].
[47] Fontenelle, *Plurality of Worlds* (1688).
[48] *Discourses*, Preface [v]. Roth, *Descartes' Discourses on Method*, 2, quoting *Voyage du Monde de M. Descartes*, Father Daniel, Eng. transl. 1692.
[49] *Autobiography*, Chap. VI, and Add. MSS. cited.
[50] *Discourses*, Preface [ii].

Although there is no evidence that Roger was a great Latinist, he had studied the language and was obviously competent in it.[51] The Preface writer on several occasions employs legal metaphors: the public 'stamps judgment and execution' on authors, and a more extended comparison is based on the language of 'the lawyers in their Deeds'. These are the verbal tricks of a lawyer—Roger. In addition, the Preface writer refers to Montaigne, and to the *Scalligerana, Pirroana,* the *Pensees* of Pascal, and Selden's *Table Talk*.[52] All these allusions are very much in character with Roger. The Preface writer uses the Latin phrase, *'ejusdem farinae',* a somewhat pompous substitute for 'more of the same thing'.[53] This quite uncommon phrase recurs only once in all the literature surrounding the Norths—and that is in Roger's autobiography.[54]

Other even closer parallels exist between the Preface and the *Autobiography*. On the question of literary style, Roger wrote the following lines in his *Autobiography*:

[Business men] keep to the business and nothing else. And that is the substantial part which outweighs all other embellishments . . .

On the other side, that which is with some a felicity, as loving to write or to speak orderly, with many proves a failing, and of a ridiculous kind that is empty wordiness. A readiness of words wheedles one to an excess of complaisance to it, and to neglect the material part, which many look first after, for we think the jargon, when apt and clever, serves the turn, whereas the other extreme, want or difficulty of words, makes men attend the matter, and strive by quintessence of that to supply their defect of clever expression.[55]

This passage could hardly resemble more closely the Preface writer's rendition of the same ideas:

[51] *Autobiography,* 17.
[52] Preface [iv].
[53] *Ibid.* [viii].
[54] *Autobiography,* 195.
[55] *Ibid.,* 197–98.

The Merchants in their policies and exchanges use no
one word but what is necessary to their point . . . because the Matter and Substance only is intended and
not the dress . . .

Words are indeed a felicity, which some have in great
perfection; but many times, like a fair face, prove Temptations to Vice; for I have known very good Sence neglected, and post-poned to an Elegance of Expression;
whereas if Words are wanted, the whole effort is made
by pure strength of Reason, and that only is relied on.[56]

Similarly, other comments by Roger on Dudley's style,
such as that he had 'a faculty of expressing himself, without show of art, or formality of words',[57] and that his pen
like his discourse was

quaint and clear . . . for he sought to be understood,
and to avoid superfluity; and never formally composed
any thing, with pretence of exactness of style, or nice-
ness of method.[58]

are similar to many judgments in the Preface, such as, for
example:

As for the Method used in these papers, there is so
little of it affected, that I am afraid some will say there
is none at all. . . . What could the formal Methodist
add?[59]

There can remain little doubt that the Preface was
written by Roger North, and that the circumstances of its
composition are accurately explained by the hypothesis set
out above. But if Roger wrote the Preface, who really developed those ideas which, though contained in the fourteen
economic maxims of the Preface, do not occur in the text?
To answer this question, we must review the relationship
between Roger and Dudley.

When Dudley left England he had just reached maturity,

[56] Preface [ii].
[57] Lives, I, 351.
[58] Add. MSS. 32,512, f. 124b.
[59] Preface [iii–iv].

while Roger was a schoolboy of nine. They probably hardly knew each other. But when Dudley returned to England eighteen years later, he and Roger were long-term guests together in Guilford's house. Roger records that they then 'grew into close alliance and friendship, which continued untainted to his death',[60] and that he 'had the conversation and friendship of . . . brother Dudley'.[61] Much of their conversation revolved around Dudley's ideas on trade, and Roger, a commercial lawyer and public official, must have been an interested and intelligent listener. In the *Life* of Dudley, Roger reports many of these conversations, and the reports bear a certain resemblance to some of the maxims in the Preface and some of the notions expressed in the discourses.[62]

This may only mean that Roger refreshed his memory, while writing his *Life* of Dudley, by reading the manuscript of Dudley's discourses. But this does not explain the origin of those of the maxims that do not correspond to the text.

It may be concluded that Roger took many of his own economic ideas from conversation with Dudley. When he came to write the Preface to Dudley's discourses, he included some ideas which he knew to be Dudley's, even though they did not appear in the text. But he included some which apparently did not derive from Dudley. This is borne out by some inconsistencies in the text of the *Discourses*. The last paragraph of the second discourse, and the last paragraph of the postscript are set off typographically, stylistically, and logically from the preceding matter. They look as though they should be, but they are not, summaries of the preceding arguments. And it is these paragraphs which form the major grounds for hailing Dudley as a great free-trader. They read as follows:

> So to conclude, when these reasons, which have been hastily and confusedly set down, are duly considered, I doubt not but we shall joyn in one uniform Sentiment: That Laws to hamper Trade, whether Forreign, or

---

[60] *Autobiography*, 189.
[61] *Ibid.*, 194.
[62] See table opposite.

Maxims	Text	Lives
1. World unified as to Trade	P. 14, para. ii	I, 352
2. Any loss of trade affects whole world	None	Ibid.
3. No trade is unprofitable to public because no private trader will continue an unprofitable trade ..	None	Ibid.
4. No trade regulation can benefit the public	Not present in same context	None
5. Trade cannot be regulated, or if it can then only in a destructive way	15, ii; etc.	None
6. Money is a merchandise; of which there may be a surplus as well as a deficit ..	13, ii Contradicted by Postscript	III, 168 None
7. There is always just enough money	Postscript, etc.	I, 352–3 III, 168
8. 'No man shall be richer for the making much Money . . . but as he buys it for an equivalent price' ..	?	?
9. Free coinage benefits a few at the cost of the many ..	18, v; etc.	III, 167
10. Debasing the coin is a fraud	Postscript (4), iii	III, 168
11. Debasing by fineness or weight are the same ..	Postscript (4), iii	None
12. Exchange and cash are the same except for the cost of carriage	17, iv	None
13. Money exported in trade increases wealth of nation; money spent in war, and in payments abroad, decreases it	13, ii 22, iii; Ps (5), iii None	None None None

	Maxims	*Text*	*Lives*
14.	'All favour to one Trade or Interest . . . is an abuse, and Cuts so much of Profit from the Publick'	None	None

Domestick, relating to Money, or other Merchandizes, are not Ingredients to make a People Rich, and abounding in Money, and Stock. But if Peace be procured, easie Justice maintained, the Navigation not clogg'd, the Industrious encouraged . . . the Stock of the Nation will increase . . .

Thus we may labour to hedge in the Cuckow, but in vain; for no people ever yet grew rich by Policies: but It is Peace, Industry, and Freedom that brings Trade and Wealth, and nothing else.[63]

The paragraphs agree on the commercial importance of Peace. The thirteenth maxim of the Preface similarly maintains: 'That money . . . spent in war . . . is so much impoverishment.' This noble sentiment appears nowhere else in the text with the exception of the two paragraphs quoted. It is probable that Roger was entirely responsible for this idea, which he inserted into the maxim and the concluding paragraphs.

The sentiments expressed in the two paragraphs and in those maxims not organically related to the text go beyond mere war-weariness; they outline a credo of free-trade. Even if Dudley North did not write these passages, he remains an important economic theorist. But since Roger very probably did write them, it is he more than Dudley who should be listed among the early free-traders.[64] Roger North, who worked to rescue his brother's memory, ought now to have the same office performed for him.

[63] *Discourses*, 22–23, and 'Postscript' [v].
[64] If the revision takes place, it would be well to verify the attribution of *A Discourse of the Poor*, 1753, published posthumously under Roger North's name, but based very largely on Sir Dudley's ideas, set forth in a manuscript to have been published as a sequel to the *Discourses* (Add. MSS., 32,512, ff. 124b–130b).

Appendix V

LOCKE'S EARLY MANUSCRIPT
ON INTEREST

(In 1668, Locke wrote out his views on interest, in his own hand. This manuscript, or part of it, was copied by someone else, the copy being sent to Coventry; it is now in BM Add. MSS. 32,094, f. 289 et seq. From 1668 to 1674 Locke corrected and added to the manuscript, whereupon the revised text was copied, partly by Brownover, Locke's secretary; this copy is Bod. Lib., MS. Locke e.8. Later on, when Locke came to compose Some Considerations, *he incorporated sheets of his original version with, of course, later changes; these are now collected in the final draft manuscript of* Some Considerations, *Bod. Lib., MS. Locke d.2, where the sheets from 1668 are, e.g. ff. 28–37.*

The transcript that follows is of the intermediate version, MS. Locke e.8. I have modernized some of the spelling and introduced punctuation, of which the manuscript is almost totally devoid.)

[ ] Square brackets indicate page numbers of original work.

[3]

*Some of the Consequences that are like to follow upon
Lessening of Interest to 4 Percent:*

It will be gain to the merchant: for if he borrow at 4 percent and his returns be 12 percent, he will have 8 percent and the usurer 4, whereas they divide it now equally at 6 percent. But this neither gets nor loses to the kingdom in the trade, supposing the merchant and usurer to be both Englishmen.

It will be a loss to the monied man 1/3 of his estate: it will be a loss to the yearly income of lands, annuities, etc. [3b] For £100 per annum will be 1/3 less worth—unless the merchant making more profit by low interest will sell his consumable commodities at 2 percent cheaper than he doth now—which is not likely as long as the consumption of England is as great, and the buyers as many as are now— which must be an effect of the good husbandry and not low use. It will be a loss to the value of land in its purchase. For whatsoever land shall be sold for under 30 years purchase will be so much loss to the seller. And 30 years purchase is not like to be given in a country where money is already scarce (and where if upon lessening of interest foreigners call home their money it is like to be scarcer) and there are more sellers than buyers. That land is at 30 years purchase in Holland, is not (I suppose) [4] from the lowness of their interest, but from their plenty of people and money in proportion to their land, which makes money cheap, and land dear. But by all this the kingdom neither gets nor loses.

It will hinder trade. For there being a certain proportion of money necessary for driving such a proportion of trade, so much of this money as lies still lessens so much of the trade. Now 'tis to be expected that where the venture is great and the gain small (as is lending in England upon low interest) many will choose rather to hoard up their money than venture it abroad on such terms. And this will be a loss to the kingdom. But all this is upon supposition that borrower and usurer be both Englishmen. [4b] If the usurer be a foreigner, by lessening interest from 6 to 4, you get to the kingdom 1/3 of the interest you pay yearly. But then upon lessening it, it's like one of these things will happen: that either you fall the price of your native commodities or lessen your trade—or else prevent not the high use as you intended. For at the time you make a law for reducing interest to 4 percent, you want money or you do not. If you do not, there's no need of preventing borrowing of your neighbours at a high rate. For there can be no money borrowed but in order to trade, for what is not employed in trade lies still, and nobody borrows for that. If you do want money, that want will still force you to borrow of your neighbours and at the rate your necessity, not your laws, shall set. Or else if there be scarcity of money, it must hinder the [5] merchants' buying and the labourers' manufactury. Now the kingdom gets or loses by this (for no question the merchant by low interest gets all the while) only proportionally (allowing the consumption of foreign commodities to be still the same) as the paying the use to foreigners carries away more or less of our money than want of money and stopping our trade keeps us from bringing in by hindering our gains—which can only be estimated by those who know how much money we borrow of foreigners and at what rate, and also what profit in trade we make of that money.

Though perhaps it will be found true upon examination that our growing rich or poor depends not at all upon our borrowing upon interest, or not, of our neighbours, but only which is greater or less, our importation or exportation of consumable commodities. [5b] For supposing two millions of money will drive the trade of England, and we have money enough of our own to do it. If we consume of our own product and manufacture, and that which we purchase by it of foreign commodities, one million, but of the other million consume nothing, but make a return of 10 percent per annum, we must then every year be £100,000 richer, and our stock so much increased. But if we import more than we export, our money must go out to pay for it and we grow poorer. Suppose therefore ill husbandry hath brought us to one million stock, and we borrow the other million (as we must or lose half our trade) at 6 percent. If we consume but one moiety, and make still 10 percent per annum of the other million, the kingdom gets £40,000 though it pay £60,000 per annum use. So that if the merchant's returns be more than his use, [6] (which 'twill certainly be or else he will not trade) and all that is so traded for in borrowed money be but the over-balance of our exportation to our importation, the kingdom gets by this borrowing so much as the merchant's gain is above his use. But if we borrow only [?] for our own expenses, we grow doubly poor, by paying money for the commodity we consume, and use for that money—though the merchant get all the while by making returns greater than his use. And therefore borrowing of foreigners in itself makes not the kingdom rich or poor (for it may do either), but spending more than our fruits or manufactures will pay for brings in poverty, and poverty borrowing.

For money, as necessary to trade, may be doubly considered: 1. As in his hands that pays the labourer and landholder (for there its motion terminates, and through [6b] whose hands soever it passes, between these he is but a broker) and if this man want money (as for example the clothier) the manufactury is not made, and so the trade stops and is lost. 2. As in the merchant's hands who buys the commodity when made, and if he want money, the value of the commodity when made is lessened and so the kingdom loses in the price. For I believe in England 'tis the English merchant makes the price.

If therefore use be lessened and you cannot tie foreigners to your terms, then the ill effects fall only on your own landholders and artisans. If foreigners can be forced by your law to lend you money only at your own rate or not lend at all, is it not more likely they will rather take it home and think it safer in their own country at 4 percent than abroad? [7] Nor can their over-plus of money bring them to lend it you on your terms, for when your merchant's want of money shall have sunk the price of your market, a Dutchman will find it more gain to buy your commodities himself, than lend his money at 4 percent to an English merchant to trade with. Nor will the Act of Navigation hinder their coming by making them come empty, since even already many that go for English merchants are but Dutch factors, and trade for others in their own names.

But that a law cannot keep your own subjects, much less strangers, from taking more use than you set (the want of money being that alone which regulates its price) will perhaps appear if we consider how hard it is to set a price upon wine or silks or other unnecessary commodities, but how impossible it is to set a rate on victuals in a time of famine. [7b] For money being an universal commodity, and as necessary to trade as food is to life, everybody must have it at what rate they can get it, and unavoidably pay dear when it is scarce.

The bankers are (I suppose) a clear instance of this, for

the scarcity of money having made it in England worth
really more than 6 percent, most of those who have not the
skill to let it for more than 6 percent and secure themselves
from the penalty of the law, put it into the bankers' hands,
where it is ready at their call when they have an opportunity
of greater improvement. So that the rate you set profits not
the lenders and very few of the borrowers, who are fain to
pay the price for money that commodity would bear were it
left free, and the gain is only to the bankers. And should
you lessen the use to 4 percent, [8] the merchant or tradesman that borrows would not have it one jot cheaper than he
has now, but probably these two ill effects would follow:
(1) that he would pay dearer etc., (2) that there would
be less money left in the country to drive the trade. For the
bankers paying but 4 percent and receiving 10 or 12 percent, at that low rate would be content to have more money
lie dead by them than now, when it is higher. By which
means there would be less money stirring in trade, and a
greater scarcity, which would raise it upon the borrower by
this monopoly. For that the bankers have not more of the
money of England in their hands than they have is because
they refuse to borrow, and not others refuse to lend to them,
there being many now who lend to them at 5½ or 5 percent
who will not lend to [8b] others at 6 percent. It would
therefore perhaps bring down the rate of money to the borrower, and certainly distribute it better to the advantage of
trade in the country, if the legal use were raised pretty
near to the natural (by natural use I mean that rate of money
which the present scarcity of it makes it naturally at, upon
equal distribution of it) for then men being licenced by
the law to take near the full natural use will not be forward
to carry it to London to put it into the bankers' hands till
they have opportunity to do so, but will lend it to their
neighbours in the country, where it is convenient for trade
it should be. But if you lessen the rate of use, the lender
(whose interest it is to keep up the rate of money) will
rather lend it to the banker at the legal interest than the
tradesman, [9] who, when the law is broken shall be sure
to pay the full natural interest or more because of the engrossing by the banker, whereas were the natural use sup-

pose, 9 percent or 10 and the legal use 8, first the usurer would not venture the penalty of the law for the gaining 1/9 or 1/5, that being the utmost his money would yield. Nor secondly would the banker venture to borrow where his gains would be but 1 or 2 percent. Nor thirdly would the monied man lend the banker what he could make better profit of legally at home.

All the danger lies in this that if your being behindhand has made the natural use so high that your tradesman cannot live upon his labour, but that your rich neighbours will so undersell you that the return you make will not amount to pay the use and afford a livelihood, [9b] there is no way to recover from this but by a general frugality and industry, or being masters of the trade of some commodity which the world must have from you at your rate and cannot be otherwhere supplied.

I think the natural use of money is raised two ways: 1. When the money of a country is but little in proportion to the debts of the inhabitants one amongst another. For suppose £10,000 were sufficient to manage the trade of Bermudas, and that the planters carried over £20,000, which they lend up and down to the several tradesmen and inhabitants of the country, who living above their gains had spent £10,000 of this money, and it were gone out of the island. 'Tis evident that should all the creditors at once call in all their moneys there would be £10,000 wanting [10] which the stock of the country could not possibly pay, and so money would be very scarce, and interest high. But this seldom happening, that all or the greatest part of creditors do at once call for their money, unless it be in some great and general danger, is less and seldomer felt than the other which follows. 2. That which most sensibly raises the natural interest of money is when money is little in proportion to the trade of a country. For in trade everybody calls for money according as he wants it, and this disproportion is always felt. If Englishmen owed in all but one million, and there were a million of money in England, the money would be well enough proportionable to the debts, yet if two millions were necessary to carry on that trade there would be a million wanting, and the price of money would be raised—

[10b] as it is in any other commodity in a market where the merchandise will not serve half the customers and there are two buyers for one seller.

The necessity of a proportion of money to trade (I conceive) lies in this: that money in its circulation driving the several wheels of trade, whilst it keeps in that channel (for some of it will unavoidably be drained into standing pools) is all shared between the landholder whose lands afford the materials, the labourer who works them and the broker (i.e. merchant and shopkeeper) who distribute them to those that want them. Now money is necessary to these three sorts of men, as serving both for counters and for pledges, and so carrying with it even reckoning, and security that he that receives it shall have the same value for it again of other things that he wants whenever he pleases. [11] The one of these it doth by its stamp and denomination, the other by its intrinsic value, which is nothing else but its durableness, scarcity and not being apt to be counterfeited. Which intrinsic value though it be not natural but is only in the opinion of men consenting to it, yet being universal has generally but not always (for we see that in a siege silver may not be of equal value to gunpowder and in a famine gold may not be worth its weight in bran) the same effect as if it were natural.

The necessity therefore of a proportion of money to trade depends on money not as counters but on money as a pledge. For since the bill, bond, or note of debt I received from one man will not be accepted as security by another, he not knowing that the bill or bond is true [11b] and legal or that the man bound to me is honest or responsible, and so is not valuable enough to become a current pledge, nor can by public authority be well made so, as in the case of assigning of bills. First, because a law cannot give to bills that intrinsic value which universal consent has annexed to silver and gold. Indeed they may pass as valuable considerations within among your own subjects but will not be taken as any part of payment by a foreigner, did not the following reason hinder, which is that they are liable to unavoidable doubt, dispute, and counterfeiting, and require other proofs to assure us they are true and good security than our eyes or a touchstone. And at best this course, if practicable, will not hinder us from being poor, but may be suspected to help to make us so by keeping us from feeling our poverty—[12] which in distress will be sure to find us with greater disadvantage. Though it be certain that it is better than letting fall any part of our trade for want of current pledges and better too than borrowing of our neighbours upon use, if this way of assigning bills can be made so easy, safe, and universal within our territories as to hinder it.

Every man therefore (to return to the business in hand and show the necessity of a proportion of money to trade) must have at least so much money, or so timely recruits, as may in hand or in a short distance of time satisfy him who supplies him with the necessaries of his life or of his trade. For nobody hath any longer those supplies than he has money or credit (which is nothing else but an assurance of money in some short time). So that it is requisite to trade [12b] there should be so much money as will keep up the landholder's, labourer's and broker's credit. And therefore ready money must be constantly exchanged for wares and labour or follow within a short time after.

This shows the necessity of some proportion of money to trade, but what proportion that is is hard to determine, because it depends not barely on the quantity of money, but the quickness of its circulation—which since it cannot easily be traced (for the very same shilling may at one time pay 20 men in 20 days, at another rest in the same hands 100 days together), to make some probable guess, we are to consider how much money it is necessary to suppose must rest constantly in each man's hands as requisite to the carrying on of trade. First therefore the labourers, living [13] but from hand to mouth, and considered as labourers in order to trade, may well enough carry on their part if they have but money enough to buy victuals, clothes, and tools, all which may very well be provided without any great sum of money lying still in their hands. The labourers therefore being generally paid once a week (if the times of payment are seldomer they must have the more money lie by them) we may suppose there is usually amongst them, one with another, at

least one week's wages. For it cannot be thought that all or
most of the labourers pay away all their wages as soon as
they receive it, and live upon trust till next pay day. This
the farmer and tradesman could not well bear, were it every
labourer's case and everyone to be trusted; and therefore they
must of necessity keep some money in their hands to [13b]
go to the market for victuals and to other tradesmen as poor
as themselves for tools, and lay up money too to buy
clothes or pay for those they were trusted for, which money
thus necessary resting in their hands we cannot imagine to
be less one with another than one week's wages.

Secondly, as for the landholder, since his tenants cannot
create their rent just at Quarter day, but must gather it up
by degrees and lodge it with them till pay day (or borrow
it of those who have it lying by them, which yet the greater
part cannot do or do gather it up by degrees, which is the
same thing) and must be necessarily so much money lying
still for some time. For all that is paid in great sums must
somewhere be gathered up by retail incomes of a trade, or
else lie still too in great sums, which is the same stop of
money or a greater. Add to this that the tenant, to pay the
creditor who lent him his rent, must gather up the sum by
degrees as the sale of his commodities shall bring it [14]
in, and so by borrowing makes two stops for one and a
greater want of money—since the borrowed money that paid
the landlord the 25th March must be supposed to lie still
some time in the creditor's hand before he lent it to the
tenant, and the money that pays the creditor 3 months after
must lie still some time in the tenant's [hand]. Nor doth the
landlord pay away his rent usually as soon as he receives it
but by degrees as his occasions call for. We cannot therefore but suppose that between the landlord and tenant there
must necessarily be at least 1/4 of the yearly revenue of the
land constantly in their hands. Indeed considering that most
part of the rents of England being paid at our Lady day and
Mich., and that that same money which pays me my rent
from my tenant 25 March or thereabouts cannot pay my
next neighbour his rent from his tenant at the same time,
much less one more remote in another country, it might
seem requisite to suppose half the yearly revenue of the

land to be necessarily [14b] employed in paying of rent. For to say that some tenants break and pay not their rent at all, and others pay not till 2—3—4—5—6, etc. months after Quarter day, and so the rent is not all paid at one time, is no more than to say that there is money wanting to the trade.

For if the tenant fail his landlord, he must fail his creditor, and he his, and so on till somebody break, and so trade decay for want of money. But since a considerable part of the land of England is in the owner's hands, who neither receiveth nor pay great sums for it at a certain day, and because too (which is the chief reason) we are not to consider here how much money is in any one man's or any one sort of man's hands at any one time—for that at other times may be distributed into other hands and serve other parts of trade—but how much money is necessary to be in each man's hands all the year round, taking one time with another [15] (i.e. having £300 in his hands one month is to be reckoned at £100 in his hands 3 months and so proportionably), I think we may well suppose 1/4 of the yearly revenue to be constantly either in the landlord's or tenant's hands. Where, by the by, we may observe that it were better for trade, and consequently for everybody (for more money would be stirring and less would do the business) if rent were paid by shorter intervals than 6 months. For supposing I let a farm at £52 per annum, if my rent be paid half yearly there is required £26 to be employed in payment of it in one entire sum (if it be paid well, and if it be not paid well for want of so much money to be spared to that purpose, then is there so much want of money and trade is still endamaged by it) a great part whereof must necessarily lie still before it come out of my tenant's chest to my hands. [15b] If it be paid once a quarter £13 will do it and less money is laid up for it and stopped a less while in its course. But should it be paid every week one single 20s. will pay the rent of £52 per annum. Whence would follow this double benefit: first, that a great deal less money would serve for the trade of a country, and secondly that none of the money would lie still, the contrary whereof must needs

happen where growing debts are to be paid at large distances
and in great sums.

Thirdly, as for the brokers, since they too must lay up
money coming in by retail, either to go to market and buy
wares or to pay at the day appointed, which is often 6
months for those wares they have already, we cannot suppose them to have less by them one with another than 1/10
of their yearly returns. Whether the money be their own, or
they be indebted so much or more, [16] it matters not, if it
be necessary they should have constantly by them, comparing one time with another, at least 1/10 of their yearly return.

To which if you add what part of the money of a country
scholars of all sorts, women, gamesters, and great men's
menial servants, and all such that do not contribute at all to
trade, either as landholders, labourers, or brokers, will unavoidably have constantly in their hands, it cannot be
thought that less than 1/52 of the labourer's yearly wages,
1/4 of the landlord's yearly revenue, and 1/10 of the broker's
yearly returns in ready money will be enough to drive the
trade of any country. And how much the ready cash of any
country is short of this proportion, so much must the trade
be impaired and hindered for want of money.

But however these measures may be mistaken, this is evident: that the multiplying of brokers hinders the trade of
any country [16b] by making the circulation the money
goes larger, and in that circuit more stops, so that the returns
must necessarily be slower, scantier, to the prejudice of
trade, besides that they eat up too great a share of the gains
of trade, by that means starving the labourer and impover-
ishing the landholder, whose interest is chiefly to be taken
care of, it being a settled unmovable concernment in the
common wealth. And therefore it would be convenient to
hinder as much as is possible anyone from selling any of our
native commodities but he that makes it. Shopkeepers in this
being worse than gamesters, for they do not only keep so
much of the money of a country constantly in their hands,
but also make the public pay them for their keeping of it.
Though gaming too, upon the account of trade (as well as
for many other reasons), may well deserve to be restrained,

[17] since gamesters in order to play keep great sums of money by them, which there lie dead. For though gamesters' money shift masters oftener than any, and is tumbled up and down with every cast of the die, yet as to the public it lies perfectly still, and no more of it comes into trade than what they spend in eating or wearing.

Here too we may observe how much manufacture deserves to be encouraged, since that part of trade, though the most considerable, is driven with the least money, especially if the workmanship be more worth than the materials. For to so much of the [17b] trade that is driven by labour and handicraftsmen, 1/52 of the yearly money paid them will be sufficient, but to a trade of commodities of our bare native growth, a much greater proportion of money is required.

[18]

Supplement

Upon a review of the foregoing particulars, I guess the third consequence should be stated thus brief: That lessening of use will very much alter the value of men's estate in land, annuities, and money, in reference to one another (by annuities I mean any estate for years to which that of lives is reducible), but will not at all alter the value of the yearly income of those lands and annuities in reference to commodities purchasable by it. The reason whereof is this, that the rate of interest is the measure of the value of lands, annuities and money in proportion to one another. But the measure of the value of money in proportion to any commodity is the quantity of the ready money we have in comparison with the quantity of that commodity and its vent, which depends upon its necessity or usefulness. For whatsoever is absolutely necessary, men give any proportion of money for it, rather than go without it; and in such things the scarcity of them alone makes their price. As for example, one ounce of silver now in England is worth one bushel of wheat. But should there be the next year a great scarcity of wheat in England and a proportionable want of all [18b] other food, ten ounces of silver would perhaps in exchange purchase but one bushel of wheat, so that money would be then 9/10 less worth in respect of food, though at the same value it was before in respect of other things that kept their former proportion in their quantity and consumption. By the like proportions of increase and decrease does the value of things more or less convenient rise and fall in respect of money; only with this difference, that things absolutely necessary for life must be had at any rate, but things convenient will be had only as they stand in preference with other conveniencies. And therefore in any one of these commodities the value rises only as its quantity is less, and vent greater, which depends upon its being preferred to other things in its consumption. For supposing that at the same time that there is a great scarcity of wheat and other grain, there were a considerable plenty of beans. Men, no question, would give far more for wheat than beans, as being the healthier, pleasanter and more convenient food. But since beans would serve to supply that absolute necessity of sustaining life, men would not rob themselves of all other conveniencies of life by paying all their money for wheat, when beans that are cheaper (though with some inconvenience) would supply that defect. It may then so happen at the same time that one ounce of silver, that the year before would buy one bushel of wheat, will this year buy but 1/10 of a bushel; and one ounce of silver, that the year before would have bought four bushels of beans, will this year still buy one bushel; and at the same time one ounce of silver that would the year before have bought 30 lbs. of [19] lead will still buy the same quantity. So that at the same time silver in respect of wheat is 9/10 less worth than it was, in respect to beans 3/4 less worth, and in respect to lead as much worth as before.

The fall, therefore, or rise of interest—making neither more or less land, money, or commodity in England than there was before, immediately by its change, but only in a long train of consequences which are not instantly felt—alters not at all the value of money in reference to commodities, because the measure of that is only the quantity and vent which are not immediately changed by the change of interest but only as the change of interest may in trade conduce to the bringing in or carrying out money or commodity and so in time varying their proportion here in England from what it was before, which is not in this place to be considered. But yet the changing of use does immediately alter the value of lands, annuities and money in reference to one another, because the rate of use is the measure of the value of these, in their mutual exchange, as will appear by what follows.

For the better clearing of this, that the rate of use is the measure of the value of money, lands and annuities one to another, but is not the measure of the value of money to commodities, we may consider: 1. That the value of land consists in this, that by its constant production of saleable commodities it brings in a certain yearly income. 2. The value of commodities consists in this, that as portable and useful things, they by their exchange or consumption supply the necessaries or conveniencies of life. 3. In money there is a double value answering to both of these. First as [19b] it is capable by its interest to yield us such an yearly income —and in this it has the nature of land, the income of one being called rent, the other use; only with this difference, that the land in its soil being different, as some fertile, some barren, and the products of it very various both in their sorts and value too, according as their quantity and vent varies, but money being constantly the same, by its interest giving the same sort of product through the whole country, is capable of having a fixed rate yearly set upon it by the magistrate, but land is not. Second, money has a value as it is capable by exchange to procure us the necessaries or conveniencies of life. And in this it has the nature of a commodity—only with this difference, that it serves us commonly by its exchange, never almost by its consumption, but has not at all a more standing settled value in exchange for any other than any other commodity hath, but a more known one and better fitted by name, number and weight to enable us to reckon what the proportion of scarcity and vent of one commodity is to another. For supposing as before that one ounce of silver would last year exchange for one bushel of wheat, or for 30 lbs. weight of lead, if this year wheat be ten times scarcer, and lead in the same quantity to its vent as it was, is it not evident that one ounce of silver will still exchange for 30 lbs. of lead, though it will exchange but for one-tenth of a bushel of wheat, and he that has use of lead will as soon take 30 lbs. weight of lead as one ounce of silver for 1/10 of a bushel of wheat [20] and no more? So that if you say that money now is 9/10 less worth than it was the former year, you must say so of lead too and all other things that keep the same proportion to money they were in before. Only this variation is first observed in money because that is the measure by which people reckon for calling that ounce of silver 5s. They are understood better when they say 5s. will now buy but 1/10 of a bushel of wheat but do not say that 30 lbs. of lead will now buy but 1/10 of a bushel of wheat, because it is not generally used to this sort of reckoning; nor do they say lead is less worth than it was, though in respect of wheat, lead be 9/10 worse than it was, as well as silver. Only by the tale of shillings we are better enabled to judge of it.

This I suppose is the true value of money when it passes from one to another in buying and selling, where it runs the same changes of higher and lower as any other commodities doth, for an equal quantity whereof you shall receive more or less of another commodity at one time than you do at another in exchange. For a farmer that carries a bushel of wheat to market and a labourer that carries 5s. shall find that the money of one as well as corn of the other shall at some times purchase him more or less leather or salt according as they are in greater plenty or scarcity one to another. So that in exchange of coined silver for any other commodity, which is buying and selling, the same [20b] measure governs the proportion you receive as if you exchanged lead or wheat or any other commodity, which is nothing else but their quantity in proportion to their vent, which vent is the ready passing of any commodity in exchange for money or anything else. If then use makes not the silver more in specie or the wheat or other commodities less, it will not have any influence at all to make it exchange for less of wheat or any other commodity, than it will have on lead to make it exchange for less wheat or any other commodity.

Money therefore in buying and selling being perfectly in

the same condition with other commodities and subject to all the same laws of value, let us next see how it comes to be of the same nature with land by yielding a certain yearly income which we call use. For land produces naturally something new profitable and of value to mankind, but money is a barren thing and produces nothing, but by compact transfers that money that was the reward of one man's labour into another man's pocket. And this is the unequal distribution of it, which inequality has the same effect too upon land that it has upon money. For my having more money in my hand than I can, or am disposed to use in buying and selling makes me able to lend, and another's want of so much money as he could employ in trade makes him willing to borrow. But why then and for what consideration doth he pay use? For the same reason and upon as good consideration as the tenant pays rent for your land. For as the unequal distribution of land—you having more than you can or will manure, another less—brings you a tenant for your land, and the same unequal distribution of our money—I having more than I can or will [21] employ and another less—brings me a tenant for my money. So my money is apt in trade by the industry of the borrower to produce more than 6 percent to the borrower, as well as your land by the labour of your tenant is apt to produce more fruits than his rents come to, and therefore deserves to be paid for, as well as land, by an yearly rent. For though the usurer's money would bring in no yearly profit if he did not lend it (supposing he employ it not himself) and so his 6 percent may seem to be the fruit of another man's labour, yet he shares not near so much of the profit of another man's labour as he that lets land to a tenant. For without the tenant's industry (supposing as before the owner would not manage it himself) his land would yield him little or no profit, so that the rent he receives is a greater portion of the fruit of his tenant's labour than the use is at 6 percent. For generally he that borrows £1,000 at 6 percent, and so pays £60 per annum use, gets more above his use in one year by his industry than he that rents a farm of £60 per annum gets in two [years] above his rent, though his labour be harder. It being evident therefore that he that has skill in traffic but has not money too, enough to exercise it, has not only reason to borrow money to drive his trade and get a livelihood, but as much reason and more to pay use for that money than he that has not land of his own, yet has skill in husbandry, has not only reason to rent land, but to pay money for the use of it, since he that rents land pays more of the income and fruit of his labours to his landlord [21b] for the use of his ground than the tradesman doth to the usurer at 6 percent for the use of his money. From whence it is clear that borrowing money upon use is not only by the necessity of affairs and the constitution of human society unavoidable to some men, but that also to receive profit for the loan of money is as equitable and lawful as receiving rent for land and more tolerable to the borrower, notwithstanding the opinion of some overscrupulous men.

This being premised, it remains now to show how the rate of interest is the measure which regulates the value of land, annuities and money in proportion to one another. Money therefore being at 6 percent, if I have £2,000 in money, and another £100 per annum land, our estates are equal; and allowing 1/6 for the hazard of my lending my money (which the creditor may run away with better than the tenant can run away with the £100 per annum land), allowing too for more useless intervals that will happen to me necessarily in letting out my £2,000 in money than to the other in letting his £100 per annum land, they will to the world's end yield annually the same income, and will always pass as of equal value one to another in exchange. But if you lessen the use of money to 4 percent, my £2,000 presently loses 1/3 of its income and comes no nearer the value of the £100 per annum land in exchange than any other parcel of land would, that being once worth £100 per annum is, by the inundation of the sea or some other way, so impoverished as not to yield now above £66 13s. 4d. per annum, which is 1/3 less worth. So that land to money is after such a lessening of use 1/3 better than it was.

The case of annuities (by annuities I mean any yearly income determinable after a certain number of years, to which estates for lives are reducible), as [22] partaking partly of the nature of land and partly of the nature of money, by the decrease of interest to 4 percent, grows worse than land, but continues better than money; and that proportionally as the grant is for a greater or lesser number of years. For the longer the term is, the nearer it comes to the nature of land and its advantages, the shorter the term is the nearer it comes to the nature of money and partakes the more of its loss. Because after the determination of those years, it is supposed to resolve again into as much money as the money paid for the purchase would upon the same measure of improvement—viz. of 4 percent or 6 percent—then mount to.

To make this clear by an instance, it is necessary to premise that

At 6 percent:
Land is worth 20 years purchase.
Annuity for 25 years absolute is worth 13 years purchase.
Annuity for 10 years absolute is worth 7 years purchase.
At 4 percent:
Land is worth 30 years purchase.
25 years absolute is worth 16 years purchase.
10 years absolute is worth 8 years purchase.

Suppose then money being at 6 percent, N. leaves to his
Sons:
{
A. £100 per annum land
B. £153 per annum for 25 years
C. [£]285 per annum for 10 years
D. £2,000 in money
}
{
Each worth
£2,000 whose
use per annum
[is] £120.
}

Presently upon the change of use to 4 percent, they thus alter their value:

A's £100 per annum land is worth £3,000, whose use is per annum £120.

B's £153 per annum for 25 years is worth £2,448, whose use per annum is £98 [22b].

C's £285 per annum for 10 years is worth £2,280, whose use per annum is £91.

D's £2,000 in money produces for its use but £80 per annum.

So that B's annuity of 25 years is worse than land £22 per annum, is better upon money £18 per annum. And C's annuity of 10 years is worse than land £29 per annum, but better than money £11 per annum or thereabouts. For I have in the calculation of these only mentioned the pounds, and wholly left out fractions, the thing I was to prove requiring no such nicety.

There only remains now to be considered whether the £100 land rent or £285 annuity will buy as much corn, cloth, or lead after the fall of use as it would before. Which that it will I guess will appear if I do but here recapitulate what I imagine I have proved already, viz.: 1. That though money when let to use hath the nature of land, yet when it is exchanged for other commodities it has presently the nature of another commodity. 2. That in exchanging one commodity for another, if any one commodity, e.g. barley, purchases less of another commodity, e.g. timber, at one time than another, it is because your barley is more in quantity than it was, or the vent of it less, or your timber less than it was, or its vent more. For the value of every commodity, compared with itself or with a standing measure, is greater as its quantity is less in proportion to its vent. But in comparing it, or exchanging it with another consumable commodity, the rise and fall of the value of that too must be allowed for in computation of their values.

But since money, if not transported out of the kingdom, is not as most other commodities consumed in its [23] use, supposing we have the same quantity of money in England this year as we had the last, though the use be changed, we shall find some things dearer this year and some things cheaper. Not that the value of money is or can be lessened in respect of one and increased in respect of the other, but as a common standard it shows us that those things that are dearer are less this year in proportion to their vent than they were the last and those that are cheaper are more this year in proportion to their vent than they were the last, and so is but as it were the common measure whereby we are able to compare and discern the present but variable values of other things in reference to one another. The worth of things in their price is but the comparing the quantity and vent of one thing with the quantity and vent of any other which you exchange for it (which is very variable) by some common measure at that time; and money, whilst it is not more or less in the kingdom, remains that common measure.

But yet there is no manner of proportion between the value of an ounce of silver and any other commodity, for sometimes it will buy a bushel of wheat, sometimes half, sometimes but 1/4, 1/16, etc., and this it does equally, whether by use it be apt to bring in to the owner 6/100 of its own weight per annum or nothing at all, it being only the change of the quantity of wheat to its vent, supposing we have still the same sum of money in the kingdom. Or else a less or greater sum of money in the kingdom—supposing the quantity of wheat in respect to its vent to be the same—that makes the change in the price of wheat; for if you alter the quantity or vent on either side you [23b] presently alter the price, but no other way in the world.

For it is not the being, adding, increasing, or diminishing of any good quality in any commodity that makes its price greater or less, but only as it makes its quantity or vent greater or less in proportion one to another. This will easily appear by two or 3 instances.

1. The being of any good and useful quality in anything neither increaseth its price nor indeed makes it have any price at all, but only as it lessens its quantity or increases its vent, each of these in proportion to one another. For what more useful or necessary things are there to the being or well being of men than air and water, and yet these have generally no price at all, nor yield any money, because their quantity is immensely greater than their vent in most places in the world. But as soon as ever water (for air still offers itself everywhere without restraint or enclosure and therefore is nowhere of any value) comes anywhere to be reduced into any proportion to its consumption, it begins presently to have a price, and is sometimes sold dearer than wine. And hence it is that the best and most useful things are commonly the cheapest, because though their consumption be great yet their production is large and suitable to it.

2. Nor does the adding an excellency to any commodity raise its price, unless it increase its consumption. For sup-

pose there should be taught a way (which should be published to the knowledge of everyone) to make a medicine of wheat alone that should infallibly cure the stone, tis certain the discovery of this quality in that grain gave it an excellency very considerable, and yet this would [24] not increase the price of it one farthing in twenty bushels, because its quantity or vent would not be hereby altered.

3. Neither doth the increasing of any good quality in any species of commodity increase its price, nor the making really better make it more worth. For though teasels be much better this year than they were last, they are not one jot dearer unless they be fewer too, or the consumption of them greater.

4. Nor doth the lessening the good quality of any sort of commodity lessen its price, which is evident in hops, which are usually dearest those years they are worst. But if it happen to be a species of commodity whose defects may be supplied by some other, the making of it worse does lessen its price, because it hinders its vent. For if the barley should any year prove generally smutty or grown, no question it would yield less money than otherwise, because the deficiency of that grain might be in some measure made up by wheat, rye and oats. But if it be a sort of commodity whose use no other known thing can supply, tis not its being better or worse, but its quantity and vent is that alone which regulates and determines its value.

To apply this now to money and its use: Considering money (as it is in itself) as a commodity passing in exchange from one to another, all that is done by interest is but adding to money by agreement or public authority a quality which naturally it hath not, viz., a faculty of increasing every year 6 percent. Now if public authority sink use to 4 percent, tis certain it diminishes this good quality in money one third, but yet this [24b] making the money of England not one farthing more than it was, it alters not the measures upon which all changeable commodities increase or sink their price, and so makes not money exchange for less of any commodity than it would without this alteration of its interest. But rather if lessening use to 4 percent does at all alter the quantity of money it makes it less either by transportation into those countries where it will yield more profit or by hoarding [?] up because of the smallness of its use, both which ways the vent of money is increased and the quantity diminished. (The sum of money you have among you as well as the quantity of other commodities not being to be estimated in proportion to its price by the mass that does exist and is in being, but by the quantity that is current in trade and lies open to be purchased by him that has a mind to it.) And so the falling of use, though it makes money—as it has the nature of land—cheaper, it makes money—as it has the nature of a commodity—dearer, i.e. a less quantity of money will change for a greater quantity of another commodity than it would before.

This perhaps will appear a little plainer by these following particulars:

1. That the intrinsic natural worth of anything consists in this, that it is apt to be serviceable to the necessities or conveniences of human life, and it is naturally more worth as the necessity or conveniency it supplies is greater. But yet,

2. That there is no such intrinsic natural settled value in anything as to make any assigned quantity of it constantly worth any assigned quantity of another commodity.

3. The value of any assigned quantities of two or more commodities are *pro hic et nunc* equal when they will exchange one for another, as supposing one bushel of wheat, 2 bushels of barley, and one ounce of silver will now in the market be taken one for another, they are then of equal worth. And our coin being that which Englishmen reckon by, an Englishman would say that now one bushel of wheat or two bushels of barley or one ounce of silver were equally worth 5s.

4. The altering of this value in respect of one another or any one standing common measure is not the altering of any intrinsic value or quality [25] in the commodity (for musty and smutty corn will sell dearer at one time than the clean and sweet at another), but the alteration of some proportion the commodity bears to something else.

5. This proportion in all commodities, whereof money is one, is the proportion of their quantity to their vent, which

vent is nothing else but the passing of commodities from
one owner to another in exchange, and is then called
quicker when a greater quantity of any species of commodity is taken off from the owner of it in an equal space of
time.

6. This vent is regulated (i.e. made quicker or slower) as
greater or less quantities of any saleable commodities are removed out of the way and course of trade and separated
from public commerce and no longer lie within the reach of
exchange. For though any commodities should shift hands
never so fast and be exchanged from one man to another, yet
if they were not thereby exempted from trade and sale, and
did not cease to be any longer traffic, this would not at all
make or quicken their vent; but this seldom or never happening makes very little or no alteration. And this [removal
of goods from the market] is done three ways: 1. By consumption, when the commodity in its use is destroyed, as
meat and drink and clothes, and all that is so consumed is
quite gone out of the trade of the world. 2. Exportation,
and all that is [25b] so carried away is gone out of the
trade of England and concerns Englishmen no more in the
price of their things one among another than if it were out
of the world. 3. Buying and laying up for a man's private
use.

For what is by any of these ways shut out of the market
and no longer movable by the hand of commerce makes no
longer any part of merchantable ware, and so in respect of
trade and quantity of any commodity is not more considerable than if it were not in being. All these three terminating
at last in consumption of all commodities (excepting only
jewels and plate and some few others which wear out but
insensibly) may properly enough pass under that name. Engrossing too has some influence on the present vent, but this
enclosing some great quantities of any commodities (for if
the engrossing be of all the commodity and it be of general
use, the price is at the will of the engrosser) out of the free
course of trade only for sometime and afterwards returning
again to sale makes not usually so sensible and gradual an
alteration in the vent, as the others do, but yet influences
the price and the vent more according as it extends itself to a

larger portion of the commodity and hoards it up longer.

7. Most other portable commodities (excepting jewels and [26] plate) decaying quickly in their use, but money being less consumed or increased—i.e. by slower degrees removed from or brought into the free commerce of any country than other merchandise (for it wastes less and goes out of the world slower than food and raiment and most other things, is not apt to be hoarded up in any great disproportion more one year than another)—and as for exportation, though over balance of trade may call for it out, yet borrowing of your neighbours at interest often keeps it in—and so the proportion between its quantity and vent altering slower than in other commodities, it comes nearest a standing measure to judge of the value of all things else, especially being adapted to it by its weight and denomination in coinage.

8. Money, whilst the same quantity of it is passing up and down the kingdom in trade, is really a standing measure of the rising and falling value of other things, not altering its own value at all. But as soon as you increase or lessen its quantity in the traffic of any country, you instantly alter its value, and if at the same time wheat keep [26b] its proportion of vent to quantity, money—to speak truly—alters its worth and wheat does not, though it sell for a greater or less price, than it did before. For money being looked upon still as the standing measure of other commodities, though by altering its value it be unperceivedly changed from it, men consider and speak of it still as if it were a standing measure; but the value or price of all commodities, amongst which money passing in trade is truly one, consisting in proportion, you alter this as you do all other proportions whether you increase one or lessen the other.

9. In all other commodities the owners when they design them for traffic endeavour as much as they can to have them vented and consumed—i.e. removed out of the reach of commerce and exchange by consumption, exportation, or laying up—which vent is sometimes slower and sometimes quicker. But money never lying upon people's hands or wanting vent, for anyone may part with it in exchange when he pleases, the endeavour of the public and almost everybody is to keep it from venting and consuming—i.e. exportation or hoarding

up which is [27] its proper consumption. The vent of money therefore being always sufficient or more than enough, its quantity alone is enough to regulate and determine its value, without considering any proportion between its quantity and vent as in other commodities.

10. Therefore lessening of use, not bringing one penny of money more into trade or exchange of any country but rather drawing it away from trade and so making it less, does not at all sink its value and make it buy less of any commodity but rather more.

11. That which raises the natural interest of money is the same that raises the rent of land—i.e. its aptness to bring in yearly to him that manages it a greater overplus of income above its rent as a reward to his labour. That which causes this in land is the greater quantity of its product in proportion to the same vent of that particular fruit, or the same quantity of product in proportion to a greater vent of that single commodity, but that which causes increase of profit to the borrower of money is the less quantity of money in proportion to trade or [27b] to the vent of all commodities taken together.

12. The natural value of money, as it is apt to yield such an yearly income by interest, depends on the whole quantity of the then passing money of the kingdom in proportion to the whole trade of the kingdom, i.e. the general vent of all the commodities. But the natural value of money in exchanging for any one commodity is the proportion of all the money of the kingdom in proportion to that single commodity and its vent. For though any single man's necessity and want either of money or any species of commodities being known may make him pay dearer for money or that commodity, yet this is but a particular case and does not at the same time alter this constant and general rule.

Sic cogitavit

1668   JL

[28]

13. That supposing wheat a standing measure—i.e. that there is constantly the same quantity of it in proportion to

its vent—we shall find money to run the same variety of changes in its value as all other commodities do. Now that wheat in England doth come nearest to a standing measure is evident, by comparing wheat with money, other commodities and the yearly income of lands in Henry VIIth's time and now. For supposing [that in the year] 1 Henry VII, N. let 100 acres of land to A. for 6d. per annum per acre rack rent, and to B. another 100 acres—of the same soil and yearly worth with A.'s 100 acres—for one bushel of wheat per acre rack rent, a bushel of wheat at the time being probably sold for about 6d. or less, it was then an equal rent. If therefore the leases were for years yet to come, tis certain that he that paid 6d. per acre would now pay 50s. per annum [for the 100 acres] and he that paid a bushel of wheat per year would pay now about £25 per annum [for the 100 acres],[1] which would be nearabout the yearly value of that land were it to be let now. The reason whereof is this, that there being ten times as much silver now in the world (the discovery of the West Indies having made the plenty) as there was then, it is 9/10 [28b] less worth now than it was at that time, i.e. that it will exchange for 9/10 less of any commodity now which bears the same proportion to its vent as it did 200 years since, which of all other commodities wheat is likeliest to do—it being in England and this part of the world, the constant and most general food, not varying with the alteration of fashions, nor growing by chance, but as the farmers sow more or less of it, which they endeavour to proportion as near as they can guess to its consumption, subtracting the over plus of the precedent year in their provision for the next, and vice versa. It must needs fall out that it keeps the nearest proportion to its consumption (which is more studied and designed in this than other commodities) of anything, if you take it for ten or twenty years together. Though perhaps the plenty or scarcity of one year, caused by the accidents of the season, may very much vary it from the precedent or the following. Wheat therefore in this part of the world, and that grain which is the constant

---

[1] [Locke's calculation is that silver having declined in value to 10 per cent of its previous value, wheat will have risen from 6d. to 60d. a bushel, which, for a 100 acre farm, would come to £25.]

universal food of any other country, is the fittest measure by which to judge of the altered value of things in [29] any long tract of time. Whence by the by it may be considered whether wheat here and maize or the bread corn of the Indies, be not the fittest thing to reserve a rent in, which is designed to be constantly the same in all future ages. But money is the best measure of the altered value of things in a few years, because its vent is always the same, and its quantity alters slowly. But wheat or any other grain cannot serve instead of money, because of its bulkiness and too quick change of its quantity; for had I a bond to pay me 100 bushels of wheat next year, it might be 3/4 loss or gain to me, too great an inequality and uncertainty to be ventured in trade.

14. That supposing an island separate from the commerce of the rest of mankind, if gold and silver or whatever else material—so it be lasting—be their money, if they have but a certain quantity of it and can get no more, that will be a standing measure of the value of all other things.

15. That if in any country they use for money any lasting material whereof there is not any more to be got and so cannot be increased, or being of no other use the rest of the world doth not value it and so [29b] is not like to be diminished, this also would be a standing measure of the value of other commodities.

16. That in a country where they had such a standing measure, any quantity of that money (if it were but so much that everybody might have some) would serve to drive any proportion of trade, whether more or less, there being counters enough to reckon by, and the value of the pledges being still sufficient because constantly increasing with the plenty of the commodity and the quickness of trade. But these three precedent [i.e. 14, 15, 16] being but suppositions that are not like to be found in the practice of the world (since navigation and commerce have brought all parts acquainted with one another and with the use of gold and silver), they serve rather to give us some light into the nature of money than to teach here a new measure of traffic. Though it be certain that that part of the world which breed most of our gold and silver uses least of it in exchange, and had found out another sort of money.

17. That in a country that hath commerce with the rest of the world it is almost impossible now to have any coin but of gold and silver; and having money of that, it is impossible to have any [30] standing unalterable measure of the value of things. For whilst the mines supply to mankind more than wastes and consumes in use, the quantity of it will daily grow greater in respect of other commodities, and its value less.

18. That in a country open to the commerce of the world and that uses money made of the same materials with their neighbours, any quantity of that money will not serve to drive any quantity of trade, but that there must be a certain proportion between money and trade. The reason whereof is this, because to keep on your trade without loss, your commodities amongst you must keep equal [to] or at least near the price in money that the same species of commodities in other countries do, which they cannot do if your money be far less than in other countries. For then either your commodities must be sold very cheap or a great part of your trade must stand still, there not being money enough in the country to pay for them (in their shifting of hands), at that high price which the plenty and consequently the low value of money makes them to be sold for in other countries. For the value of money in general is the quantity [30b] of all the money of the world in proportion to all the trade of the world. But the value of money in any one country is the present quantity of money in that country in proportion to the present trade of that country. Supposing then that we had now in England but half as much money as we had seven years ago, and yet had still as much yearly product of commodities, as many hands to work them, and as many brokers to disperse them as before, and that the rest of the world had as much money as they had before (for tis likely they should have more by our moiety shared amongst them), tis certain that either half our rents should not be paid, half our commodities not vented, and half our labours not employed, and so half the trade be clearly lost, or else that every one of these must receive but half the money for their commodities and labour they did before, and but half so much as our neighbours do receive for the

same labour and same natural product at the same time. Which, though it will make no scarcity of our native commodities amongst us, yet it will have in use ill consequences: [31] 1. It will make our native commodities vent very cheap; 2. It will make all foreign commodities very dear; both which will continue and increase our poverty. For the merchant making silver and gold his measure—and considering what the foreign commodities cost him (i.e. how many ounces of fine silver) in the country where money is more plenty, i.e. cheaper, and considering too how many ounces of silver it will yield him in another country—will not part with it here but for the same quantity of silver, or as much as that quantity of silver will buy here of our commodities, which will be a great deal more than in other places. So that in all our exchange of native commodities for foreign, we shall pay almost double the value that any other country doth where money is in greater plenty. This indeed will make a dearness and in time a scarcity of foreign commodities, which is not the greatest inconveniency it brings upon us, supposing them absolutely [31b] necessary. But 3., it endangers the drawing away your subjects, both artisans and soldiers, who are apt to go where their pay is best, which will always be where there is greatest plenty of money, and in time of war must needs carry with it great danger and distress.

BIBLIOGRAPHY

Acts P. C. (Col.)	*Acts of the Privy Council (Colonial)*
Add. Mss.	Additional Manuscripts, British Museum
Andrews	Andrews, C. M. *British Committees, Commissions, and Councils of Trade* (1908)
	Aubrey, John. *Brief Lives* (1898)
Autobiography	See North, Roger
B.M.	British Museum
B.O.	See Child, Josiah
	Bacon, Francis. *Works* (ed. Spedding, Ellis, Heath; 1857–59)
Concerning Coining	Barbon, Nicholas. *A Discourse*
Coining	*Concerning Coining the New Money Lighter . . .* (1696)
Discourse	B[arbon], N[icholas], M.D. *A Discourse of Trade* (1690)
Bod. Lib.	Bodleian Library, Oxford
	Boyle, Robert. *Works* (1772)
Brett-James	Brett-James, N. G. *Growth of Stuart London* (1935)
Burnet	Burnet, Gilbert. *History of My Own Time* (Airy ed., 1897)
C.J.	*Journals of the House of Commons*

C.S.P. Col.   Calendar of State Papers Colonial

C.S.P.D.   Calendar of State Papers Domestic

C. Treas. Bks.   Calendar of Treasury Books
Cannan   See Smith, Adam. Wealth of Nations
B.O.   Child, Josiah. Brief Observations (1668)
N.D.T.   Child, Josiah. New Discourse of Trade (1693; 1698 ed.)
                           Clark, G. N. Science and Social Welfare in the Age of Newton (1949 ed.)
                           Coke, Roger. England's Improvements . . . Treatise III (1675). [For 'Treatises I and II', see Coke, A Treatise . . . (1671; Kress 1287)]
Coining   See Barbon, Nicholas
Plea   Collins, John. A plea for bringing in of Irish cattle and keeping out of fish caught by foreigners (1680)
Salt and Fishery   Collins, John. Salt and Fishery . . . (1682)
Concerning Coining   See Barbon, Nicholas
Considerations   See Locke, John. Considerations . . .
Correspondence   See Petty, William. Correspondence . . .
Craig   Craig, Sir John. The Mint (1953)
Cranston   Cranston, Maurice. John Locke (1957)
Ct. Bk.   East India Co. Court Book, India Office Library, London
                           Davies, K. G. Royal African Company (1957)

Discourse	See Barbon, Nicholas. *A Discourse of Trade*
Discourses	See North, Sir Dudley
Evelyn	Evelyn, John. *Diary* (de Beer ed., 1955)
Examen	See North, Roger
Gregory	*James Gregory Tercentenary Memorial Volume* (ed. H. W. Turnbull, 1939)
H.M.C.	Historical Manuscripts Commission
Horsefield	Horsefield, J. Keith. *British Monetary Experiments 1650–1710* (1960). [Horsefield numbers, when given with bibliographic data for pamphlets, refer to Horsefield's bibliography, pp. 277 ff. of his volume.]
Hull	Hull, Charles Henry (ed.). *The Economic Writings of Sir William Petty* (1899)
Hunter	Hunter, William Wilson. *History of British India* (1900)
JPE	*Journal of Political Economy*
Khan	Khan, S.A. *East India Trade in the XVIIth Century* (1923)
Kress	Kress Library (Harvard). *Catalogue Through 1776* (1940)
Kress S. ⎫ Kress Supp. ⎭	Kress Library (Harvard). *Supplementary Catalogue* (1956)
L.J.	*Journals of the House of Lords*
Lives	See North, Roger
	Locke, John. *Essays on the Law of Nature* (ed. W. von Leyden; 1954)
	Locke, John. *Of Civil Government* (1690; Laslett ed., 1962)

Considerations	Locke, John. *Some Considerations of the Consequences of the Lowering of Interest and Raising the Value of Money* (1691). In Locke, *Works* (1823; 10 vols.), V.
	Locke, John. *Works* (1823; 10 vols.)
London Bibliography	*London Bibliography of the Social Sciences* (v.d.)
	Lowndes, William. *Report containing an essay for the amendment of the silver coins . . .* (1695)
Luttrell	Luttrell, Narcissus. *A Brief Historical relation of State Affairs, from Sept. 1678 to April 1714* (1857).
M.B.	Ms. Minute Book of 'Committee concerning . . . Trade, 1669', in House of Lords Record Office, H. L. Papers (1669), No. 215
	McCulloch, J. R. *Select Collection of Early English Tracts on Commerce* (1836)
	McCulloch, J. R. (ed.). *Select Collection of . . . Tracts on Money* (1856)
Mallet	Mallet, C. E. *A History of the University of Oxford* (1924–27)
Mss. Locke	Locke Mss. in Bodleian Library
Mun	Mun, Thomas. *England's Treasure by Forraign Trade* (1664)
N.D.T.	See Child, Josiah
Autobiography	North, Roger. *Autobiography* (ed. A. Jessopp; 1887)

Examen	North, Roger. *Examen* (1740)
Lives	North, Roger. *Lives of Francis . . . Dudley . . . and . . . John North* (1826; 3 vols.)
PRO	Public Record Office, London
Pap. Mem.	Papillon, A. F. W. *Memoirs of Thomas Papillon* (1887)
Hull	*The Economic Writings of Sir William Petty* (1899; 2 vols.; ed. C. H. Hull)
Petty Correspondence ⎱ *Correspondence* ⎰	*The Petty-Southwell Correspondence 1676–1687* (1928; ed. Lord Lansdowne)
Petty Papers	*The Petty Papers* (1927; 2 vols.; ed. Lord Lansdowne)
Rigaud	Rigaud, S. P. *Correspondence of Scientific Men of the Seventeenth Century* (1841)
Salt and Fishery	See Collins, John
	Schumpeter, Joseph. *History of Economic Analysis* (1954)
Scott	Scott, W. R. *The Constitution and Finance of . . . Joint-Stock Companies to 1700* (1910–12)
Shaftesbury Mss.	Mss. of first Earl of Shaftesbury, in Public Record Office, London
	Smith, Adam. *The Wealth of Nations* (1776), (Edw. Cannan ed., 1904)
Some Considerations	See Locke, John
Some of the Consequences . . .	See Locke, John
Strauss	Strauss, E. *Sir William Petty* (1954)
	Swift, Jonathan. *Works . . .* (1824; Scott's second ed.)

TED
Tudor Econ. Docts. } Tawney, R. H., and Power, Eileen. *Tudor Economic Documents* (1924; 3 vols.)

Vickers, Douglas. *Studies in the Theory of Money 1690–1776* (1959)

W.o.N. See Smith, Adam. *Wealth of Nations*

Wood   Wood, Alfred C. *History of the Levant Company* (1935)

INDEX

Admiralty, commissioners of the, 21

African Company, 26 n., 98, 176 n., 199, 200, 200 n.

Albemarle, Duke of, 24 n.

Albin, Benjamin, 26

Algebra, Petty's views on, 140

Allestree (London bookseller), 115

Allington, Lord, 175 n.

Alum Farmers, 111, 115

Anderson, Adam, 235 n.

Andrews, C. M., 4 n., 5 n., 17 n., 26 n., 27 n., 175 n., 177 n.

Andrews, Sir Mathew, 179

Anglesey, Earl of, 24 n.

Anglo-Dutch Wars, 42, 110, 111, 176

Anonymity, 96–98

Apprentices, 6–7, 10, 34, 46

Aquinas, St Thomas, 189

Arber, E., 86 n., 287 n., 288 n.

Archimedes, 140

Aristotle, 90–91, 162, 184, 185, 233

Arlington, Lord, 24 n.

Asgill, John, 58

Ashe, Sir Joseph, 37

Ashley, Lord. See Shaftesbury

Ashley, Sir W. J., 278

Ashton, T. S., 262, 268

Aubrey, John, 125, 152, 271 n.

Austin, William, 109

Bacon, Francis, 105, 125, 131–38, 139, 187, 193, 210, 223, 227

Baker (author of tract on Smyrna trade), 117 n.

Baker, Thomas, 112 n., 113 n., 114, 117 n.

Baltic trade, 6

Banks, Sir John, 28 n., 178

Banks, 101 f.
Bank of England, 56, 58, 59, 76
goldsmiths of London, 7, 9, 262
in Holland, 7
Land Banks, 58–59, 77, 94
Orphan's Bank, 94

Barbon, Nicholas (1637–1698):
Apology for the Builder, 60
as builder, 53–56, 60, 102
contributions to economic theory, 66 ff.
Discourse Concerning Coining, 78–81, 101–2
Discourse of Trade, 60–64, 78–79, 231–32
economic writings, 60 ff., 77 ff.
education, 53
insurance enterprise, 56–57
land bank, 58–59
and Locke, 77–81
methodology, 52, 61 ff., 78–81, 101–3, 159
objectivity of, 94, 101–3
parentage, 52–53
and Petty, 155 n., 157
views:
on banks, 58, 101–2

WILLIAM LETWIN, Associate Professor of Industrial History at the Massachusetts Institute of Technology, has published many articles and reviews in learned and popular journals. He is also the author of *Sir Josiah Child, Merchant Economist* (1959) and *A Documentary History of American Economic Policy Since 1789* (1961).

Mr. Letwin attended the University of Chicago and did graduate work there and at the London School of Economics. After receiving the degree of Doctor of Philosophy from the Committee on Social Thought at the University of Chicago, he remained at the university as Postdoctoral Fellow in the Economics Department and then as Research Associate in the Law School. He has been at M.I.T. since 1955 and was a Visiting Member of the London School of Economics during 1959–60.